PROGRAMS FOR THE GIFTED

A Case Book in Secondary Education

COMMISSION OF YEARBOOKS OF THE JOHN DEWEY SOCIETY,
ARCHIBALD W. ANDERSON, CHAIRMAN

All yearbooks of the John Dewey Society
are prepared under the general co-ordination of the Commission on Yearbooks.

FIFTEENTH YEARBOOK OF THE JOHN DEWEY SOCIETY

PROGRAMS
for the
GIFTED

A Case Book in Secondary Education

EDITED BY

SAMUEL EVERETT, *1898 -*

Associate Professor of Education
The City College of New York

HARPER & BROTHERS   PUBLISHERS   NEW YORK

Library of Congress catalog card number: 61-6330

In Memoriam

Miles E. Cary,

EDUCATIONAL PHILOSOPHER AND FRIEND OF ALL MANKIND

YEARBOOK COMMITTEE

CHRISTIAN O. ARNDT, Professor of International Education Relations, New York University

HERBERT L. COON, Principal, The University High School, The Ohio State University

JEAN FAIR, Associate Professor of Education, Wayne State University

WILLIAM HEARD KILPATRICK, Professor Emeritus, Columbia University

HAROLD A. KLEINER, Principal, U. S. Grant High School, Portland, Oregon

LLOYD S. MICHAEL, Superintendent, Evanston Township High School, Evanston, Illinois

GLYN MORRIS, Director of Guidance, Board of Co-operative Educational Services, Lewis County, Port Leydon, New York

HOWARD G. SACKETT, Executive Officer, Board of Co-operative Educational Services, Lewis County, Port Leydon, New York

HENRY SCATTERGOOD, Principal, Germantown Friends School, Philadelphia, Pennsylvania

ALEXANDER TAFFEL, Principal, Bronx High School of Science, New York City

GOODWIN WATSON, Professor of Education, Columbia University

CLIFFORD W. WILLIAMS, Supervisor, Gifted Child Program, Portland Public Schools, Oregon

MARGARET WILLIS, Associate Professor and Core Teacher, The University High School, The Ohio State University

PAUL WITTY, Professor of Education, Northwestern University

SAMUEL EVERETT, Chairman, Yearbook Committee, and Associate Professor of Education, The City College of New York

Contents

Foreword

THIS volume deals with a current problem of grave concern to the American public. The John Dewey Society, through committees of educators selected in each instance because of special competence and interest, has always used the Yearbook as its means of carrying forward its intention "to foster the study of democratic education in its relationship with the culture, and to promote thorough and systematic inquiry and investigation in the social foundations of education." This writing—addressed as it is to the difficult problems, first, of locating talented young people and, second, of providing for the cultivation of their special gifts within practices that exemplify and strengthen the democratic aspiration— is no exception to this aim.

The interest of the Society in bringing to the public the results of the thoughtful study of educational and cultural problems in their inescapable relationships has been in no way diminished by its decision to replace the Yearbook series with a new venture, a series specifically addressed to the exploration of educational theory. It will also continue to publish the John Dewey Lecture annually.

Archibald W. Anderson, Chairman of the Commission of Yearbooks of the John Dewey Society and editor of *Educational Theory*, the journal the Society sponsored in 1950 in cooperation with the College of Education of the University of Illinois, stated the purpose of the Society in changing its publication pattern when he wrote that it did so in the hope of ". . . fostering the creative thinking about education which the present situation demands."[1]

---

[1] "Fostering Study in the Theory of Education: The Development of New Approaches to Basic Educational Problems," *Educational Theory*, IX, No. 1, January, 1959, p. 22. This article is so developed that one of its achievements is to present the history of the publications program of the John Dewey Society.

Yearbooks dealing with problems arising from the interaction of education with the social, economic, and political areas of the culture, important as they have been in the publishing history of the Society, no longer seem to be fully appropriate for dealing with the questions arising on the frontier of educational theory. For this reason the new series noted above have been projected. Professor Anderson described them as follows:

One of these is the *John Dewey Society Series in Educational Theory.* This is to consist of books, published annually, in which one or two authors make a vigorous and searching study of some significant problem in, or contributing to, the theoretical foundations of education.

The Second of the new series is the *John Dewey Society Lectureship Series.* This is to consist of the printed version of an annual lecture to be delivered by some outstanding individual, either in or outside the field of education, whose ideas could be regarded as one of the thought resources to be explored by those seeking to advance the theory of education.[2]

Two of the lectures have already been presented in cooperation with the National Society of College Teachers of Education at general sessions in its annual meetings. Each has been published by Harper & Brothers. The first, *The Climate of Learning: A Constructive Attack on Complacency in Higher Education* (1958), was given by Dr. Ordway Tead, editor of social and economic books for Harper & Brothers, as well as a vice president and director of Harper & Brothers. The second, *John Dewey's Challenge to Education: Historical Perspectives on the Cultural Context* (1959), was given by Professor Oscar Handlin, professor of history at Harvard University, editor of the Library of American Biography, and winner of a Pulitzer Prize for his historical writings. The initial publication of the newly created Commission of Publication, now under the chairmanship of Professor Arthur Wirth of Brooklyn College, will be the first replacement of the Yearbook series and is projected for 1961.

Reasons entirely beyond the control of Archibald W. Anderson made it impossible for him to bring this manuscript to publication, as he had expected to do. The present writer, having full knowledge

[2] *Ibid.,* p. 22.

of the editorial standards Professor Anderson has established, substituted for him reluctantly. This act provides him the opportunity, however, to express the appreciation of the John Dewey Society to one who has served it, and the profession of which he is a part, faithfully and well. Dr. Anderson has always labored beyond the call of duty. We salute him for the high standards he has set and maintained as Chairman of the Commission on Yearbooks of the John Dewey Society and rejoice in his continued editorship of the journal of *Educational Theory*.

The present volume has been prepared under the leadership of Dr. Samuel Everett of the City College of New York.

The John Dewey Society is indebted to Professor Everett both for his proposal that it authorize a cooperative study of the problems involved in the education of the gifted and for his willingness to bring the study to completion. It is appreciative also of the contributions made by the many authors who assisted Professor Everett. And, finally, this writer is appreciative of the editorial assistance given him by Frank Zidonis, an instructor in the teaching of English in the College of Education at The Ohio State University.

H. GORDON HULLFISH
The Ohio State University
President, The John Dewey Society

April 1960

Preface

THIS book is concerned with the education of gifted students in American high schools. For purposes of exposition the terms "talented," "unusually able," and "gifted" are used to designate the entire group of students with whom we are concerned.

Man has made the present society and can alter it through thought and effort. We can change certain conditions which affect the lives of all, including our potential leaders. We are not automatons subject to immutable forces of nature but can as free men do much to direct and control human effort.

In schools the gifted must be challenged again and again to accept and prepare for responsibilities of social leadership. They must learn to value knowledge and to work hard in its pursuit. They must develop those qualities of persistence, concentration, and objective appraisal of which they are capable. Perhaps, most of all, they must learn that society needs them.

Our old leisurely ways in regard to appropriate education for our best-qualified youth are gone for good.

This volume presents ideas and programs for educating able youth at the secondary level. All the contributors are devoted to promoting democratic values in which respect for the individual and experimentalism are central. Because of their experimental orientation they differ as to how the gifted should be educated and the way in which democratic values should be implemented. As to what these values are, however, there is general agreement.

Most of the contributors believe in the comprehensive school for all American youth. Yet they are willing to consider special programs for the gifted. "Experimentalism" has been interpreted to mean that no dogmatic position should be taken on the moot subject of grouping—heterogeneous or special. Though the contributors have preferences, they seek to explore, believing that there may be more than one promising road to democratic objectives.

In Part I desirable objectives, the nature of giftedness, and contemporary American society are examined, as are conditions affecting the growth of people and of society. The assumption is both stated and implied that we can do a better job of educating our able youth if we but put our minds and considerable resources to the task.

Part II looks at secondary education abroad. Confidence in our democratic values should make us unafraid of a closer look at educational practices based on class traditions or communism. We should be objective enough to recognize good teaching and learning where they exist, regardless of differences of ideology, and intelligent enough to sift out those foreign practices appropriate for democratic comprehensive schools.

The chief emphases in Part III are upon curricular provisions and the learning process. Other aspects—organization, teaching staff, testing, guidance, evaluation—are presented in the context of curriculums which are broadly interpreted.

The high schools included in Part III were chosen for a variety of reasons. Large and small institutions are represented, as are private and laboratory schools. There is a specialized high school for the gifted, a core curriculum, as well as a school offering the core as an alternative to an otherwise subject curriculum. Also covered are programs in the fine arts, in science, mathematics, and the academic subjects. Geographic location is also considered.

In some major respect each school selected is unique: a dynamic group of teachers produced an educational program of special value; a school had had for years a sound program which included, as a matter of course, a concern for able students; a program demonstrated unusual maturity in planning and execution; a school enjoyed a reputation for the superior quality of its graduates; a program showed great promise as one of a number in a school system; an experiment in the education of rural youth was realistic and imaginative.

The members of the Yearbook Committee never met. Their work

was co-ordinated by the chairman through correspondence and limited personal contact. The individual chapters are therefore the specific responsibility of those who produced them. There is no over-all responsibility other than that assumed by the chairman in conceiving the project and carrying it through as best he could under the circumstances. He alone assumes over-all responsibility for limitations of design and execution.

SAMUEL EVERETT
Associate Professor of Education
The City College of New York

PART I
ORIENTATION

I

The Gifted in American Society

Samuel Everett
The City College of New York

THERE was a time in the history of America when the ablest men in all sections of the colonies sought and achieved positions of social leadership. Two lasting products of the period of the Revolution, the Declaration of Independence and the United States Constitution, represent the best thought of a group of brilliant and experienced men. The Declaration sets forth the goals—the rights of man—which inspired the people to achieve freedom: "We hold these truths to be self-evident, that all men are created equal, that they are endowed by their Creator with certain unalienable Rights, that among these are Life, Liberty and the Pursuit of Happiness."

The Declaration still has the power to thrill those who love freedom as it has thrilled and inspired a multitude before us. Though we may no longer accept the theory of natural rights, we recognize that this document has been inspired by greatness.

Big business and huge industrial combines did not exist in that simple agrarian society, so they could not attract a majority of the ablest persons as they do today. The small economic and social organizations made possible the quick recognition of ability. Gifted men engaged in many creative activities in addition to business. Benjamin Franklin, for example, not only was an astute businessman but also conducted original experiments, served his country as a foreign diplomat, wrote, and actively participated in the immediate community life. Other able men similarly, if less spectacularly, engaged in trade, commerce, writing, and government.

3

Unfortunately too few of our ablest men today are providing social leadership. How many elected congressmen are the most brilliant and able persons in the states from which they come? How many appointed officials are among the ablest in our society? Similar questions can be asked concerning people in public life in other fields of social service. The answers are obvious.

The Organization Man

In huge economic and social organizations today there is considerable evidence that many superior men and women do not achieve to their potential abilities.

William H. Whyte, Jr., develops the thesis that in industry and large-scale scientific research, group decisions are often allowed to dominate the individual.[1]

In this view "How good an organization man are you?" becomes the primary question. Junior executives hesitate to express ideas. Or, if expressed, these ideas are often lost in the hierarchy of command. It is safer for a man of ability to play the game of being a good organization man. In this process one's integrity as a person and his urge for creative achievement may be lost.

Where the major test is conformity to the decisions of the people at the top or to group appraisal, the development of science in industry, in private foundations, and in higher education suffers. Likewise, governmental decisions which require group agreement at policy making and administrative levels may lose all creative insight.

About the plight of creative scientific research in America Lancelot Law Whyte states:

During the past hundred years Europe produced some fifteen or twenty men of high originality in theoretical physics, who evolved new ideas, not merely better mathematics, but the United States only one: J. Willard Gibbs (1839–1903), the great physical chemist, a lonely figure who did not found a school.[2]

The plight of unusually able persons in pure scientific speculation only mirrors that of superior individuals in business and other large

[1] William H. Whyte, Jr., *The Organization Man* (New York: Simon & Schuster, Inc., 1956).
[2] Lancelot Law Whyte, "Can We Grow Geniuses in Science?" *Harper's Magazine,* June, 1957, p. 46.

impersonal social organizations. Individuality tends to be buried in the dominant emphasis upon immediate, practical problems and a line and staff organization which values loyalty more highly than ideas.

The dilemmas faced by gifted people in adult society must be explored at the high school and more advanced levels by those who will themselves assume positions of leadership. In schools youth must be presented with significant social problems and encouraged to speculate on alternative solutions. This approach requires thinking at a higher level than is commonly the case. But it is a level which our ablest young people are capable of reaching. To do less than to present an honest picture and explore hypotheses as to at least partial solutions is to miseducate our future leaders.

THE PLIGHT OF FREEDOM

Henry Steele Commager considers the importance to society of free minds.

. . . first rate men and women will not and cannot work under conditions fixed by those who are afraid of ideas.

We do not encourage dissent for sentimental reasons; we encourage dissent because we cannot live without it. . . .

It is correct to say that a people like ourselves, with our traditions, our history, our habits, our attitudes, our institutions of democracy and freedom, our general enlightenment, must have freedom if we are to survive. Only if we actively encourage discussion, inquiry, and dissent, only if we put a premium on nonconformity, can we hope to solve the enormously complex problems that confront us. Only if we do this can we enlist the full and grateful support of all our people and command the respect of our associates abroad.[3]

In any society the right to dissent is subject to qualification in the interest of the general welfare. The acid test as to the applicability of this general notion to individual instances, however, must be the consequences. We must ask, for example, if the consequences will promote freedom of intelligence or an authoritarian standard of orthodoxy.

Millions of American Negro children continue to attend separate

[3] Henry Steele Commager, *Freedom, Loyalty, Dissent* (New York: Oxford University Press, 1954), pp. 15, 18, 36.

schools, which have been judged in a unanimous decision of the United States Supreme Court to be in fact unequal. Public agencies, including state legislatures and, at Little Rock, the state troops, have been marshaled in the Deep South to preserve these unequal schools. The plight of superior Negro youth, caught in this unhappy struggle, is obvious.

In the North and West Negro youth go to the same schools as white boys and girls. But prevailing community segregation practices concentrate Negroes in certain schools which are often not as good as those in more favored sections.

In many communities members of minority groups are unable to find teaching positions. A political liberal may be considered "as bad as a communist" and certainly the type of person who cannot be trusted to educate American youth. A teacher's serious exploration of weaknesses as well as strengths in both our private enterprise economy and government may at any time be publicly attacked.

The right to dissent is theoretically granted but in practice is fraught with danger. Teachers are in an exposed position. In our schools, and particularly in high schools where subject matter content is comparatively adult, teachers are subject to harassment when handling major controversial areas. When dealing with the Soviet Union, they are expected to make clear that American achievements are superior to those of the U.S.S.R. Otherwise they may be called to account by local "patriots" or demagogues to be judged by an unpredictable public opinion.

Limitations on freedom of teaching are quickly sensed by superior and gifted students. When idealistic American youth find that their mentors are "unrealistic," or "covering up" or "do not pursue the truth as they see it," they become resentful. General cynicism coupled with determination to pursue selfish ends provides an easy escape. Many turn away from creative tasks and personal intellectual enthusiasms which are potentially rewarding to the life of the individual and conducive to creative social leadership.

THE PURPOSES WE SEEK

The purposes we seek are not unique to the gifted. They are good for all men. In *The Sane Society* Erich Fromm states universal values in terms of the mental health of all mankind:

Mental health is characterized by the ability to love and to create, by the emergence from incestuous ties to clan and soil, by the sense of identity based on one's experience of self as the subject and agent of one's powers, by the grasp of reality inside and outside of ourselves, that is, by the development of objectivity and reason.[4]

In our American tradition democracy stresses the values espoused in *The Sane Society*. Respect for the individual person, which is central to a democratic philosophy, implies the same basic approach to life. As Fromm points out, this is essentially the outlook which has been voiced by thinkers and great religious leaders throughout history. The good life is equated with the ability of man to develop himself and improve the lot of the people around him.

Any program, in the field of education as well as in the larger society, will necessarily reveal basic values. Programs for the gifted are no exception. The development of the individual, in terms of mental health or of some broad social philosophy, is central to our task. In accepting the individual as primary, and freedom as necessary, we should be conscious that the decisions we are making in the education of youth help to determine whether we are to move toward a sane society in which democratic values can flourish.

EDUCATIONAL DETERRENTS

A limited approach to the task of developing programs for gifted students would be to concentrate on the mechanics of the job. Costs will increase. Higher salaries will be needed to attract and hold able people. Libraries will require special books. Classes must be smaller. Teachers of intellectually heterogeneous classes will need assistants. More expert personnel and equipment will be needed.

In a period of high competitive salaries in industry, rising costs, and tremendous rises in school enrollments, adequate material support for our schools is increasingly important. Everything possible should be done to improve the efficiency of every phase of education. But to limit our efforts to essentially financial factors will prove futile unless we concentrate also on putting other parts of our house in order.

The present concern for educating the gifted can serve as the motivating force for a thoroughgoing reappraisal of existing ideas

4 Erich Fromm, *The Sane Society* (New York: Rinehart & Co., Inc., 1955), p. 69.

and practices. What are some of the professional deterrents to the development of adequate programs for the gifted? Perhaps the major one has to do with misconceptions about the meaning of democracy.

In education the honor accorded the common man has been reflected in the development of free schools from the kindergarten through the publicly supported university. With the major exceptions of American Negroes and poor whites in the South, the school has become the American road to culture and to personal success. And major social forces are even now concentrated upon extending these opportunities to all.

In our concern for giving the best and most appropriate education to the mass of students, our attention and resources have often focused on pupils at the lower end of the ability range. In the process the talented in many communities have been neglected. Special small remedial classes are established for slow learners but not for advanced ones. Teachers do not always trouble themselves with able students who easily achieve the subject matter goals set for the majority. They are often more concerned with saving mediocre learners who find academic achievement difficult.

Our special concern for the common man in society has too largely become a special concern for the common student in our schools. Respect for the individual also means providing conditions favorable for the growth of each and every person and each and every pupil, not only those who have difficulty with academic subjects.

If special groups and special teachers are justified for slow learners, they are justified for fast learners as well. The needs are different, but the principle is the same. Our able people are important and merit at least equal attention.

Additional misconceptions have to do with the processes of democracy. Adjustment, cooperation, and majority decisions are too often accepted in our schools as ultimate democratic goals. As a result the right and responsibility to dissent are not sufficiently respected. The dominant concern for conformity and adjustment in society, revealingly expressed in *The Organization Man,* thus finds its counterpart in schools.

The Lonely Crowd distinguishes between independent personalities and those dominated by the group as the difference between those who are "autonomous" and those who are "other-directed."[5] Riesman finds that teachers stress desirability of adjustment in a group or conformity to established patterns in taste and behavior, rather than originality and basic knowledge.

Thus the children are supposed to learn democracy by underplaying the skills of intellect and overplaying the skills of gregariousness and amiability—skill democracy, in fact, based on respect for ability to do something, tends to survive only in athletics.[6]

Conformity certainly takes many forms. Social ostracism may be suffered by teachers who do not go along with the administration. Students who always ask questions may disturb the teacher's complacency, and ways are found to discourage their intellectual curiosity.

The current emphasis upon group thinking and group decisions, important as these are in the democratic process, too often leads to conformity at the expense of intellectual excellence and personal conviction. Giving up without adequate exploration is frequently justified through recourse to the principle of respect for majority decision. Creative ideas are often disregarded in majority decisions. Fundamental challenges may be overlooked for extraneous reasons, such as the objectionable personalities of the people who express them. The slow of mind may not grasp the significance of higher criticism. Considerable time is needed for basic thinking. Moreover, it is easier to go along with the mainstream of opinion than to combat it especially if such action is justified as being democratic.

The majority can be unthinking and even tyrannical, as many minority groups know. Where we do not show respect for ideas, mediocrity results. Cooperation can thus be a stultifying process; it can even lead to the tyranny of a determined minority.

Where there are misconceptions as to what is most significant in the democratic process, conformity can easily become pervasive. The current emphasis on social development is a case in point. One may be termed a good school citizen when he meekly adjusts to the established school and community mores. One may be

[5] David Riesman, Nathan Glazer, and Reuel Denney, *The Lonely Crowd* (New York: Doubleday and Company, Inc., 1950), pp. 276–79.
[6] *Ibid.*, p. 84.

termed a bad school citizen when his perception leads him to penetrate beneath the surface of these mores.

It is the nature of giftedness to evaluate, explore, and challenge.
Little can be accomplished in the development of gifted students
unless conditions are established which are favorable to nonconformity. Only then can creativity flourish.

Two additional deterrents to the development of excellence are
the acquiring of money and the achieving of security. Certainly
both are important to one's well-being. But intellectual and artistic
creativity is killed where primary allegiance is given to material
goals.

The educational profession must seek to change the current mores
here as elsewhere. Able boys and girls tend to accept, as do others,
the predominant motivations in our culture. The majority come
from homes in which artistic and intellectual interests are not
valued. Creativity, unless it carries a price tag, may actually be
frowned upon. Thus for many the intellectual adventure of search
and discovery must be learned in school if it is to be learned at all.

Teachers and administrators in America come mainly from lower
middle income families in which education is valued, though the
necessary rigorous self-discipline may not be understood. A teaching
position frequently offers members from this class more security
than does one in business. It may even provide them with a higher
income than their parents have enjoyed. Teachers, as well as their
students, carry material values with them to school. These may be
subconscious commitments which are sensed by students, particularly by able students. Or they may be consciously externalized and
taught as worthy ideals around which to mold a life.

Devotion to special fields of knowledge also has its pitfalls.
Teachers can become so specialized in schools—as people are in
society—that they have no realization of the larger significance of
what they teach. It is easy to lose touch with the movements and
problems of society.

Educational Opportunities

Numerous new programs for the education of gifted youth are
needed in all sections of the country. The welfare of society requires

them, as does the democratic tenet of the maximum development of each individual.

In the American structure of education no national authority gives directives on the details of what is to be done at the local level. Educational departments in individual states exercise power over local schools through state legislation. State control over local schools emphasizes adequacy of finances and administration. Curricular requirements usually stress minimum essentials and not detailed content. Local programs for gifted students are thus largely free of domination by external authorities.

Extralegal regional organizations, such as the North Central Association, have been established by secondary schools and colleges. These organizations accredit the schools in their region and so may exercise more direct influence than the individual states over programs for students who plan to enter higher institutions of learning. Professional regional and national associations are especially concerned with the quality of teaching and learning in member secondary schools. Local schools can therefore expect from these sources encouragement of, and sometimes considerable assistance in, efforts to improve the education of superior students. Where somewhat unorthodox high school courses or procedures are proposed, regional association representatives may well be consulted. Where plans are well prepared for any new ventures, local schools in most situations can expect sympathetic cooperation.

Since the Eight Year Study of the Progressive Education Association in the 1930's, higher institutions have shown increasing desire to liberalize the conventional Carnegie-unit type of entrance requirement.[7] The nation-wide Early Admission and Advanced Standing programs are doing much to break down rigid patterns.

Though there has long been a movement in American education which has stressed the importance of the education of gifted students, results have been sporadic. Many studies of the gifted and of the nature of giftedness have been made without generally affecting practice. Where individual secondary schools and school systems are in the process of building programs for unusually able youth, knowledge regarding the nature of giftedness is essential.

7 Wilford M. Aikin, *The Story of The Eight Year Study* (New York: Harper & Brothers, 1942).

The education of superior students requires a high degree of personal maturity and social awareness on the part of teachers. The potentially most promising teacher may at first fight the hardest to preserve unfounded beliefs. Many more are wary of new ideas which disturb complacency.

Fortunately, however, almost every high school has one or more exceptional teachers or an administrator committed to intellectual and artistic values. On these people rests the responsibility of building programs for gifted students who have potentialities for leadership.

Young minds may be led to discover that intellectual honesty is more demanding than commonly accepted versions of honesty. Speculative ideas often carry one far afield of practical considerations. Social awareness can lead an individual to become emotionally involved in the welfare of people foreign to his own experience. Leadership requires a quality of realism and character many stages removed from the popularity contest. Artistic quality may imply departures from commonly accepted criteria of beauty. New perceptions and new goals are required.

American high schools have a job of reorientation and rebuilding to do which will call forth the best that is in them. Developing programs for the gifted will require time for learning and relearning. Most of all, it will require a working conception of individuality and freedom too rarely found in American life and American high schools.

2

The Nature and Needs of Gifted and Superior Adolescents

Paul Witty
Northwestern University

SINCE the appearance of Sputnik I, there has been a resurgence of interest in superior pupils. Investigations of such students and their needs, and appraisals of the nature and extent of educational opportunities available to them, have led to conclusions not greatly different from those advanced by L. M. Terman, Leta Hollingworth, and myself about thirty years ago.

A BROADER DEFINITION OF GIFTEDNESS

There is, however, one conspicuous difference in current discussions. A broader concept of giftedness is now frequently endorsed. It was formerly believed that giftedness was revealed reliably by a single measure—the intelligence test. A very high I.Q. was associated positively with every kind of outstanding attainment. For example, the role of the gifted person in society was described as follows: "Individuals of surpassing intelligence create national wealth, determine the state of industry, advance science, and make general culture possible."[1]

It was believed, too, that the I.Q. was stable within narrow

1 Leta S. Hollingworth, *Gifted Children: Their Nature and Nurture* (New York: The Macmillan Co., 1926), p. 297.

limits. Accordingly, a high I.Q. in childhood was considered an indicator of high ability at later times. Thus, it was stated:

The new knowledge thus accumulated, and the new tests invented in the twentieth century, afford us the modern approach to the study of the gifted. We can now study gifted children and learn eventually all we care to know about extraordinarily able persons, their education, and their place in civilization.[2]

Today a different point of view recognizes that intelligence test results are affected by a number of factors which influence their validity. For example, expression is blocked in some gifted children by emotion or by insecurity traceable to deprivations at home. In communities which offer children meager opportunities, the expression of intelligence may differ from that in more fortunate areas. Moreover, there are children whose abilities in art, music, or writing, though rare and distinctive, cannot be discovered through intelligence testing.

A high I.Q. is no longer closely associated with creativity in areas such as art, music, and writing. Robert Havighurst, Eugene Stivers, and Robert DeHaan state:

From what we know about the nature of talent we suppose that there is relatively little connection between the various kinds of talent. While it is true that there is a tendency for gifted people to be talented in more than one area, there certainly are a great many people with talent in only one area and no more than average ability in most other areas.[3]

Consequently a broader definition of giftedness is recommended.

Again, Robert Havighurst and his colleagues state:

A meaningful definition of the gifted would then not be a narrow one but might include every child, who, in his age group, is superior in some ability which may make him an outstanding contributor to the welfare of, and quality of living in, society.

Programs operating on this basis seek to develop such a variety of gifts and talents as:

---

[2] *Ibid.*, p. 40.

[3] Robert Havighurst, Eugene Stivers, and Robert F. DeHaan, *A Survey of the Education of Gifted Children* (Supplementary Educational Monographs, No. 83 [Chicago: University of Chicago Press, November, 1955]), p. 4.

(a) General intellectual ability (ability to think abstractly and to do other kinds of relational thinking) and its various components, such as reasoning, verbal skill, mathematical skill, and spatial imagination.

(b) Ability in such useful areas as science, mechanics, social leadership, and human relations.

(c) Talent in creative arts, such as graphic art, music, creative writing, and dramatics.[4]

Within the past decade the American Association for Gifted Children has promoted a broader concept of giftedness. The following concept was adopted too for the *57th Yearbook of the National Society for the Study of Education:*

> The talented or gifted child is one who shows consistently remarkable performance in any worthwhile line of endeavor. Thus, we shall include not only the intellectually gifted but also those who show promise in music, the graphic arts, creative writing, dramatics, mechanical skills, and social leadership. Although most of the attention of educators has been directed toward the intellectually gifted . . . we think of such special attention to the intellectually gifted as a weakness or shortcoming in the kind of program for gifted children that we would like to see in existence.[5]

The foregoing discussion should not lead one to minimize the attempts to provide more adequately for children who are gifted in abstract or verbal intelligence. But it is important to remember that there are many pupils whose giftedness in other areas will not be discerned through intelligence tests. Efforts must be made to identify these pupils and to foster their full development.

In this chapter we shall describe several types of gifted pupils and discuss their needs. The types we examine will include pupils (1) whose abstract or verbal intelligence is high, (2) those who show promise in science, (3) those who show creativity in the arts, and (4) those who are potential social leaders.

---

[4] *Ibid.*

[5] Robert Havighurst (chairman), "Education for the Gifted," *57th Yearbook of the National Society for the Study of Education,* Part II (Chicago: University of Chicago Press, 1958), p. 19. The concept of giftedness advanced by the writer of this chapter appeared in *The Gifted Person* (by Paul Witty), Chapter III of "Education for the Gifted." Adaptations from Chapter III of the *57th Yearbook* are found in parts of the present chapter.

CHARACTERISTICS OF PUPILS OF VERY HIGH I.Q.

With the development of the intelligence test and its widespread use, the gifted were defined in terms of high I.Q. L. M. Terman referred to those children whose intelligence quotients were 130 or higher as "gifted." In his early studies he found that about 1 per cent of the elementary school population had an I.Q. of 130 or higher.[6] For many years the intelligence test was the generally established method of identifying the gifted. This method is still widely followed, as may be seen by its use in selecting pupils for classes recently initiated in Indianapolis and St. Louis. Additional factors are sometimes considered, but the I.Q. continues to play a major role in the selection of the gifted. In the case of high school students, it has been proposed that the delimiting I.Q. be lower— perhaps 120. Another proposal is to designate two adolescent groups: the moderately gifted, I.Q. 120 to 137; and the highly gifted, 137 and above.[7]

Numerous investigations reveal that the typical gifted pupil (I.Q. 130 and above) is physically superior, attractive, and rather well adjusted—not the physical weakling and social misfit often pictured.

The gifted pupil excels generally in his school work. His educational growth progresses at such a rapid rate that by the time he reaches the upper elementary school, he has acquired knowledge and skills which surpass those of children two or three grades above him.

Studies show that the typically gifted pupil continues to display superior academic ability throughout high school. Nearly ninety per cent of a group studied by L. M. Terman went to college and about 70 per cent graduated.[8] Over 60 per cent of the college graduates enrolled in advanced courses. Although the members of this group as a whole did superior academic work, a rather large number failed to

[6] Recent studies suggest that the I.Q. delimiting the upper 1 per cent is nearer 135.

[7] Paul Witty (ed.), *The Gifted Child* (Boston: D. C. Heath and Company, 1951). See also *Education of the Gifted* (Educational Policies Commission of N.E.A. and the American Association of School Administrators, N.E.A., 1950).

[8] Lewis M. Terman and Melita H. Oden, *The Gifted Child Grows Up* (Stanford: Stanford University Press, 1947).

achieve in accordance with their earlier promise. Among the many causes of failure in such pupils, L. M. Terman and M. Oden cite the "absence of educational procedures adapted to children of exceptional ability." Nevertheless these writers assert that "the prognostic significance of superior childhood I.Q. has been established beyond question."

In several studies it became clear that the gifted adolescent required a curriculum enriched and developed according to his rapid learning rate and his particular needs. That he seldom was the recipient of such educational opportunities was revealed again and again. Similarly, many college students of high ability were shown to be unchallenged by their courses. L. M. Terman reported that, objectively measured, the overlapping of educational attainment was so great that in certain colleges about 20 per cent of the gifted sophomores and 15 per cent of the gifted freshmen reached or exceeded the median scores of seniors. These students needed stimulating courses, which were not often provided. Reasonably, he proposed that we "quit accrediting colleges and accredit instead the individual student."[9]

Studies Showing Failure of Superior Students to Continue in Education

The need for greater stimulation and guidance of the gifted throughout high school and college is suggested by some early studies of Gilbert Wrenn. This investigator reported a follow-up of the top 16 per cent of a group of 1938 Minnesota high-school graduates.[10] Nine years after high school graduation, "only 45 per cent (of this top group) had received baccalaureate degrees, and 8 per cent had earned advanced degrees. In approximate figures only 4 per cent of the high school graduates with I.Q.'s of 125 and above had earned advanced degrees."

The National Manpower Council estimated in 1951 that one fourth of our eighteen-year-old youth had I.Q.'s of 110 or above. Of

9 Lewis M. Terman, "The Gifted Student and His Academic Environment," *School and Society,* January 21, 1939, pp. 65–73.

10 C. Gilbert Wrenn, "Potential Research Talent in the Sciences Based on Intelligence Quotients of Ph.D.'s, *Educational Record,* January, 1949.

this fourth, 60 per cent did not enter college and 20 per cent did not complete high school. Of the 40 per cent who entered college, only about one half graduated.[11]

Recent studies have also revealed the failure of many gifted students to continue their educational careers. According to a newspaper report, President Henry of the University of Illinois, after pointing to the "gross under-utilization" of some of the nation's highest talent, stated in *The Sun-Times,* September 23, 1955:

Of 2,250,000 young people who reach the age of 18 each year, 152,000 or over 7 per cent have a rating of ability higher than that of the average college graduate . . . only a little more than half of them enter college, and fewer than half finish. Two per cent receive doctor's degrees.

In 1960, the neglect continues, but the situation is improved. Thus, Dale Wolfle reports that "Of the top 30% in general intellectual ability—nearly 60% enter college, and close to 40% earn bachelor's or higher degrees."[12]

Many articles have been devoted to the neglect of potential scientists. This neglect was cited in *The Gifted Child* in 1951. And it was stressed in numerous articles and books during the decade before Sputnik I.[13] These earlier accounts pointed out that secondary school curriculums did not sufficiently challenge many superior students.

THE ACADEMICALLY TALENTED STUDENT—HIS NATURE AND NEEDS

One way to meet the academic needs of the superior secondary school pupil is to extend and enrich the curriculum. A conference in Washington in February 1958 considered this problem. James B. Conant, who served as chairman, stated:

Throughout the conference, we used the phrase, "academically talented" to refer to that 15 to 20 per cent of an age group who have the ability to study—effectively and rewardingly—advanced mathematics, foreign

11 *Student Deferment and National Manpower Policy* (National Manpower Council [New York: Columbia University Press, 1952]).

12 Dale Wolfle, "Diversity of Talent," *The American Psychologist,* Vol. 15, No. 8, Aug. 1960.

13 R. H. Knapp and H. B. Goodrich, *Origin of American Scientists* (Chicago: University of Chicago Press, 1952).

language, physics and chemistry. Obviously the gifted would be included in this broad definition.[14]

The following is a description of the academically talented student:

He is in the upper 15 to 20 per cent of the secondary students in the United States. In your school he and his academically talented fellow students may constitute 90 per cent of their class or five per cent.

He is usually a rapid learner, a good organizer, and a skilful thinker, as a rule he is about average in his use of vocabulary and in his reading skills. He is probably creative, curious, persevering, and capable of considerable independent study. He usually possesses more than the normal amount of stamina, is physically above average, and is fully capable of profiting by unusual academic challenges.

But he may not be easy to identify. He may have been born and may live in almost any kind of circumstances. He may be any one's child; hidden under almost any of a number of guises—indifference, resentment, under-achievement, frustration, delinquency. He may be beset with problems, arising from over-ambitious parents, indifferent parents, or a society whose values are oriented to unnecessary conformity.[15]

The conference recommended that a comprehensive high school program be made available for the academically talented student. This program should require: (1) four years of English, (2) four years of one modern language, (3) one year of a physical science and one year of a biological science, (4) one year of American history, one year of history other than American, and one additional year of some other aspect of social science, and (5) three years of mathematics.

The need for more comprehensive programs in the high school was emphasized again and again as a result of studies of superior pupils made in the twenties and thirties. Meager opportunities are offered gifted students today in many high schools. Lack of challenge, traceable to impoverished offerings, is undoubtedly one reason for the failure of many capable students to go to college as well as for others to drop out of school.

14 James B. Conant, "Education of the Academically Talented," *School and Society*, May 10, 1958.
15 "Finding and Educating the Academically Talented Student in the Secondary School" (N.E.A. Bulletin; undated brochure published by the N.E.A. on conference held in 1958).

FORD FOUNDATION PROGRAMS TO MEET THE ABILITIES AND NEEDS OF THE GIFTED

To foster the development of superior pupils, the Ford Foundation has sponsored programs designated to bridge the gap between high school and college. In a sense these programs involve acceleration. In 1951 the Fund for the Advancement of Education sponsored an experiment involving superior high school students. Under the Early Admission Program 420 boys and girls—most of them sixteen or under—who had completed at least the tenth grade and seemed ready both academically and in terms of personal maturity to enter college, were given Ford scholarships to any one of 11 colleges. In 1952 a twelfth college joined the program, and 440 scholarships were awarded. Additional grants in 1953 and 1954 brought the total of Ford scholars to 1,350.

Another plan sponsored by the Ford Foundation provides college level work in high school leading to advanced standing in college. This program is now also sponsored by the College Entrance Examination Board. The board provides high schools with descriptions of courses in 12 fields, and prepares examinations in them. Students who pass the examinations may apply for college credit. Students thus admitted with advanced standing can complete college in less time, or they can take more advanced work or venture into fields they might otherwise not explore. In 1953–1954, the first year of the program, 18 secondary schools and 532 students participated. Many more students are currently participating.[16]

These programs have already proved successful. Elbert Fretwell has shown that the students are not only successful in college courses, but also well adjusted and socially effective. Moreover, these students are assuming leadership in school activities and are causing instructors to raise their standards.[17] Apparently one of the great needs of mentally superior pupils is more challenging educational opportunities.

[16] "Bridging the Gap Between High School and College" (Ford Fund for the Advancement of Education, June, 1953). See also *They Went to College Early* (Ford Fund for the Advancement of Education, 1957).

[17] Elbert Fretwell, "Challenge of the Gifted," *Journal of Higher Education,* June, 1957.

The National Merit Scholar—His Nature and Needs

Another effort to challenge the academically gifted student has centered on increasing the number of scholarships. A number of plans already in operation—including the Westinghouse Science Talent Search—have offered substantial help to qualified students. Recently a more comprehensive search for highly talented high schools students was undertaken. The National Merit Scholarship Corporation conducted its first screening program for this purpose in 1956, with the objective of granting 556 four year scholarships.

As a first step, 58,158 high school seniors ranking in the top five per cent of their class were nominated as participants by high school principals throughout the United States including Alaska, Hawaii, and Puerto Rico. This sample was given a preliminary screening test measuring verbal and mathematical aptitudes. Next, a sample of 5,078 students of finalists was secured from the large participant sample by selecting the highest scoring students on this test from each state in proportion to the size of the high school senior population for that state. . . .

Last, a selection committee composed of 8 educators made the selection of 556 students from the sample of 5,078.[18]

These scholars in many ways resemble the gifted adolescents of other studies. Here is a description of the typical male scholar:

The typical male scholar is about 18 years of age, comes from a heavily populated state and a large high school graduating from 101 to 500 students per year. He possesses superior scholastic ability and especially quantitative ability. His socio-economic status is relatively high since his father is usually employed in a skilled trade, clerical, semi-professional or professional position. Within his own family, he is most frequently the oldest child or the only child. If there are other children in the family, he has one or two siblings. The male scholar rarely comes from a large family.

The male scholar plans to enter a scientific field after graduation from college. His vocational motivation for the social sciences, business and arts is almost minimal. His hobbies and extracurricular activities are in the main consistent with the patterns found for scientists since they

18 John L. Holland and Ruth C. Stalnaker, "Descriptive Study of Talented High School Seniors, National Merit Scholars," *The Bulletin of the National Association of Secondary School Principals*, March, 1958, pp. 9-21.

reflect a greater concern with things and intellectual problems rather than an emphasis in sociality or social activities. His life goals are characterized by his practical outlook on life, doing a competent job, achievement through working, desiring new experience, and dominance (leadership and supervisory roles). These goals tend to support the latter generalization; that is, his motivation appears practical and directed at self-development and directed at securing new experience rather than an interest in people *per se*. This is not to say that the scholar is not concerned with human values and social activities, but rather his desire for intellectual and scientific problems outweighs his concern for social problems and events.

It is of interest to note similarities to and differences from the foregoing sketch in the following description of the girl scholar:

The female scholar is about 17 years of age, comes from a heavily populated state and a large high school graduating from 101 to 500 students per year. She possesses a superior scholastic ability and is characterized more by her verbal skills than by her quantitative abilities although she ranks high on both. Her socio-economic status and family characteristics are essentially identical with those of the male scholar.

The female scholar plans to enter either a teaching or a scientific field, and like her male counterpart, she displays little motivation for other vocational areas. Her hobbies and extracurricular interests reflect a variety of intellectual and esthetic activities. Compared with the male scholar, she appears more concerned with the arts and social activities and less concerned with more physical active and aggressive activities such as athletics and debate.

Her life goals describe a similar feminine pattern. She is concerned first with establishing a meaningful marriage and second with practical work goals. Knowledge and education are considered important goals in their own right. Her need for achievement and other self-oriented goals is much less than that for males. Like the male scholar, she is not concerned with security as a goal.

Many other awards now available reflect a growing recognition of the role of intellectually superior persons in scientific accomplishment and progress.

THE GIFTED STUDENTS IN THE AREAS OF SCIENCE

Mentally gifted young people drop out of high school and college so frequently that serious shortages in superior personnel may be anticipated. Accordingly, educators and scientists are concerned about the possibility that in the future the United States may have too few outstanding scientists and scholars of high ability to compete successfully with leaders in other countries.

But who are the potential scientists? Paul Brandwein has offered some valuable suggestions for identifying them:

> Three factors are considered as being significant in the development of future scientists: a Genetic Factor, with a primary base in heredity (general intelligence, numerical ability and verbal ability); a Predisposing Factor, with a primary base in functions which are psychological in nature; an Activating Factor with a primary base in the opportunities offered in school and in the special skills of the teacher.[19]

As he develops, the potential scientist will also display the following characteristics:

> The characteristics grouped under the Predisposing Factor . . . include a spectrum of traits which the writer places under the head of *Persistence*. This is defined as consisting of three attitudes. (1) A marked willingness to spend time, beyond the ordinary schedule, in a given task (this includes the willingness to set one's own time schedules, to labor beyond a prescribed time, such as from 9 to 5). (2) A willingness to withstand discomfort. This includes adjusting to shortened lunch hours, or no lunch hours, working without holidays, etc. It includes withstanding fatigue and strain and working even through minor illness, such as cold or a headache. (3) A willingness to face failure. With this comes a realization that patient work may lead to successful termination of the task at hand.[20]

Although it is desirable perhaps to emphasize the identification of promising scientists in high school, such abilities and qualities can in some cases be observed earlier. The child who has a flair for mathematics, who constructs apparatus and engages in experimentation at home, who reads many biographies about scientists, and who turns frequently to scientific presentations in various printed sources, is thus revealing some characteristics which foreshadow outstanding endeavor in this field.

In high school the promising student may display the following characteristics:

19 Paul Brandwein, *The Gifted Student as Future Scientist* (New York: Harcourt, Brace & Co., 1955), p. xi.
20 *Ibid.*, pp. 9–10.

Here, then, is a brief and generalized profile of a typical student in the High School of Science. He wants to go to college and make science his career; however, he is not too definite in his interest. He is a year younger than the average high school student of the same grade; but he knows the fundamentals of arithmetic and spelling. He reads extensively in many kinds of books and periodicals. He is alert to current issues and is capable of profound loyalties. He complains about too much homework but puts a considerable amount of time on daily study. He spends much spare time in his home laboratory and on other hobbies. Because he is eager and vocal, he is sometimes difficult to control in class. He is hard on the teacher and can spot at once the one who "doesn't know his stuff." He has achieved an early sophistication in the importance of marks and is aware of short cuts to high grades. His mental and physical health is excellent. He welcomes the advent of girls with typical adolescent enthusiasm. Though young, he is proficient in athletics, participating in and supporting baseball, soccer, swimming, basketball, tennis, hardball, and track. He may work after school and during the summer. He joins many clubs. His IQ is exactly at the median for the school; it is 140! He offers his teachers the greatest possible challenge, spiritually and professionally.

His parents may come from any one of many economic levels and be engaged in one of many types of work or professional activities. In any case they are keenly interested in his school and in his progress there.[21]

Potentially gifted pupils in the area of science are typically characterized by high verbal ability, high mathematical ability, superiority in various aspects of science which may be revealed on tests, a determination to use their abilities, and a searching, inquiring attitude. And they are, of course, interested in various aspects of science.

Some of these abilities are nurtured in a classroom where a capable teacher offers suitable motivation and varied opportunities for development. In this connection a serious problem arises because of the shortage of well-trained teachers. Not only is there a shortage of good teachers of science, but there are too few high schools equipped with the materials and laboratories necessary for an effective program in science. There is a great need for more adequate science offerings in high schools throughout the United

21 Morris Meister, "A High School of Science for Gifted Students," *The Gifted Child, op. cit.,* p. 222.

States. To provide them, the services of a comprehensive high school are necessary especially to offer challenging and rewarding experience to superior students.

THE GIFTED STUDENT IN CREATIVE ENDEAVOR

We have stressed the importance of a definition of giftedness which includes promise in the arts. How can such pupils be identified? What are their characteristics?

Several efforts are being made to locate such pupils. I have discussed some potentialities in the use of films to promote creative expression as well as to identify pupils gifted in creative writing.

The symbolic and imaginative short film, *The Hunter in the Forest*, prepared by Arne Sucksdorff, was shown in many schools. At the beginning of the picture, the section "A Story Without Words" provides an introduction for the pupils, who are invited to write their own stories about the film.[22]

Over 2,000 pupils wrote stories after viewing the film. These compositions were judged according to the degree to which the pupils displayed (1) genuine feeling; (2) sensitivity to the value of particular words, phrases, and larger units in expressing their reactions; (3) recognition of the film maker's intent and his use of symbol; and (4) appropriate and effective use of English.

Compositions of unusual quality were received from pupils in grades two to twelve. Some of the most outstanding products were obtained from fifth and sixth grade pupils, although the film technique was effective for adolescents as well as for younger pupils. The following is an example of the compositions at their highest level. Note the unusual use of language as well as the originality of interpretation:

Once upon a time there was a beautiful forest. In it were the graceful deer, the comical grouse, and the beauty of flowers and trees. Near this

[22] Paul Witty, "The Use of Films in Stimulating Creative Expression and in Identifying Talented Pupils," *Elementary English*, October, 1956, pp. 340-44. See also: Victor Lowenfeld, "Current Research on Creativity," *National Education Association Journal*, Vol. 47, No. 8, November, 1958; Paul Witty, James B. Conant, and Ruth Strang, *Creativity*, New York: Teachers College, 1959; Jacob W. Getzels & Philip W. Jackson, "The Meaning of Giftedness," *Phi Delta Kappan* XL. November, 1958.

forest lived a hunter, oblivious of these things. He was out for sport. He walked through the beautiful forest, crushing the tender blossoms, and breaking boughs of lovely trees. He saw a grouse, done up in feather finery, and killed it. He then put one of its tail feathers in his hat. Then he went home, satisfied with the day's kill. Then a rain came. The flowers, sprinkled with shining diamonds, did their exotic rain ballet. The trees swayed, too, with the gentle beat of the rain. The next day, the hunter again went into the forest. He set up a net for some unwary animal. Then something caught his eye. It was a deer family, grazing peacefully by the water. His hand touched the trigger. Just then something wonderful happened. As a flower opens, slowly, slowly, so the hunter's heart and eyes opened, slowly, slowly. The hunter, the destroyer of nature, awoke. Why, this wasn't something to destroy. It was something beautiful, sacred, it was the unspoiled, perfect beauty of God and nature. The hunter took down his net, lowered his gun and started home. Instead of a stalk, his steps were light and springy. The birds chirped. The squirrels chattered. Why hadn't he seen this before? He threw down the grouse feather, the symbol of his slaughter and put in its place a delicate flower. He walked along whistling. It was thus that the hunter found what so many long to find, a new world, a heaven on earth, a paradise. It's everywhere. It's beauty, purity, exotic grace. It is beauty of Venus, the kingdom of Pan, the haunts of Diana. Here, there is no past, no future, just now. Beautiful, happy now.[23]

Many other compositions were similarly remarkable. Throughout these compositions, written by elementary and secondary school pupils, originality of presentation and beauty of expression were found. They were the products of pupils who appeared to be potentially gifted in writing.

Many pupils who write effectively do not have intelligence quotients in the categories which would classify them as gifted. In fact, there appears to be only a slight relationship between the I.Q. and this type of creativity. The most superior writing, however, is generally by pupils with I.Q.'s above 110.

The pupil who has a potential gift in another field may reveal his promise by comparable, consistently superior performance. In some areas of creativity, gifted pupils may also make high scores on tests. But such tests are often unreliable. They may, however,

23 By Susan Dorris, a fifth grade pupil in Public School No. 23, Elizabeth, New Jersey.

supplement performance as a means of identifying the pupil of promise. A fundamental need of the gifted pupil is an opportunity for the release and development of his varied abilities in classrooms characterized by an atmosphere conducive to original expression.

THE GIFTED STUDENT IN THE AREAS OF SOCIAL LEADERSHIP

The pupil gifted in leading others may show an inclination to serve as an effective guide of different groups. Thus, fourteen-year-old Jane was selected on each of three successive years to be the leader of a state-wide organization for young people. Her ability to organize and direct groups was recognized in many local activities, too. She showed tact and understanding as she encouraged groups to differentiate between desirable and undesirable goals. She also displayed skill in helping others to decide upon the most appropriate, practical, and effective ways to achieve various goals. Her enthusiasm, interest, and competence in group pursuits served as an inspiration to other pupils. By her performance she demonstrated her talent for social leadership.

Thus, students gifted in social leadership may be recognized by their performance.[24] Their potentiality may be suggested further by sociometric measures, opinionaires, and nominating devices employed in the classroom. An "interest inventory" may also provide additional help in locating such pupils.

Student councils, widely used in high schools, offer an opportunity for enrichment of pupils' social experience. They may also become agencies for the identification of potentially gifted pupils in social leadership. Concerning these councils, Earl McWilliams writes:

Student Council organizations enable pupils to develop social leadership. These councils all across the country are grappling with the same type of problems, and it is encouraging to witness the democratic manner in which most of these organizations operate. The school government in Skokie School in Winnetka, Illinois, is outstanding both in the degree to which it really governs the life of the school and in the unique

---

24 Jack Kough and Robert F. DeHaan, *Identifying Children Who Need Help, Teachers Guidance Handbook,* Part I (Chicago: Science Research Associates, 1955). See also Paul Witty "The Gifted Person," *op. cit.*

structure of the school society of which it is a part. This school program offers a unique experience to its pupils, who live in a school environment which closely approximates our highly organized society, with a multitude of opportunities for gifted leadership to operate.[25]

That there is a low positive relationship between intelligence test results and social leadership has been suggested in studies of pupils of high I.Q. Relatively little is known, however, regarding the intelligence of various types of social leaders. Some writers believe that the group leader must not be too far removed in intelligence from the people he leads. This hypothesis should be examined carefully.

Relatively little has been done in the identification and study of the potentially gifted pupil in various types of social leadership. In several projects, however, such as those in Quincy and in Portland, criteria are being sought for identifying such pupils. And efforts in their behalf are being undertaken. But much remains to be accomplished.

MENTAL HEALTH

Every gifted pupil is an individual who needs guidance and sympathetic help. Difficulties and problems in his case, as in others of less marked ability, are traceable in large measure to a deprivation of basic needs. Since optimum conditions for human development are rarely found, basic needs are inevitably thwarted, and satisfying and socially desirable human relationships are many times precluded. Accordingly, the gifted pupil, like other pupils, encounters many obstacles to sturdy growth.

Pupils of high I.Q. are usually above average in mental health. They are somewhat more stable emotionally than their typical classmates. Their relative superiority persists through adolescence and young adulthood.[26]

There are, of course, many gifted pupils who experience serious

25 Earl McWilliams, "Enrichment Programs for Gifted Junior High School Pupils," *Bulletin of the National Association of Secondary School Principals,* September, 1956, pp. 72–81.

26 Lewis M. Terman and Melita H. Oden, "The Stanford Studies of the Gifted," in *The Gifted Child, op. cit.,* p. 25.

difficulties in personal and social adjustment. Some fail to realize their potentialities as students and consequently develop keen feelings of disappointment and inadequacy. Others are unsuccessful in social relationships, and still others display serious emotional maladjustments resulting from home conditions or parental expectations that are undesirable or unrealistic. Of course, various combinations of difficulties are found. In my early studies, failure in school work was found frequently among bright children who were withdrawn and socially inadequate, or indifferent and uninterested, or aggressive and antagonistic. C. M. Louttit listed these items among others as possible sources of difficulties in the gifted:

1. Lack of teacher's recognition of superiority leading to an antagonism toward the school as an institution.

2. Lack of parental recognition of superiority with resulting lack of stimulation or positive discouragement.

3. Superiority over available associates so marked that social adjustment is extremely difficult.[27]

And Lewis M. Terman and Melita H. Oden made this observation concerning individual differences in the patterns of personality problems:

. . . Gifted children do not fall into a single pattern but into a definite variety of patterns. One can find within the group individual examples of almost every type of personality defect, social maladjustment, behavior problem, and physical handicap; the only difference is that among gifted children the incidence of these deviations is, in varying degrees, lower than in the general population.[28]

Of interest is a report by Douglas Thom and Nancy Newell, who studied children with I.Q.'s above 130 who were referred to the Massachusetts Division of Mental Health.[29] About half of these children had been repeatedly punished, and more than half had been subjected to inconsistent discipline. Some parents were overprotective; others tended to exploit their children. Still others were inclined to thwart or discourage expression of interests and gifts.

27 C. M. Louttit, *Clinical Psychology* (New York: Harper and Brothers, 1936).
28 Terman and Oden, *op. cit.*, p. 25.
29 Douglas A. Thom and Nancy L. Newell, "Hazards of the High I.Q.," *Mental Hygiene,* January, 1945, pp. 61–77.

Nor had the school provided the guidance which these children appeared to require. Rarely indeed were opportunities offered for enriched experience and varied expression of creative ability. As a result of these conditions, a variety of behavior and emotional problems developed.[30]

The havoc resulting from the lack of a wholesome environment in early childhood is clear. Problem behavior is largely a result of failure to achieve a reasonably successful fulfillment of basic needs. Every child needs to feel that he and his attainment are acceptable—this feeling will nourish his future achievement and promote his growth. He needs to feel that he is a necessary, contributing member of his group. And he needs to love and be loved by persons he respects. Fulfillment of basic needs is necessary for desirable adjustment during adolescence as well as in childhood.

Some special types of problem are found somewhat frequently among gifted adolescents. These will be discussed briefly.

Problems Resulting from Lack of Challenge

A school whose curriculum provides only meager opportunities and makes few persistent demands on high ability is likely to be associated with attitudes of indifference or lack of interest on the part of the gifted. Lack of incentive is a primary cause of the gifted student's failure to develop an ideal of self that includes recognition of his high ability. Certainly "lack of college goal" has proved to be characteristic of many superior students who drop out of high school or fail to go to college.

Charles C. Cole has reported questionnaire results for 32,750 seniors, who were a random sample of students in public high schools. In addition to answering the questionnaire, these students also took a brief academic aptitude test. Analysis of the data for those in the upper 30 per cent of the aptitude test (9,689 seniors) yielded some significant facts regarding the desire to go to college and reasons for not planning to go.

Twelve per cent of the high scoring group indicated that *the* most important reason for not planning to go to college was financial

---

30 Ruth Strang, "Mental Hygiene of Gifted Children," in *The Gifted Child, op. cit.* See also Paul Witty "The Gifted Student in the American High School," *California Journal of Secondary Education,* Nov. 1958, Vol. 33, No. 7, p. 398 f.

need. Many others stated that financial need was an important consideration. But other considerations were also cited. The importance of "lack of college goal" was stressed.

About 25 per cent of the high-scoring boys and 45 per cent of the girls cited the lack of a college goal as possibly an important reason for not continuing their education. This suggests that there is considerable validity in believing that, despite the importance of financial need, lack of motivation for college is a stronger deterrent to college-going among those of high ability who do not go to college. About nine per cent of the boys and eighteen per cent of the girls say that they have no interest in higher education.[31]

The high frequency of little interest in school work is characteristic of drop-outs among the gifted. There have been several attempts to ascertain the characteristics of the unsuccessful gifted student as compared with the most successful student of comparable ability. A recent study sought

. . . to discover the circumstances and conditions which apparently influence some high school pupils of superior ability to a high level of academic accomplishment, while others of equal ability for some reason or reasons fail to realize proportionate accomplishment.[32]

In this study 237 superior high school pupils in Long Beach, California, were studied, and matched groups of low and high achievement were contrasted. Comparisons led to the following conclusions:

A pattern of circumstances was found which seemed to be closely related to high-level pupil achievement. The pattern was made up of six circumstances. The pupil associated with the complete pattern of circumstances could be described as a pupil (1) who is satisfactorily adjusted personally and socially, (2) who includes college in his plans for the future, (3) who has a fairly specific vocational choice of plan, (4) who indicates that his parents expect him to go to college, (5) who feels no parental disagreement with his vocational plans, and (6) who senses an inspiration or source of inspiration or encouragement to succeed.

31 Charles C. Cole, "Current Loss of Talent from High School to College, Summary of a Report," *Higher Education*, November, 1955, pp. 35–38.

32 Leslie J. Nason, *Academic Achievement of Gifted High School Students* (Southern California Education Monograph, No. 17, 1957).

The study concluded further: "The pattern of circumstances concerning the superior pupil's concept of himself and his orientation toward the future was closely related to his achievement."

The pattern above was clearly revealed in the boy of high achievement, who is described as follows:

A typical boy in the highest quintile of achievement was a boy who had satisfactory scores on a test of personality, who included college in his educational plans, who had fairly specific vocational plans, and who sensed the presence of inspiration or a source of encouragement to success; his parents expected him to go to college and did not oppose his vocational plans.

A number of factors thus contribute to the gifted pupils' success and satisfaction in school: favorable parental attitudes, high expectations, and successful personal and social adjustment.

L. M. Terman and Melita H. Oden compared the most successful with the least successful in a large group of young men who had all been identified as gifted children.[33] The successful group was designated as the A Group and the less successful as the C Group. The parents of the A Group were above those of the C in vocational status and cultural background. Moreover, the A Group had more books in their homes, and their parents had given home instruction somewhat more frequently. The members of the A Group were less often from broken homes. And they were three times as likely as the C's to have a father who was graduated from college.

Our own studies suggest the importance of early recognition of gifts on the part of parents and the importance of opportunities and stimulation for expression in the home. The pupils, too, need schools which continue to offer stimulation, encouragement, and varied opportunities for the expression and development of gifts.

Difficulties Traceable to Relative Speeds of Mastery of Different Tasks

Very bright youngsters may display marked feelings of inadequacy. These feelings are sometimes associated with physical size

[33] Lewis M. Terman and Melita H. Oden, *The Gifted Child Grows Up* (Stanford: Stanford University Press, 1947).

and development. Gifted pupils often choose older associates. They are somewhat accelerated in school. Hence their physical development is less advanced than that of their older classmates. Accordingly, they have abundant opportunities for unfavorable comparisons of their own relative success in physical feats. Because of his physical size, the gifted child may also be rejected socially. A feeling of inadequacy may result, too, from a pupil's realization of his own slowness in mastering a physical skill in contrast to his extremely rapid accomplishment of intellectual tasks.

Failing to receive recognition in physical and social pursuits, the gifted pupil sometimes will devote excessive time and effort to his studies. Yet his feeling of success in school work may not compensate for his deep feeling of inadequacy, since increased scholastic success may accompany increased separation or even isolation from his group. Perhaps this condition may account for the findings reported by J. W. Musselman, who discovered that in one group of bright high school pupils a good adjustment was associated with high average attainment, while poor adjustment was associated with the very highest attainment.[34]

Some pupils who are greatly accelerated in school suffer from feelings of loneliness and loss of social status. Much younger than their peers, they continue to feel a sense of social or physical inadequacy. Ruth Strang calls attention to the opinions of 56 gifted youngsters who had entered high school at eleven years of age.[35] They felt that thirteen was the best age to enter, for by that time a pupil would be able to hold his own. Much depends, in the case of acceleration, upon the particular nature of the pupil. To avoid unhappiness and disappointment, it is desirable to recommend acceleration only after a thorough case study is made and the conditions affecting each pupil are thoroughly explored. Human happiness and welfare depend not only on a pupil's ability to succeed academically but also on his success in achieving social recognition and acceptance.

[34] John M. Musselman, "Factors Associated with the Achievement of High School Pupils of Superior Intelligence," *Journal of Experimental Education,* September, 1942.
[35] Ruth Strang, "Mental Hygiene of the Gifted Children," in *The Gifted Child, op. cit.,* p. 137.

Social Maladjustment Associated with Parental Expectation

Parents of gifted children often expect them to maintain a very high level of scholarship. During the early years superior school records can usually be achieved by the gifted pupil without marked emotional disturbance. Harvey Zorbaugh points out, however, that as competition increases throughout the high school years, greater deprivations are exacted if excellent scholarship is to be maintained. He believes that many adolescents maintain their high educational status at a great emotional cost:

> While we have observed frequent exceptions, many [gifted pupils] show evidences of maintaining their level of function at increasing emotional cost. Some show a diminution of social interest, creativity and productivity. Still others, like the third of the children reported by Hollingworth, show no indication of marked constructive originality. A few remain remarkable only in that they continue to achieve high scores on intelligence tests. Exploration of these children's feelings about themselves convinces us that such changes, in the children in whom they occur, reflect an increasing absorption of emotional energies within themselves, which in turn result from an increasingly stressful social adjustment.

> We have had the opportunity to achieve a deeper insight into the emotional dynamics of the families from which highly gifted children come than had Terman or Hollingworth. These families, predominantly upper middle class, exhibit all the drives for advancement of their social status and for competitive success that Warner[36] has found characteristic of the upper middle class as a whole. Of superior intelligence, they hold high standards for themselves, and high expectations for their children. At the same time, they reveal more awareness of the disparity between what life might be and what it is, more frustration in themselves, and more apprehension for their children.

> This becomes doubly significant when related to the fact that these children are likely to have an unusual emotional value for their parents.... This is particularly true within upper-middle-class families. When we consider that highly gifted children tend to come from exceedingly small families the implications of this fact become obvious.[37]

---

[36] W. L. Warner, Marchia Meeker, and Kenneth Eells, *Social Class in America* Chicago: (Science Research Association, Inc., 1949). Cited by Harvey Zorbaugh and others.

[37] Harvey Zorbaugh, Rhea Kay Boardman, and Paul Sheldon, "Some Characteristics of Highly Gifted Children," in *The Gifted Child, op. cit.,* pp. 99–100.

The gifted adolescent needs guidance and experiences that will enable him to develop harmoniously and to work out an individually suitable ideal of self.

Difficulties Traceable to Differences Between Intellectual and Emotional Development

We have pointed out that the gifted pupil's rapid mental development is not accompanied by similarly accelerated physical, social, and emotional growth. As his understanding of play activities outstrips his ability to participate in them, so, too, his intellectual development usually surpasses his emotional development and control.

Again, conflict may be created within the highly gifted child's personality by the discrepancy between his intellectual and his emotional maturity. As Hollingworth noted, highly gifted children from an early age through adolescence into maturity, are concerned over the meaning of the world and their destiny in it. Such concerns may prove exceedingly stressful in view of the child's relative immaturity emotionally—may create active anxiety where family and school fail to provide the child the supporting security of warm and understanding relationships.

As the adolescent's world expands, he seeks increasingly for security within widening relationships: he feels the need of orienting his life in accord with social values which will give him satisfaction. But our culture is exceedingly heterogeneous, characterized by innumerable inconsistencies and conflicts among values, standards, conceptions of behavior, and ways of life. The need to work through and resolve these inconsistencies and conflicts is one of the major sources of adolescent stress in America.

The higher the adolescent's intelligence the more insistent is this need. At the same time, the higher the intelligence the more difficult the problem.[38]

The gifted adolescent often undergoes emotional conflict as he attempts to reconcile the behavior of man in a world of war and threat of war with the values he has been taught to revere. Insecurity and conflict over such issues are often experienced by the gifted. When the primary emphasis in the school is upon his academic attainment with little recognition of his emotional need, the pupil may experience serious anxiety. Such anxiety accompanied

[38] Harvey Zorbaugh and others, *op. cit.*, p. 103.

by other conflicts has been reported with unusual frequency among adolescents in the very highest categories of intelligence (I.Q. 180 plus). Certainly there is a great need to supplement the current interest in academic challenge for the gifted student with a similar concern for his personal, emotional, and social adjustment during the critical adolescent years.

The pupil of high verbal ability displays fewer emotional problems than his more typical classmates. Problems in meeting life's needs occur among all types of gifted pupils. Among children having special gifts in fields such as music and art, the incidence of such problems may indeed be higher than among the verbally gifted. The available data do not, however, provide a basis for reliable conclusions in this respect, though we do know that all gifted adolescents need patient counsel and appreciative guidance to achieve or maintain optimum development.

Conclusion

The intelligence test does not enable us to identify all gifted pupils. There are students whose outstanding potentialities in the arts or in social leadership can be recognized chiefly through their performance. Hence, our definition of giftedness should be revised to include any pupil whose performance, in a potentially valuable line of human activity, is consistently or repeatedly remarkable. This definition is being increasingly accepted.

The actual meaning of intelligence test results should be clearly understood. Both parents and teachers are often misled and attach too much significance to test results. It is unwise to regard a high I.Q. as more than an indication of possible accomplishment in one important area of human development. Outstanding accomplishment is a product of various other factors; some of them, such as drive or persistence are difficult to measure.[39] Nevertheless, the in-

[39] Paul A. Witty and Harvey C. Lehman, "Drive—A Neglected Trait in the Study of the Gifted," *Psychological Review,* 1927, pp. 364–76; Witty and Lehman, "Nervous Instability and Genius: Some Conflicting Opinions," *Journal of Abnormal and Social Psychology,* January, 1930, pp. 486–497; Witty and Lehman, "Ability Versus Effective Ability," *Psychological Review,* January, 1928; Paul Witty, "Interest and Success: The Antidote to Stress," *Elementary English,* December, 1955, pp. 507–13.

telligence test, wisely and widely used, will help us to identify one type of gifted pupil. We should seek out such pupils and provide the home and school opportunities merited by their abilities.

We should not neglect other types of gifts, however. We should strive on a widespread scale to identify gifted youth who have great promise in the arts, in social leadership, in mechanical ability, and in other areas. And we should aim to provide for all of them the varied opportunities essential to their full development.[40] For we need, in the United States, men and women of superior ability as leaders in business, art, education, journalism, labor, scientific research, and government. To realize their youthful promise, the gifted require appropriate educational opportunities, and they need also guidance and encouragement in order to develop stable personalities. Superior ability alone does not qualify an individual for outstanding accomplishment or leadership; training is required suitable to the responsibilities of various types of endeavor. In addition, the gifted should be encouraged to develop desirable character traits and to appreciate their social responsibility.

We are failing to develop fully the ability and talent of many potential leaders. To remedy this situation, we need not only the constructive endeavor of school people, but also the cooperation of informed parents and citizens generally in a determined effort to conserve ability and talent.

The problem of caring more adequately for the gifted pupil is closely linked with the larger problem of providing more suitable opportunities for all pupils. We should redouble our efforts to enable every boy and girl to attain his optimum development in accord with his unique nature and needs. Concerning this problem, as related to the education of the gifted student, John Hersey writes:

It is time to restore perspective to our views on help for the gifted. Educational practice is a set of slow pendulums. Just now the gifted child is in fashion—and in a little danger, too. . . .

The work of the Manhattan Project on the atomic bomb seems to have convinced many people that all that is needed to unlock extreme mysteries,

[40] For a study of current educational practice, see Paul Witty, "Our Schools Can Do Much for the Gifted Child," *The Nation's Schools*, February, 1956, pp. 65–72.

such as those of atomic energy or cancer or talent, is an act of Congress, or the banding together of many vast agencies and the expenditure of a huge sum of money.

But the job of freeing talent does not lend itself to this kind of attack. Talent is elusive, fragile, manifold, fast-moving, luminous, tantalizing, and incredibly beautiful, like aurora borealis on a cool September night. Who would give a weatherman a bag of money and tell him to go out and catch some northern lights?

The danger is that a "crash-program" approach to the problem of our country's need for talent may (a) not release talent, and (b) therefore produce disappointment and revulsion which would cause the pendulum to swing away from special help for the potentially talented.

The perspective that is needed is this: Our uncertainty about exactly how to develop talent is only one part of the greatest unsolved problem in American education—the problem of how to help every child realize his maximum potential; the problem indeed of individual differences.[41]

41 John Hersey, Chapter I, *Education for the Gifted*, *57th Yearbook of the National Society for the Study of Education*, Part II, pp. 4–5.

3

A Philosophic Viewpoint and a Suggested Program

William Heard Kilpatrick
Professor Emeritus, Teachers College, Columbia University

SINCE our American civilization is avowedly democratic, it follows that American education must prepare youth for democratic living. The aim will accordingly be to help each pupil to develop to the fullest what in him lies, for both his own happiness and the common good. In other words, this democratic education will stress the individual development of each child. We start with each one where he now is and help him as best we can to develop into a growing, self-directing, responsible, and creative personality.

Since our existing civilization is not perfect, a further major aim will be to improve our civilization. We thus stress creative and responsible citizenship—creative in that helpful new features may be devised for our growing civilization, responsible in that each new proposal may be reliably tested as to whether it makes for the common good.

Children and young people of school age are found to get on best in groups. Twenty-five is a good upper limit to the size of a school class. While children work best in groups, each child also has his own individuality; no two children are exactly alike in sensitivity or in ability. It is psychologically possible to make a group reasonably like-minded along some one chosen line, but there can be no such thing as an entirely homogeneous class group, for its members will differ in other respects.

39

A primary problem, probably *the* primary school problem, is (1) how to conduct a class as such and at the same time (2) take care of the individual needs of the class members. To cope successfully with this problem the teacher must study each child as fully as possible so as to learn his peculiar sensitivities, interests, attitudes, abilities, and tendencies. It will probably help such study if a teacher stays with the pupils of a particular class more than one year, but how many years is best we do not yet know.

A specific help in such study of an individual will be the approved standardized tests. For each pupil there should be a year-after-year abiding folder in which successive teachers put pertinent data of all kinds to help size up his tendencies and abilities.

The fact that children of school age are found to get on best when they work in groups is not to be understood as meaning that all individual work must be in groups. For many reasons each individual also has to learn to work alone. For class work it may be well for all to work together for part of the day and separately and individually for another part of the day. I suggest that the teacher experiment by having the class work as a group for two thirds of the time and as separate individuals for one third of the time. If the school can afford it, helpers for the teacher might well be added during the time of individual work so that each pupil may receive the specific help that he needs.

A few words about the curriculum may now be appropriate.

In the traditional school the curriculum was prepared in advance and given to the teacher. The content was usually written down in textbooks, divided by the teacher into "lessons," and thus assigned to the pupils for study and subsequent recitation and examination. For such courses as history or rhetoric the teacher would assign a lesson—perhaps a chapter, perhaps the next ten pages. A typical way of studying was for a pupil to read a lesson and try to repeat it with the book open until he could repeat it with the book closed. In the recitation the pupil would repeat whatever the teacher called for.

This kind of teaching-learning represented the Renaissance with its feudal class system and its strong interest in scholarship, its fundamental aim being to develop scholarliness in a selected few. The hope was that what was thus memorized would in time be understood; that what was understood would in time be appreciated; and that what was appreciated would be joined with other appreciated and pertinent content to form "learning." This was what Festus had in mind when he said, "Paul, thou art beside thyself, much learning [literally, many books] hath made thee mad."

In democratic America from such teaching-learning only a small proportion at the top attain any high degree of scholarship; the majority forget what they have "learned" soon after the examinations are over.

A NEWER CONCEPTION OF EDUCATION

A quite different and not fully understood conception of education has developed in America within recent years.

1. The aim of education is not to be primarily book knowledge or learning, but rather, more inclusively, living the good life, living the life good to live. And the word "good" is (though that is perhaps the most essential part in it) but the consummating good, like a good apple or a good book or a good road, in which "good" means *good for the purpose under consideration*. A good apple is an apple good to eat; a good book is a book good to read; a good road is a road good to travel.

2. A second aim of education, which is *means* to the good life *as end*, is to support, promote, and improve our civilization. Preparing pupils increasingly to understand our civilization, to learn how to make it work, and if possible to improve upon it is a more concrete aim than that of living the good life. As it is more concrete, it is more immediately and more surely understood by the pupils. Attaining this second aim is a long and gradual process. The child begins upon it almost as soon as he is born; each day brings its addition. Parents and teachers must help the child digest his successive experiences so as to form appropriate concepts and generalizations. The child learns. He becomes intelligent as he grasps the connection between what he does and what happens in consequence. In this way effective intelligence is developed. It is also in this way that the individual, if fortunate, acquires the habit of "learning to learn."[1]

3. The third aim of education is to help each pupil to develop in the best possible way those traits of character which are needed for attaining the two preceding aims.

[1] Adapted from J. L. Childs, University of Michigan School of Education Bulletin, May, 1958, p. 116b.

4. The fourth aim of education is to find and use such teaching-learning procedures as are mostly likely to develop those human traits which are needed for the three preceding aims.

Some people may say that for education to aim at the good life is at best a theoretical objective, not a practical one. There does remain, however, a large area of the good life about which the wisest among us are in substantial agreement: bodily health, the well-adjusted personality, effective intelligence, moral integrity, respect for the rights and feelings of others, regard for the common good, favorable attitudes toward art and literature, moral and healthful pastimes. All such the school must try to teach.

A fair conception of the good life helps us to define "morality," "democracy," and "education": morality is the obligation to act and live so as to bring the good life as best possible to all affected by one's acts and life; democracy is the effort to run society on the basis of bringing the good life equally to all by letting them inclusively manage the common life; education is the effort to lead the young —and all of us—to learn and live the good life.

THE TEACHER-LEARNER PROCESS

Any proposal along this line must meet two essential require-ments. It must be scientifically defensible. It also must be the best known way for building the human traits described under the third aim.

Fundamental to the older conception of school learning was memorization. Plutarch, writing in the second century A.D., said that "the memory of children . . . is, as it were, the storehouse of all learning; . . . nothing doth so beget or nourish learning as memory." We now have a different definition of the verb "to learn":

Anything—a thought, an attitude, a bodily movement, any phase or aspect of an experience—has been learned in the degree that it will stay thereafter with the learner to get back at the right time into his life experience to play there its appropriate part.

And how is such learning effected? The answer is that we learn to behave a certain way by behaving that way wholeheartedly, accepting that way of behaving as one's own. To learn anything we have to live that thing:

I learn what I live and I learn it as I accept it to act on. I learn it in the degree that I live it, in the degree that I feel it important for me and to my values and in the degree that it is interrelated with what I already know and value.

With this definition of "to learn" and this statement as to how learning takes place, we can go back to an earlier statement that probably *the* primary problem of the teacher is how to take care of the individual learner, how to take him as he now is and help him to put heart and soul into what he is doing so that he will *grow* from each succeeding experience to other creative experiences.

EDUCATION FOR THE GIFTED

Many people tend to discuss only the intellectually gifted. But we must not so limit our conception of the gifted. We must also include all who show consistently remarkable performance in any worthwhile line of endeavor. The term *gifted* must include not only the intellectually gifted but all who show promise in music, the arts, creative writing, dramatics, mechanical skills, and social leadership. This broader definition is needed because it serves better the common good by involving both more people and all the different kinds of useful ability.

What education is desirable for the gifted child? It must include the fullest possible development of the specific gift, for both the satisfaction of the child and the social contribution that he can make. In our democratic society it must also prepare him to fill his place as a citizen and as a member of the social group to which he will belong. Some people have tended to limit the education of the gifted solely to the development of their specific gifts, but democracy cannot be content with such narrowness.

How—considering the democratic principle of "equal rights for all, special privileges for none"—can we give each gifted child the peculiar development that his gift demands? How can the teacher help each individual in his class to develop his special personal gifts while at the same time he lives as a pupil in the surrounding class and community?

Possibly the best way of examining specific answers to these questions is to start with a typical school in a typical American city.

THE TYPICAL ELEMENTARY SCHOOL LEADING TO THE JUNIOR HIGH SCHOOL

The school system of this typical, not too large city has a number of elementary schools, a smaller number of junior high schools, and a still smaller number of comprehensive senior high schools, the whole being arranged on the 6-3-3 plan. The system has one or more general supervisors in the elementary schools and one or more special supervisors in art and music. These, both general and special, help new teachers get adjusted and give special attention to classes where supervision is needed. Their special duty is to encourage the teachers to study their classes to find those who call for special attention, whether among the less gifted or among the more gifted. Properly chosen standardized tests can help here.

Suppose 123 pupils enter the first grade in a single year. This will mean five first grade teachers, since no class should have more than 25 pupils. These 123 pupils can be arranged in alphabetical order and divided into five groups, two of 24 each, three of 25 each, and three going to the most promising teachers. The alphabetical division will make probable an average choice for the classes. The next year the principal, in conference with the supervisors, can choose which teachers can best go on to second grade with their classes. If a particular teacher has not done a good job, it would seem fairer to her pupils to give them a better teacher the second year. In this case the superintendent will have to choose the incoming teacher and decide what to do with the less successful one.

Under the principal's guidance the teachers will meet from time to time to make a desirable "map of values" for each of the several grades, having in mind (1) the continuous development of these pupils from six to thirteen years of age and (2) the appropriate subject matter for each grade. This is a perpetual problem, and the resulting map of values must not unduly limit the freedom of each teacher to choose with the class its own succession of activities through which to attain the values set forth in the map. An instance of subject matter for the third grade might be long division. Suppose the year is running out and some teacher is behind on long division. He could guide the next choice so that that activity will involve long division. The teacher might explain that long division is on the required list and ask the class to help find an activity that involves it. Analogous efforts are possible along other lines. To allow for desirable teacher-class freedom, however, the map should not be too exacting.

Let us now choose the fourth grade in which to consider more particularly the study of the pupils and the treatment of the gifted. Suppose that this is the second year the teacher is to be with these pupils. Before the school year opens he secures the folders for all his pupils and studies them carefully. For the first day he puts on the wall and table some of the best specimens of third grade work done during preceding years. He encourages the pupils to notice these as they come in. When the class starts, he can ask the pupils to tell what they did on their vacations; hoping thereby to get some suggestions for the beginning activity of the year. After they have talked of vacations awhile, he will shift attention to the conscious choice of the initial activity, and write various more promising suggestions on the board. As he thinks of the first choice, which the pupils are to make under his guidance, he has in mind four desirable features: (1) it must not be too easy, for that would fail to stir their best efforts; (2) it must not be too difficult, for that would bring frustration and discouragement; (3) it must lead toward one or more items on the school's map of values for the fourth grade; and (4) it must enlist the active interest of as large a proportion of the class as possible.

With these in mind the teacher directs the class discussion around which, if any, of the proposed activities to choose. As the children get older, these four aims may well be given to them to get them more fully "into the game" with the teacher. Of the four, the last will probably most often prove the most important, but divisions of interest tend to disappear the more a class works successfully along these lines and once it has made a reasonably good choice and has actively begun to map out the attack.

The class must now map out the steps of a program with which to carry out the activity. In this, as well as in choosing the activity, the teacher guides not so much by making positive proposals as by asking pertinent questions. It would be disastrous for the pupils to form the habit of waiting for the teacher to make constructive proposals. What we seek as absolutely necessary is active and creative interest from the pupils. The more fully they give themselves to what they are doing and the more creative they are in carrying out the activity, the more surely will they learn and the more constructively will they think and relate what they are now doing with what they remember from the past. In this way they build conceptions, attitudes, and generalizations; out of these they build responsible characters—desirable all-round characters to prepare them for all the varied aspects of life. This is essential in a world which is changing as rapidly as ours, especially in this country where the changes have brought us world responsibilities, for which we are not yet adequately prepared.

A map of values leads the pupils into social activities. In the class itself we have already seen discussion and decisions. Pupils have to learn to discuss issues constructively. Many adults get angry at opinions opposed to theirs; we must bring up a generation able and disposed to think constructively in response to contradictory opinions. This is a basic value in the social scene, but there are many others. A class is itself a social body and must learn to act accordingly. A class is also part of the larger school whole, and it must act according to this social whole. Also, there is the surrounding community. This fourth grade must plan trips into the community, to learn more fully what the community is and how it acts. When the pupils are old enough, they may find opportunities to share in community activities. This is a significant educational possibility.

But, someone may ask, what about the gifted? So far little if anything has been said about them.

Some of the gifted will be prominent in the class discussions. The intellectually and socially gifted pupils, especially those who are overt and outgoing, will take a leading part in the activities of the group as a whole, as well as those involving drawing and painting, or music. Those notably good along these lines will be prominent.

But it is in the period of individual work that the gifted will especially work. Each one will now have the opportunity to follow his particular interest. This may show itself in reading, history, art, science. In later high school years, however, science and mathematics are most manifest.

In thus helping gifted pupils to learn, much will, to be sure, depend on the teacher. If he does not know much more than the bright pupil who is working along a particular line, he will have little opportunity to help him learn. This is presently perhaps the greatest single obstacle to providing effective education for the gifted. Most teachers are not prepared to help the advanced gifted child. If we are to succeed with the education of the gifted, our colleges and schools of education must make special efforts to prepare teachers to help the advanced gifted.

THE HIGH SCHOOL TREATMENT OF THE GIFTED

We are still considering the school system in a not too large city. The high school, whether junior or senior, offers two special opportunities to the gifted—the *core work program* and the *elective system*. In the core program a special teacher is in charge of the common work of all the pupils of a grade, or several such, if there are enough pupils in that grade to make several sections. The teacher of the sixth grade has all-day charge of the all-round education of these children, and this sixth grade all-round education was common to all. By contrast, the high school brings in for the first time a division in what is taught: some is common to all, but some is chosen by each pupil with the advice of guidance personnel, the principal, and his parents.

The common learnings are under the direction of the core teacher. We have not yet had enough experience of core work to be sure how much time the core teacher should have. The following proposal is a proposal for experimentation: the seventh grade core teacher should have the pupils for three fourths of the school day. His work resembles that of the sixth grade teacher, the main differences being that the sixth grade teacher has his pupils for the whole school day, and the seventh grade is a year older than the sixth grade. In all other respects the sixth grade teacher and the seventh grade core teacher have the same duties—to help each pupil to full development as best as possible; and to help each pupil learn all the common learnings belonging to that age for which the school holds itself responsible.

In the eighth grade the core teacher should have charge for 70 per cent of the day; in the ninth grade, 65 per cent; and so on to the twelfth grade, where 50 per cent of the time will be devoted to core activities.

No one is fit to teach a core class who did not major in core work in his college preparation. Some people will ask whether we can expect a twelfth grade core teacher to know all the common learnings expected of the twelfth grade. If the pupils can learn them, surely the teacher should be able to do so.

It is here suggested—again for experiment—that the core teacher's work day be divided into the same two parts as the sixth grade teacher's, namely, two thirds of the day given to the group working all together, and one third to work by the class as individuals. This period for individual work offers great opportunity for each gifted child to pursue, under teacher guidance, his own special interests and talents.

No one teacher can give adequate care to 25 separately working high school individuals. Each core teacher should have one or more assistants—perhaps student teachers from a teachers college, possibly some advanced students who themselves expect to teach and would like this beginning experience, or perhaps hired helpers. In any case these teachers will need help.

High School Elective Work

With the core teachers carrying more than half the high school work, the elective work can be better adjusted to the individual needs of each pupil. The less capable students can choose according to their needs and interests so that more exacting courses can be left to the more capable students. In this way such courses as physics and mathematics—to mention two now in the limelight for the gifted—need not have the laggards that in the past have plagued them. With the core teachers taking care of the common needs and a variety of electives, sorting out all according to their needs and interests, elective courses can give to every variety of gifted each his opportunity at a course designed specifically for his needs. The needs of the gifted are thus well met, partly by individual work of the successive cores and partly by the elective courses expressly designed to meet them.

A special word can be added regarding the teaching of elective courses. The thoughtful careful work counted desirable for the third and fourth grades was earlier discussed. The teachers of the high school electives should use equally creative thought and skill in directing the work of their classes. I can testify from personal experience that creative work with all high school mathematics pays rewarding dividends. As a high school teacher I found this particularly true of algebra and geometry. One student, for instance, who was previously considered too dull to learn arithmetic, grew under a specific creative effort to be the most beautifully sensitive reasoner of all my high school and college students. Creative teaching is not limited to mathematics; there are great possibilities along all lines of academic work and at all levels of teaching. Thoughtful creative work pays in teaching as it does in all other activities of life. We cannot commend it too highly, and most of all for the teachers of the gifted that they may in fact rise to their highest potentialities.

Special Classes or Special Schools for the Gifted

The pro and con of having special classes or schools for the gifted with different type of communities is well discussed by Robert J. Havighurst in Chapter XVII of the fifty-seventh yearbook of the National Society for the Study of Education.

Democracy demands equal treatment; each pupil fit to go to school shall be educated to the best that in him lies. The program set forth above will, if properly carried out, take reasonable care of the gifted. It does, however, require better educated, more devoted, and more discerning teachers, both elementary and secondary, than most communities now have. It requires core teaching of a kind and a degree seldom attained. It requires, finally, for the individual period of the core work, helpers of a kind not usually available.

Now we face a new problem, namely, shall we favor special

classes for the gifted? And more, shall we have special schools for the gifted?

Fundamentally the general temper of the American people seems to be against such. To be sure, we have always had some who take exactly the opposite ground. In the Federalist days many claimed special privileges for themselves as "the wise, the rich, and the good." Few have used such plain words since those days, but the temper persists.

There is, however, a valid reason for bringing together the selected gifted to work as a school class. It seems to be true that the gifted when so brought together stimulate each other to higher levels of accomplishment than under any other conditions.

If we compare the separation of the gifted with the X, Y, Z grouping which was common in our country some three decades ago, a real difference appears. The grouping then was into three parallel groups—the more capable, the average, and the less capable. At that time both educators and parents came to reject this grouping. No matter what name was officially given to the less capable group, all the rest of the pupils looked down upon them contemptuously and called them names. This seemed, as stated, too strong a violation of American democracy to be tolerated, and the X, Y, Z grouping was almost completely abolished.

Now, however, we see a difference. If the gifted are separated from the rest, the least gifted still remain in the group with the average students; and, as Havighurst says explicitly, parents in large cities do not object to such selected classes or even to selected schools as they do in small cities, especially in suburbs. New York City has a very successful high school of science and a similarly successful high school of music and art.

Possibly the United States will carry these two opposed views continually in the different kinds of communities. Possibly we can meanwhile study the problem more thoroughly. In rural areas it remains difficult. At best, school buses allow the schools of a large district or a small county to be so consolidated as to approximate the efficiency of a small city; but as matters now stand, most rural high schools are too small to provide sufficient elective courses for the gifted. So that in any probable future the gifted in rural districts[2] will suffer in comparison with the rest of the country unless some new plan is put forward to seek them out and provide scholarships for them in special boarding schools. But this does not now seem likely.

2 Chapter 7 should be consulted to see how one rural community is approaching its problem.

PART II

PROGRAMS
FROM ABROAD

4

Ideas from Secondary Education in the U.S.S.R.

Goodwin Watson
Teachers College, Columbia University

It is ironical that current efforts on behalf of gifted youth in the United States should have been stimulated especially by recent achievements in a country which resists the idea of any distinctive program for secondary school pupils of outstanding ability. To understand why a book like this would be unlikely to appear in Soviet Russia, it is necessary to review some features of their quite different social and psychological orientation.

Forty-two years ago, in the Revolution of October 1917, councils (or soviets) of factory workers and peasants, led by a handful of fanatical Marxist theorists, took over the power of the state. Most of the bourgeois intellectuals, who had furnished what educational leadership Czarist Russia had known, were exiled, executed, alienated, or suspect. Lenin, Krupskaya, Lunacharsky, and their colleagues faced the herculean task of creating intellectual leadership for all the arts and sciences of the complicated modern world from a working-class population more than 80 per cent of whom were illiterate.

In theory the Marxists held that the backwardness of the peasants was due not to any innate limitations but to barriers imposed by the exploiting classes. The old rulers—political, economic, and religious —were regarded as superior not in endowment but only in educational privilege. These theories led in practice to emphasis upon *universal* education: universal literacy; a universal four year school; later, a universal seven year school; today, a universal ten year school; in the future, an eleven or a twelve year school open to everyone.

Psychological theory in Soviet Russia must accord with the dialectic materialism which is basic in Marxist doctrine. Pavlov has become the great exemplar of the correct approach. Since mind is not an "idealistic" entity, but is simply the product of constant interaction between the physical organism of man and our material environment (however culturally elaborated), individual differences are to be attributed basically to differences in the cumulative interactions. An ideological controversy led in 1935 to abolition of intelligence tests in schools of the U.S.S.R. It was argued that the scores obtained on such tests reflected background and opportunity to date, not future potential.

Soviet psychologists I have interviewed recently contend that if a secondary school pupil has difficulty with algebra or with the Chinese language, it does no good to blame his low I.Q. It is far better, they believe, to try to find out where he has missed some essential learning at an earlier stage. Perhaps he failed properly to connect number or language symbols with his experience of concrete objects. The task of the teacher and the psychologist is to diagnose and to remedy the specific gap in the learning sequence. It is assumed that all minds are essentially alike in their capacity to learn. The problem is to provide suitable learning opportunities and powerful motives.

Emphasis upon the gifted seems, from the Soviet viewpoint, a kind of rationalization of a class-structured society. It is but a short step, as they see it, from viewing certain pupils as innately superior to viewing a privileged class as entitled by inheritance to own the instruments of economic production and to employ at wages as low as feasible the menials not so favored by heaven. In short, the concept of the gifted is a useful rationalization of inequalities of economic position.

It remains true, nevertheless, in Russia as in America that some pupils do get better school marks, do show more musical talent, and do prove more effective as leaders. Our purpose in the remainder of this chapter will be to examine the provisions actually made in Russia for these abler adolescents. In each instance we shall try to evaluate the suitability of such an activity for the American high school.

AMERICAN IDEAL

The most important difference in educational policy between the best American high schools and their opposite numbers in the Soviet Union has been the wider range of electives provided in the schools of the United States. The formal curriculum of the high schools of the Soviet Union is essentially uniform, for bright or for dull, for girls or for boys, for city or for rural youth, from Kiev across all the 8,000 miles to Kamchatka. It matters not whether the individual has much or little aptitude for art or mathematics or mechanics or foreign languages; he studies the same school textbooks for the same number of hours and must be prepared to answer the same written and oral examinations.

It is popular in some circles in America at present to criticize our schools for the rich range of electives, decrying courses in such nonacademic areas as homemaking, automobile mechanics, fashion design, recreational swimming, retail salesmanship, and beauty parlor techniques. These contemporary critics appear to prefer the more austere, traditional, and rigid Soviet curriculum. One may agree that in some instances American pupils have been permitted to coast along through a program of not very intellectual activities, to the detriment of their habits of prolonged study, mental effort, and critical judgment. At the same time we should be careful not to discard courses and projects which have real educational value for many other pupils.

We in America have been correct in our basic assumption that pupils do differ in their interests, abilities, and purposes. We have been right to assume further that educational content can and should be adapted to such differences. If all gifted pupils have not been continuously challenged to give their best efforts, that laxity can be remedied without depriving the modern high school curriculum of its broad range of resources.

TEN FEATURES OF SOVIET EDUCATION

Ten features of Soviet education contribute to the high quality of performance by able students.

1. The intellectual challenge of the stiff academic curriculum.
2. The social climate of respect for intellectual achievement.
3. The social climate of hard work.
4. Cooperative work within the school class.
5. Enrichment assignments for abler pupils.
6. Projects in Pioneer and Komsomol circles.
7. Correlation of academic subjects with complicated practical activities (polytechnics).
8. Highly competitive selection for advanced study.
9. Economic subsidies for most students in higher education.
10. Special schools for certain kinds of talent.

Each of the practices above will be described briefly and evaluated for its applicability in American secondary schools.

The Stiff Academic Curriculum

The curriculum in the upper years of the Russian ten year school is more difficult and intellectually challenging than that of typical public or private secondary schools in the United States. In mathematics all seventh year pupils in Moscow are expected to complete algebra factoring problems which would be regarded as difficult for capable ninth-graders in Detroit or Denver. All tenth year students are now given trigonometry, binomial theory, combinations and permutations, and are soon to be expected to master calculus. The biological sciences (biology, botany, zoology, anatomy, physiology, and psychology) begin at age eleven and continue for seven years. Physics begins in the third grade and continues for seven years. Chemistry runs for six years. Science and mathematics make up nearly half the curriculum. A foreign language begins—in some new-type Russian schools—in the second grade, and in those schools pupils are expected to be able to use the foreign language for the study of other subjects during the last two years of high school. Russian pupils learn more of world geography, world history, and world economics (from the Com-

munist angle, of course) than do most students in American secondary schools. Art, music, and physical education are not neglected.
This curriculum keeps able students challenged; it must seem
overwhelming to below-average adolescents. It is possible that the
Russians will eventually reduce their demands upon slow learners;
the reforms of 1959, however, propose merely to spread out the study
over a longer period during which work and school are combined.

Respect for Intellectual Achievement

Marx and Lenin, whose pictures adorn the walls of almost every
Russian school, were intellectuals. Among the highest paid and
most honored workers in the Soviet Union today are the professors
—especially those elected to the status of "Academician." Adult
education was developed in the fight for literacy and continues to
engage millions of adult white collar, factory, and farm workers.
Parents as well as children are studying. The daily newspapers
most widely circulated—*Pravda* and *Izvestia*—contain serious essays
of the kind read in the United States by only the tiny minority
who peruse journals of opinion.

In this Russian climate of opinion able pupils choose teaching in
preference to less honored and less well-paid careers in business,
law, or medicine. It is common for a gifted high school pupil in
America to recognize certain of his teachers as more slow-witted
and less well informed than he is. By paying the average teacher
less than we pay the average factory worker, we in the United
States run the risk of filling the ranks of the teaching profession
with people unable to get admitted to other professional schools
or with girls interested in a temporary occupation before marriage.
Fortunately we do still find some first rate minds and able scholars
making a lifetime teaching career in our high schools; the proportion of such talented and skilled professionals is, however, notice-
ably higher in the U.S.S.R. today.

Another consequence—or evidence—of the different climate of
opinion is the high respect which Russian pupils themselves seem
to give to those who win high academic grades. While sports and
social activities are normally encouraged as part of all-round development, the prestige of leaders in these fields is reported to be

lower than that awarded to good scholars. The choice of leaders in the Pioneer Circle and the Young Komsomols—first steps on the ladder of political power in the Soviet Union—is usually dependent upon a high academic average. Soviet teachers do not seem to feel that they have to contend with anti-intellectual mores in the peer group.

Hard Work Is Habitual

A group of parents in a comfortable suburb on Long Island Sound asked me why American adolescents do not go to school six days a week as the Russian youth do. An answer necessarily takes into account the style of life of the parents. We value the leisure time interests that have been made possible by our shorter work week and high standard of living. In the early days of the Soviet Union, men and women, driven by economic necessity and political pressures (internal and external), worked 14 or 15 hours a day at one or two jobs and did "social work" as "volunteers" in the remaining hour or two of waking time. During what Russians call the "Great Patriotic War," residents of Stalingrad, Leningrad, and many other Soviet cities were under siege, short on goods and manpower, and driven to toil night and day for defense. By comparison, a 48 hour week now seems luxurious relaxation.

When both father and mother are accustomed to long hours and only one rest day, it seems reasonable enough to Russian pupils to go to school six hours a day, six days a week, and to have two or three hours of homework every evening. Actually the Russian child, in his 10 year school, gets more classroom hours and more homework hours than do American pupils in the 12 years from first grade through high school. It is likely that the universal school will be extended in the near future to 11 or 12 years, giving the typical secondary school graduate in Russia the time equivalent of American students completing junior college. This heavy time load is carried by teachers as well as by pupils.

Cooperative Work Within the School Class

Current studies in the psychology of teaching in the U.S.S.R. emphasize the importance of the school class as a unit. One investigator has reported that pupils learn better from a science demonstration performed by one of their own familiar classmates than from one performed by a stranger. An effort is made to keep the whole class together for the ten years from school entrance until graduation. Since families are much less mobile in the Soviet Union than in the United States, more classes remain intact. Pupils are encouraged to help one another. Performance is graded on a more or less absolute scale, not "on the curve"; a grade of "5" ("A," or excellent) given to one pupil is not supposed to reduce the others' chances of also getting "5." All that is required is letter-perfect mastery of the assignment. More advanced pupils are expected to help the slower learners. The gifted thus become assistant teachers in their class. Often a pupil understands his classmate's explanation better than he would the teacher's. As he explains to his classmates, the able pupil notably increases his own grasp of the subject. Many a teacher has said, "I never really understood this until I had to teach it!"

Enrichment

Soviet teachers generally report that they do expect more work from some pupils than from others in the same class. A Moscow teacher of high school English, for example, used a textbook containing excerpts from stories by Jack London, Charles Dickens, Theodore Dreiser, and numerous other British and American writers. She was satisfied if the slower pupils mastered the selections in the textbook, but she kept unabridged copies of the original books in English in the library so that faster learners could read them.

A Moscow exhibit of selected projects worked out in science classes (the exhibit was being used to give in-service teachers advanced training in improving their own techniques) showed that abler students had worked with their teachers in developing some extraordinary apparatus and charts. Art and craft exhibits showed similar opportunities for special achievement by the specially talented within the regular school class. "We respect our young people," said one Russian educator, "and to respect is to make demands!"

Pioneer and Komsomol Circles

Extraschool activities for youth are fostered by the Young Pioneers (ages 9 to 14) and the Komsomols (Young Communist League, ages above 14). Almost all school children belong to these organizations. In larger cities a "Pioneer Palace" houses the numerous activities: sports, musical, dramatic, technological, nature study, et cetera. Each Pioneer belongs to a certain platoon and troop but may, in addition, choose from among many clubs (called "circles") one which especially interests him. He may join a circle which runs model railroads (large enough for young riders), produces ballets, constructs television sets, plays chamber music, or arranges tours and excursions. We saw an excellent little planetarium in Leningrad built and operated by a youth circle. Gifted young people thus have, outside the school, a rich set of opportunities for the cultivation of intellectual and aesthetic interests.

In larger cities club activities are led by specially trained professional workers. If other school teachers take on such leadership after school hours, they receive extra pay. The Komsomols publish the school newspaper and serve as the equivalent of a student council in supervising pupil activities. The school Komsomol organization appoints its ablest members to be leaders of Young Pioneer platoons. Thus again we see gifted adolescents enlisted to help the younger children.

City, regional, and All-Union festivals celebrate anniversaries of national history, world culture, and science. Exhibitions are arranged for orchestral, choral, painting, sculpture, dance, and numerous athletic competitions. In many centers there are well-equipped stations which serve as laboratories and workshops for the out-of-school interests of young naturalists, geologists, chemists, aviators, et cetera.

In addition to two hours of homework, an able adolescent, in school from 9 A.M. to 3 P.M., may have on two or three days a week four to six hours of activity in his Pioneer or Komsomol organization or special interest circle. One reason for infrequent juvenile delinquency in Russia may be the heavy schedule of school and extraschool activities. Pupils who fall behind in their school work must drop out of club activities. Fellow members in the Pioneers and fellow classmates join in the effort to enable slower students to keep up with the heavy load of work.

Polytechnics

Soviet educators, proceeding from materialistic premises concerning the nature of intelligence and from equalitarian views of a classless society, have consistently emphasized practical work alongside the learning of theory. When the Soviet technology was primitive, the school curriculum included simpler manual activities such as woodwork and metalwork. Today, as agriculture has become scientific and as automatic machines operate in factories, school polytechnics has kept pace and is often highly complicated. One psychologist commented that as technology advances, "practical work" demands more and more of the higher levels of science and mathematics.

Soviet teachers are expected to establish cooperative two-way relationships with the agriculture or industries of their neighborhood. Farm and factory experts come into classrooms, and pupils go out into the practical setting to observe, to study, and, where possible, to help. School subjects include assignments correlated with practical operations. One argument for extending the present ten year school to twelve years is that, without reducing academic content, more time could be given to practical training.

One consequence of strong emphasis in school upon the skills and insights of polytechnics is that the pupils with high verbal abilities are not allowed to neglect the development of mechanical and other practical skills. The Soviet Union is trying to prepare all of its pupils for effective life in the modern world. Therefore, everyone must study trigonometry and a foreign language; everyone must be able to use tools and to repair a motor.

Pupils who graduate with high grades and who score high on the university entrance examinations may go on directly to college. Others are expected to work for two or three years on farms or in factories before they can be admitted to higher education. This requirement, like polytechnical training, serves to reduce the gap between the ordinary worker and the intellectual elite.

Premier N. S. Khrushchev, in September 1958, called for increasing stress on practical preparation for work. This was followed by policy decisions of a like nature in the Supreme Soviet in December, 1958.

Competitive Selection for Higher Education

Some selection goes on as pupils drop out because of the stiff demands of the Russian secondary school. The present ideal is that most pupils shall finish the ten year school. This is a new expectation, and in the effort to meet it teachers appear to be conducting final examinations with some leniency toward weaker pupils. Since major examinations are oral and individual, this can be done without lowering demands upon the better students. The Ministry of Education of the Russian Republic reports that in the cities 90 per cent of pupils now complete the ten year school.

The really strenuous competition in Russia comes with the attempt to get into college. High school graduation is not in itself sufficient for admission. All institutions of higher education conduct their own entrance examinations, both written and oral. Only "gold medal" graduates of the secondary school are excused from entrance exams. Current figures for the Russian Republic indicate that 22 per cent of the graduates of all ten year schools enter higher institutions for full-time study, while an additional 15 per cent take up advanced study at night or by correspondence. In a fairly typical pedagogical institute in Moscow, the entering class of 100 was selected from about 1,000 applicants. While Moscow may be more popular, colleges in more than 200 other Soviet cities also select from an excess of applicants. One basis for Khrushchev's current criticisms is that universities have room for only one out of three or four graduates of the secondary school.

Reduce Barriers to Higher Education

One reason for the popularity of higher education is that it is almost wholly subsidized. A student who is accepted for university work receives from the government a stipend which covers the cost of board, room, tuition, and incidentals. Need is one factor in the award of subsidies. Students with high grades receive about 25 per cent additional subsidy. If grades fall down to "3" ("C" level) or include any "2's," students can remain in college only at their own expense. Over 80 per cent of the students in higher education receive subsidies.

In some remote areas, where the sparse population does not justify local secondary schools, pupils receive subsidies for travel and living costs at boarding schools. The Soviet Union thus tries to develop all of the potential talent of its youth. In other countries some able pupils fail to get to high school because they live too far away, and many fail to go on to college because they can not afford the expense. The U.S.S.R. strives to eliminate geographic and economic barriers to higher education. Sex and race also constitute barriers in some countries. Racial discrimination is illegal in the U.S.S.R., and the reduction of sex prejudice is indicated by such facts as these: most physicians are women; half of the students in physical sciences and higher mathematics are women; there are about half a million women engineers in the Soviet Union; and 40 per cent of the members of Academies of Science are women. By drawing upon reservoirs of talent among low income families, women, residents of remote areas, and members of minority ethnic groups, the U.S.S.R. can build up a larger population of well-educated specialists than would be found in countries which perpetuate traditional barriers to higher education.

Special Schools

Education of the especially talented, in most lines of achievement in the U.S.S.R., is not differentiated until after they are seventeen or eighteen years of age. Throughout the elementary and secondary school, Russia's future leaders in science, business, literature, and politics all study in a class which contains a fair cross-section of the local community. Specialized training comes only with higher education.

In a few fields early specialized training is needed. Expert musical and ballet performances, for example, seem to require early cultivation. In these and other performing arts a few residential schools have been established. The special school attached to the ballet company of the Bolshoi Theater in Moscow receives about 1,000 applications from talented six-year-olds each year. From these, 15 boys and 15 girls are eventually selected for admission. All expenses for living and tuition are provided for these gifted youngsters. They now take eleven years to complete the ten-year curriculum and supplement the regular academic program with concentrated training in dance. Similar opportunities are provided in a few special dramatic schools connected with theaters, music schools connected with conservatories, and art schools connected with institutes of fine arts.

ADAPTATION TO AMERICAN SCHOOLS

How far can American schools, with our political system, ideals, history, and school practices, make use of ideas from Russian education? A slavish imitation would be even more silly than complete disregard of achievements abroad; any sound development in American education must grow naturally from our own soil and climate. While keeping our roots firmly in American traditions and community life, our high schools may be expected at this time to profit in a number of ways by study of developments in education in the U.S.S.R.

1. The teachers in many American communities have for some time stood almost alone in placing a high value upon excellent scholarship. It is gratifying today to find some newspapers, magazines, and community organizations giving increased recognition to the importance of intellectual achievement. Some of this, to be sure, is only a panicky desire to keep ahead of Russia in the weapons race. There may be a chance, however, to use the present concern to modify the anti-intellectual atmosphere which pervades some youth groups. This will be no easy task, especially in lower-class areas, rural and urban, where the parents have had only limited opportunities and the media of mass communication feature dimensions of achievement quite unlike the school honor roll. Some upper-class cliques, for different reasons ("brains can be hired cheap"), are also contemptuous of scholarship. Schools alone cannot expect to change the community atmosphere and standards. Teachers in the U.S.S.R. undoubtedly get more support in their values from the rest of the community. Teacher prestige, teacher salaries, and the pressure to enter teaching will all increase if the social climate in America becomes more respectful of academic

learning. If this should occur, special provisions for the gifted will be easily arranged.

2. If American society generally shows increased concern for the mastery of difficult subject matter, it will be a simple matter to make the high school curriculum tougher. The danger at the moment is that youth will be made the scapegoat for the intellectual laziness of American adults. While grown-ups spend their evenings watching prizefights or variety shows on television, they hope that their children are sweating over conjugations of foreign language verbs and the solution of quadratic equations. It is unlikely that youth education can move far without a parallel development in study by adults.

3. It should be entirely possible in school classes to cultivate a greater spirit of cooperative endeavor to help every pupil reach certain minimum standards of mastery. Bright youngsters can assist the teacher in helping their classmates and in work with younger children.

4. Enrichment for bright students—extra responsibilities, challenges, and projects—can be extended in every subject area.

5. After-school club programs can enlist the free time and energy of bright pupils in innumerable projects which will advance their intellectual and personal growth. The advisability of a separate staff for the beyond-school club activities is worth considering.

6. It is interesting to contrast the Russian view that everyone should have both theoretical and practical training with the practice in some high schools of giving academic subjects only to the gifted and practical work mainly to the slow learners. Would a better balance be more valuable for both groups?

7. Would oral examinations, supplementing the written tests on which we have chiefly relied, give a better basis for discovering how thoroughly pupils have mastered their work? Would such individual examinations lead here, as they have in some cases in Russia, to the identification of some pupils whose mental processes are very promising, although limited opportunity has thus far curtailed their achievements?

8. Surely America is in the best position of any country in the world to subsidize higher and other forms of specialized education. We have the tradition of equality of opportunity and the economic

resources to afford the investment. We are making progress toward reducing barriers of race and sex which have interfered with the discovery and cultivation of many talented young people.

A fair conclusion is that most of the advantages of Russian schools over American schools lie not in pedagogical techniques but in the climate of public opinion. Any time the adult citizens of America want to give high priority to intellectual achievement in their own use of time, in selection of outstanding teachers, and in subsidies for scholarship, the public and private high schools will be more than ready to maintain high standards.

5

Ideas from the German Gymnasium

Christian O. Arndt

New York University

DEEP-SEATED in German life is the disposition of the individual to identify himself with his work, particularly if its execution demands superior skill.

In Germany the attempt to do things other than one's specialty has frequently brought public opinion "to a jell" and the judgment, "Shoemaker, stay by your last" has been pronounced. This pronouncement is direction-giving, and has served to put the would-be deviationist in his place. He might continue his vagaries, but not with public approval.

The long-term effect of this public endorsement of superior workmanship in a single field is that the management of government and the military has been left to professed craftsmen in these strategic areas. The devastating results of this arrangement live on vividly in the memory of the preceding and present generations.

NATURE OF GERMAN GYMNASIA

German Gymnasia fall into three categories: the Modern Language, the Mathematics Natural Science, and the Classical. Because of its traditional orientation toward the past the Classical Gymnasium will not here be discussed.

Gymnasium programs extend over nine years and are based upon the completion of four years of primary education. The courses offered in both Gymnasia are similar, differing only in that the

Modern Language Gymnasium stresses foreign languages and the Gymnasium for Mathematics and Science, while offering the same number of foreign languages, devotes less time to them and emphasizes mathematics and science instead. The number of subjects studied during the nine year program is fifteen for both Gymnasia.

1. The Modern Language Gymnasium. The foreign languages taught are Latin and two modern languages (English, French). The sequence varies. Usually the first foreign language studied is a modern language, Latin the second. There are, however, some schools patterned after the old type Realgymnasium, which begin with Latin. In turn, Latin may at times be the third language studied.

School year	5	6	7	8	9	10	11	12	13
Religion	2	2	2	2	2	2	2	2	2
Philosophy									
German	5	5	4	4	4	4	4	4	4
History and Sociology	2	2	3	4	3	4	4	4	4
Geography	2	2	2	2	1	2	1	2	
Foreign Language (1) (modern)	6	6	4	4	3	3	3	3	
Foreign Language (2) (Latin)			5	5	4	3	3	3	3
Foreign Language (3) (modern)					4	4	4	4	4
Mathematics	4	4	4	4	4	4	3	3	
Physics					3	1	1		
Chemistry					2	1	3	3	3
Biology	2	2	2		1	3			
Music	2	2	2	2	1	1	2	1	1
Art	2	2	2	2	2	1	1	2	1
Physical Education	3	3	2	2	2	2	2	2	2
Total hours per week	30	30	32	33	34	35	32	33	29

2. The Mathematics Natural Science Gymnasium. This type of Gymnasium has the same program as the Modern Language during the first six years. The third foreign language, which is begun in the fifth year, may be dropped in the last two years or may be continued as an elective. In place of two modern languages, one modern language and Latin may be chosen. Mathematics and science are given a larger emphasis in this

Gymnasium than in the Classical Gymnasium and the Modern Language Gymnasium.[1]

School year	5	6	7	8	9	10	11	12	13
Religion	2	2	2	2	2	2	2	2	2
Philosophy									
German	5	5	4	4	4	4	4	4	4
History and Sociology	2	2	3	4	3	4	4	4	4
Geography	2	2	2	2	1	2	1	2	
Foreign Language (1)	6	6	4	4	3	3	3	3	
Foreign Language (2)			5	5	4	3	3	3	3
Foreign Language (3)					4	4			
Mathematics	4	4	4	4	4	4	4	4	4
Physics				3	1	1			
Chemistry					2	1	6	6	6
Biology	2	2	2		1	3			
Music	2	2	2	1	1	1	2	1	1
Art	2	2	2	2	2	1	1	2	1
Physical Education	3	3	2	2	2	2	2	2	2
Hours per week	30	30	32	33	34	35	32	33	29

Since education in the German Federal Republic today is the responsibility of the eleven states and not of the federal government, there are some differences in the organization and content of educational programs among the Gymnasia. The secondary school programs of West Berlin, for example, are otherwise organized.[2] The preceding tables are, however, essentially accurate for most Gymnasia.

Gymnasia are selective. Since they are designed for the gifted, admission is conditioned upon a good grade average, examinations, and the recommendation, ex officio, of the administrative official of the student's elementary school.

In some states of Germany a week of test instruction (*Probeunterricht*) is set aside for candidates who wish to enter the Gymnasium. This test instruction is conducted by the *ad hoc* elementary school teacher and a gymnasium teacher appointed for the purpose. Care-

[1] Franz Hilker, *Die Schulen in Deutschland* (Bad Nauheim: Im Christian-Verlag, 1957), pp. 43–44.
[2] J. F. Cramer and G. S. Browne, *Contemporary Education* (New York: Harcourt, Brace & Co., 1956), p. 457.

ful evaluations of each pupil are made. Factors in selection are interest, evidences of perception, and facility in verbal expression. In addition, two or three smaller compositions are required of each pupil, the written work providing further material for evaluation. The joint judgment of the two teachers is an important factor in determining admission to the gymnasium.

The first three months of the first year in the Gymnasium are considered probationary; should the pupil fail to meet the standards, he must return to the elementary school. In this event he will have the opportunity, if his record warrants, of entering the Gymnasium at a later date. In the further years of study pupils are continually re-evaluated; they are always on probation. Evaluation of the intellectual growth of students and knowledge of subject-matter, is carried out systematically and vigorously during each of the nine years of the Gymnasium's program. There is no letup in the pressure to learn.

The school day usually begins at 8:00 A.M. and continues until 1:00 P.M., or shortly thereafter. A double shift is yet operative in some schools.

Upon completion of the Gymnasium, a student must sit for the *Abiturium* (abbreviated *Abitur*) examinations if he wishes to enter a university. If he passes successfully and has a satisfactory Gymnasium record, particularly during the senior year, the student has the right to enter a university. Actually, only 20 or 25 per cent of the entrants to the Gymnasium proceed to the Abitur,[3] according to Cramer and Browne. This estimate appears quite low, 30 per cent and above being more likely.

As I have indicated already, the Gymnasium acquires its students through a carefully designed process of selection. The faculty and administration reserve the right to drop any student if after admission he fails to continue to do superior work. Pressure on the part of parents to keep in school children who are failing is of no avail.

Today most gifted youth from all levels of German society are eligible to attend Gymnasia. Educational grants-in-aid for the gifted are made by the State governments:

[3] *Ibid.,* p. 456.

The new Constitutions of the several states again make it legally possible that grants be given if the income of the person responsible for the child does not exceed a certain limit. The number of these grants and the amounts paid are not yet sufficient to justify the statement that adequate support of all gifted and needy children has been attained. Additional grants-in-aid are available for adolescents from refugee families if these young persons attend advanced or vocational schools.[4]

The immediate result of the highly selective process of determining the student body of a Gymnasium is that the quality of instruction can be so fashioned as to challenge not only the student of middle academic ability, but also the student of highest ability. Obviously this procedure results in a climate of endeavor in the classroom which is stimulating intellectually. Operative is an upward reach in terms of thinking; the standards are high. There are casualties, but even so standards are not lowered.

COMMITMENT TO HIGH ACADEMIC STANDARDS

The commitment to high academic standards is, practically speaking, an almost inevitable outcome of the highly selective process of admission to the Gymnasium.

The Gymnasium fosters high academic standards by the long period of years during which such key subjects as mathematics, science, social studies, and foreign languages are taught. To illustrate, in the modern language Gymnasium, German and one foreign language are taught for nine years and are supplemented by two other languages for seven and five years, respectively. Given five to nine years with four different languages, it is possible not only to develop the ability to communicate in and through these languages but, moreover, to engage in a study of comparative linguistics.

The system of protracted study is operative for all subjects studied in the Gymnasium. Mathematics is studied each semester for eight or nine years, biology for about two hours weekly for five years. The social sciences, music, and art are similarly studied throughout the nine years.

---

[4] Erich J. Hylla and Friedrich O. Kegel, *Education in Germany* (Frankfurt am Main: Hochschule für Internationale Pädagogische Forschung, 1954), p. 30.

An important principle of learning is thus operative, namely, to require of the student long-term application to and study of each subject. This principle has been widely discussed in recent German educational literature, and most educators hold that, with so much knowledge available today in so many fields, the Gymnasium should strive not to increase the number of subjects but rather to give depth to those already in its program. This procedure, it is held, will best develop the approach necessary for the study of any field of knowledge in later life.

Here is an example of a program designed to integrate knowledge. Two basic questions were asked of students:

What are the operative forces of the eighteenth century?
What is enlightenment?

The advanced classes of the school were divided into the following groups, each of which approached the theme from the vantage point of its particular subject field.

1. The German language group studied the literature of the eighteenth century from Brockes to Lessing.

2. The group on religion studied the optimistic world view of Leibniz to *Chr.* Wolff up to the concept of tolerance in Lessing. This group pointed out the narrowing of faith to morality, using as examples the Protestant church hymns of the time.

3. The group on history examined the changeabout of the political and social thinking and the functional historical forces from the period of Absolutism to the French Revolution.

4. The French language group concerned itself intimately with the struggles of the Encyclopedists and disputations within the French thought world.

5. The art group attempted to penetrate the confusing diversity of thought during the century through formative art. One of its special themes was "What was man like during the period of Enlightenment (La Tour)?"

6. The group on biology set forth the first comprehensive attempts to systematize (Linné) and pointed to the introduction of mechanistic principles in the study of the animal and human body.

7. The group on chemistry studied the dissolution of alchemy through scientific chemistry, particularly through the revelation of the first elements and the introduction of the quantitative method (Lavoisier and Gay-Lussac).

8. The mathematics and physics group concerned itself with the development of the laws of analytical functions, tracing their twofold root: the philosophical in Leibniz and the physical in Newton.[5]

Unfortunately the number of such integrated courses or studies is not great. Such courses are found more often in private than public schools.

Germany has been firmly committed for many years to high academic standards. This commitment developed from the structure of society that prevailed during the nineteenth century and that, in a much weakened form, continues today. Tradition has lent its sanction to the high standards of the Gymnasium, and they have emerged from the period of occupation after World War II relatively unchanged.

DEVELOPMENT OF A NEW SOCIAL EDUCATION

Concern has been expressed over the socially induced disposition of many Germans to assume responsibility only for their own work or profession. This reluctance to assume responsibility for social and political improvement at community and national levels was recognized educationally during the Weimar Republic. It has been attacked vigorously in recent years, as the nation once again became self-governing.

Apart from international relations work in the social sciences, some Gymnasia are cooperating with UNESCO in its international experimental program in Education for International Understanding. UNESCO's Interim Report of Activities in 1955 and 1956 lists the following Gymnasia as presently cooperating in the experiment: Helene Lange Schule, Hamburg; Städtisches Albertus-Magnus-Gymnasium, Köln; Albert Schweitzer Schule, Hofgeismar, Hesse; Bismarckschule, Hannover; Gerhard-Rohlfs-Schule, Bremen; and Landerziehungsheim Schondorf, Oberbayern. Here is a description of work done with the United Nations' Universal Declaration of Human Rights in the Helene Lange Schule:

It has often been wondered how human rights could be brought within the understanding of school children. This would seem to imply that, in

5 Translated freely from Kurt Zier, *Colloquium und Gesamtunterricht*, Odenwaldschule, Hesse, pp. 9–11.

any such attempt, indifference and even difficulties would be encountered. It is the very breadth of the theme that makes it difficult to handle. School curricula already provide for the study of the Universal Declaration, and every school is expected to develop in its pupils an independent judgment and habits of unprejudiced thinking.

At the Helene Lange School advantage was taken of a favorable opportunity for distributing the text of the Declaration to pupils in the upper classes, but it was not thought necessary to study the articles systematically, one after the other. The earlier instruction received by the pupils, the history teaching given them in previous years, and the reading done by them in the modern language lessons—excerpts from the works of Hobbes, Locke, Montesquieu or Rousseau—are all factors enabling the teacher to decide how far he should illustrate the evolution of human rights in his lessons by the use of a few characteristic examples, and how far the pupils can themselves take part in this illustration. . .

1) Example taken from a history lesson in Class XIII.

Preparation for the lesson:

In connection with current political questions, mention was made of the United Nations. In the chronological study of history up to 1776, attention was drawn to the Bill of Rights of 1688 and to the political implications of the philosophical movement of the 18th century (*Aufklärung*).

Homework: The development of the War of Independence.

Reading of the text of the Virginia Bill of Rights.

2) The actual lesson:

a) Brief discussion to establish and explain the facts relating to the origin and development of the War of Independence up to the proclamation of the Virginia Bill of Rights.

b) Explanation of the articles of the Bill, taken one by one, together with an attempt to see whether the ideas and demands expressed therein have already been met with in the history of various countries. In this way the fact emerges that the novelty of the Bill did not lie in the various demands it enshrined but in the fact that the State acknowledged that those claims were based upon natural law and thereby admitted their legal sanctity.

Following an analysis of the Declaration of Independence, the French Declaration of the Rights of Man (1789), the Declaration of Fundamental Rights of the Bonn Constitution, the Universal Declaration of Human Rights and the European Convention of Human Rights, the main features of these texts and the differences between them, together with the evolution of which they are expression, can be traced in subsequent lessons.[6]

6 UNESCO/ED/149, Paris, February 4, 1957, pp. 27–28.

A more recent report states:

UNESCO is encouraging 80 member-states to give instruction in secondary schools in international affairs. Seven schools and two teachers' training colleges are already engaged in the program in Germany. Among the themes offered by UNESCO, the most popular is the study of the achievements and problems of foreign countries: one of the schools is specializing on the Near East, Pakistan, and Ceylon, another on the British Commonwealth, the United States, Japan and the Arab countries. It is also hoped to arrange contacts with school children from the countries being studied.[7]

The individual states of the Federal Republic, through their ministries of education, enjoin their Gymnasia to teach about the United Nations and other organizations dedicated to the building of world peace. They also urge teaching about the responsibility of the individual toward his community, state, and nation, as illustrated below in the *Richtlinien* for Hannover. The *Richtlinien* is actually a suggested state program of study for the Gymnasia of the state:

Individual themes for the twelfth year (junior year of the Gymnasium). Transnational organizations, particularly the United Nations as a world peace organization.

   a) Organization, goals and methods of operation of the U.N. and its specialized agencies, particularly of UNESCO and the International Labor Organization.
   b) International Law Courts.
   c) The International Red Cross.
   d) Armament, disarmament, and security. Industrial and military pact systems.

Class 13 (senior year of the gymnasium).

General theme: Man in society and state of the present-day world.
   1. Single theme: Man under law in his state.
      a) Basic rights and obligations of the citizen in the Federal Republic. Political freedom and social responsibility according to the Universal Declaration of Human Rights of the United Nations dated October 12, 1948. The history of human rights, their natural and Christian foundations.
      b) The cooperation of the citizen in the building of political opinion

---

[7] *Cultural News from Germany* (Bonn: Inter Nationes, Marienstrasse 6, January, 1959), pp. 20–21.

through periodically recurring elections to community and state positions as well as to the Bundestag. Questions of election rights and the limitations of political cooperation. Equal rights for women; the legal basis for these rights.

c) Political parties; their goals and achievements.

d) The influence of nonparliamentary organizations upon the political education of the people.

e) The work of parliaments; the formulation of government and law in a parliamentary democracy.

2. Single theme: Dialectical theory.

a) The basic thought underlying the dialectic of Hegel, dialectical materialism, and the results thereof for the concept of man.

b) Basic thesis of materialism; the classic personalities of Marxism, their mutual relationship; the social theory of Marx-Engels; the change from Marxism to Leninism and Stalinism.[8]

From these themes and topics one sees that a considerable body of knowledge is assumed and notable intellectual sophistication is required of both students and teachers. Obviously this is material for gifted youth. Noteworthy also is the breadth and scope of the study, ranging as it does from the world level to the local community. Also, the rights of women are not forgotten.

Finally, the new social education includes practice in student government, which operates in varying degrees among the Gymnasia, with responsibility vested in the director and faculty of the school. The following quotation is drawn from the annual report of the Director of Leibnizschule in Hannover. This school is housed in an entirely new complex of buildings. Its enrollment is approximately 1,300 students, a small number of whom are girls.

Student Co-operative Government and School Organizations: The experiences of recent years have shown that co-operative student government can always be activated if real problems are entrusted to it. During the last school year there has been no shortage of problems. Our new buildings, moving and school furnishings called for attention. Thus, the phrase "take hold and help" was ever present. It may truthfully be said that our students, in full knowledge that they had been given one of the first new schools in the State, and one so beautiful, did not shrink in their

[8] *Richtlinien fur die politische Erziehung und Bildung, Richtlinien für den Unterrichtan den Schulen des Landes Niedersachsen,* Hannover, April, 1958, pp. 26–27.

efforts to help the builders, carpenters, gardeners, and others do their work. . . .

In developing and setting up new house orders for the new buildings, a number of students had already lent important assistance to the administration. When we moved into the new buildings, supervisory arrangements had to be effected for class movements during break-periods. Many other supervisory functions had to be organized. This work largely became the responsibility of students from the upper classes.[9]

A later report gives further information about the work of parents:

Once again it can be stated for the 1957–58 school report that co-operation between the school and parents was live and intimate, as it has been in other years. This statement applies to gatherings between parents and teachers of the several classes as also for the Parents' Council. The latter was led with energy and understanding by the chairman, Professor Wagener. He and the two other officers of the Parents' Council, Director Schrieves and Dr. Preuss, maintained close contact with the Director of the school and members of the faculty during the entire year.

On April 26, the first day for members of the fifth class, the Director addressed the parents of the latter and spoke of the requirements and problems of the school.[10]

Students share responsibility also for numerous clubs, for the organization of class or group excursions, and for visits to the school's country home. Extensive opportunity is given to students to share in the multiple tasks of school administration.

PUBLIC RESPECT FOR HIGH INTELLECTUAL ACHIEVEMENT

Scholarship and intellectual achievement enjoy high esteem in German life. This is not a new phenomenon; it reaches back into history for centuries. Goethe in his magnum opus made Faust a scholar and pictured him as a man committed to an eternal quest for new knowledge. It was this tireless drive for learning—which later in the drama takes the form of a major effort to improve the lot of human beings—that made him a candidate for redemption.

[9] Rudolf Brennecke, *Jahresbericht der Leibnizschule*, Hannover, 1954, p. 21 ff.
[10] Rudolf Brennecke, *Jahresbericht der Leibnizschule*, Hannover, September, 1958, p. 12.

This, incidentally, was the first time in the history of the drama that a Faust was otherwise than damned. The reason given for Faust's salvation was precisely his studious endeavor, for in the words of Goethe: *Wer immer strebend sich bemüht, Den können wie erlösen.* ("Who, ever aspiring, struggles on, for him there is salvation.")

During the nineteenth century and until World War I, German universities enjoyed world renown. Many Americans attended these universities during this period because of both the *Lehrfreiheit* and the *Lernfreiheit* ("freedom to teach" and "freedom to learn") which prevailed there. Democracy in administration was notably developed. Professors elected both the deans and the Rektor of the university. The qualities of teaching and research, particularly the unique combination of the two, also attracted serious students.

It was the responsibility of the Gymnasium to prepare students adequately for university work by developing their proficiency in such subjects as languages, history, and mathematics. The universities then took over, allowing freedom to attend or not to attend classes, but providing seminars which introduced students to research methods under competent professors. This functional relationship between students and professors accounted for the quality of scholarship which developed in so many and so diverse fields. Again, there developed a tradition of individual student responsibility coupled with an ever fostered quest for learning. The drive to become identified with significant contributions to scholarship was nurtured by the professor-student relationship.

The public at large, busy and content with the specialized tasks to which the structure of society had accustomed each individual, was satisfied to know only that its scholars were doing superior work. The man on the street, insofar as he understood this societal arrangement, approved and supported it.

IMPLICATIONS FOR EDUCATION IN THE UNITED STATES

Pervasive in most United States social institutions is the resolve to have them serve as agencies for the development of the basic tenets of democracy. This is to us a matter of principle which has grown out of a national need. These tenets of democracy include respect for the uniqueness of the individual as a fundamental principle. They include also the principle of developing the good citizen, who is concerned with and shares responsibility for the welfare of the community, the nation, and the world in which he lives. Finally, they include the principle of reaching a decision by the scientific method. Granted that these are principles which we strive to realize, but which we rarely achieve completely, they are nonetheless direction-giving and have been so from the beginning of our national history. They are the sinews which serve to give vitality to what we think of as the American way of life.

The United States made a basic educational decision toward the end of the nineteenth century. The decision was that education should be for all American youth, whether gifted or not. Elementary education was not enough; secondary education, too, was to be made available for all. With this achieved, we are now trying to provide junior and even senior college for all. Our societal structure did not permit differentiation between social classes (with lamentable exceptions in the case of certain minority groups). In this giant endeavor, academic standards suffered. Public opinion, influenced inevitably by our historical opposition toward rule by royalty in any form, did not want separate publicly supported secondary schools to be established for the gifted.

The latent fear that children from economically privileged families might evolve into a privileged social class served to confuse public opinion. This confusion must be clarified today. Better education is not recommended for academically gifted children alone; nor is the same education recommended for all American youth, since this would result in a revengeful disinheritance of those who happen to have superior academic gifts. Rather, the best education is recommended for everybody according to his gifts, whether these be vocational or academic.

The establishment of special public secondary schools for the gifted in this country is generally held to be unwise. However, such high schools as the Bronx High School of Science or the High School of Music and Art, both in New York City, are recommended for large population centers where the sense of community is vague and where diverse educational opportunities for all youth are readily available.

The sporadic efforts presently under way in various parts of the country to strengthen curricular offerings for the gifted should be extended and fortified through special classes and programs specifically designed for them. These classes and programs need to be organized not only in science and mathematics, but also in languages, social studies, and the arts. Present-day occasional efforts must become widespread. They need to begin in the local community but must be extended to state and national levels.

Special courses and programs for the gifted should be offered under the same roof and within the same school as classes for less gifted students. School assemblies, discussion groups concerned with social and political questions, and such courses as physical education and health should be shared by all students, so that the gifted may interact with other students.

Our universe has changed significantly, and we find ourselves placed in the position of leadership of the free world. No longer can we think only of what is desirable for our present population. We must think in larger terms or forfeit the prospects of freedom in our world. Those are the *de facto* conditions which now obtain. Our most talented youth must be trained to become scientists who discover, engineers who build, artists and men of letters who create, and diplomats who speak the languages of the countries with whose people they need to work.

The German Gymnasium, although concerned with relatively few subjects, requires that foreign languages, mathematics, and science be studied over a period of many years. Instead of spending one year upon physics or chemistry, our secondary programs for the gifted should devote two or three hours a week for two or three years to each of these subjects, instead of the five or seven hours a week for a single year which is presently the vogue in many schools. This longer exposure to the study of a subject means fuller absorption of its content. In foreign languages the present two years of study is largely a waste of time since the intention is not to develop a functional use of the language, but rather to meet a college entrance requirement. The Gymnasium, concerned only with gifted youth, begins foreign language study when a child is ten. Eight or nine years of a language makes it possible to develop a truly functional facility in it.

The present practice in the United States is to give a grade in each subject at the conclusion of the first semester and a final grade upon completion of the subject at the close of the school year. Presumably the student's obligation insofar as evidence of knowledge of a given subject is concerned, is terminated when this final grade is given. In some states, Regents examinations or other special entrance examinations to college call for further evidence of knowledge.

Final examinations before high school graduation in at least those subjects which a student intends to pursue in college will serve to motivate him to keep active his knowledge.

In America today public respect for intellectual achievement leaves much to be desired. Parents can help to effect a change in the quality of our secondary school education if they evince strong interest in educational, ethical, and moral questions within the family circle. Specifically, parents need to encourage their children to read books of quality by doing so themselves and by developing discussion at the table or elsewhere in the home. Parents need to involve their children in enterprises aimed at community improvement. They need to help alter some of the general public's anti-intellectual ideas, including the one that intellectuals should not run for public office.

SUMMARY

As a product of German historical and social forces, the Gymnasium was designed from the outset to provide secondary education for the intellectually gifted. In point of fact, however, these gifted youths came largely from the socially and economically privileged families. Even so, some provision was made to subsidize gifted youth from poor families or to exempt them from tuition. Today intellectual ability and good character are the sole conditions for admission. The several states of the Federal Republic make a strong effort to provide grants-in-aid to needy gifted youth of good character.

The significant features of the Gymnasium selected for consideration were: opportunity to work exclusively with the intellectually gifted; commitment to high academic standards; evaluation of intellectual ability and character; development of a new social education; and public respect for high intellectual achievement.

Since only the intellectually gifted are admitted to Gymnasia, high academic standards can be set and maintained. Desirable as these standards are, it is, with some exceptions, not appropriate or sound to establish special schools for the gifted in the United States. Political and socio-economic factors firmly established in our history and traditions generally militate against such schools.

The comprehensive high school can best provide for educating the gifted through special classes and programs while daily interaction between all students is furthered through school assemblies, discussion groups concerned with social and political questions, and such courses as health and physical education. Since all youth, gifted or less gifted, will need to live and work together as adults tomorrow, they should spend a longer period of time together in their youth.

Commitment to high academic standards is in need of serious attention from secondary schools in America. Examples drawn from Gymnasia gave evidence of high standards which have been fostered the more readily because of their selective features. More time spent upon fewer subjects is a necessity in classes and programs for gifted youth. Each subject should be studied over more years so that a pupil might become really proficient in it. Five hours per week of Spanish for two years yields a far lower return than four years of study for two to three hours per week.

Evaluation of intellectual ability and character is a highly desirable feature of the Gymnasium. One such element is the practice of holding all Gymnasium students to the *Abitur*. High school students in the United States should be required to pass final examinations in all those subjects they plan to pursue in college. Such a requirement should actuate the student to keep his knowledge in active form for future use.

The development of a new social education is under way in the Federal Republic of Germany. This is apparent from an analysis of state syllabuses in the area of social studies per se, but it is revealed also by an emphasis upon human rights and international relations studies in a growing number of schools.

The low level of public respect for high intellectual achievement is one of our greatest national weaknesses. Too many of us have become indolent, preferring entertainment to creative thought. More parents need to develop a greater interest in intellectual pursuits. Reading about and discussion of the important problems of today and yesterday should find a larger place in the family circle. If radio and television are to be followed extensively, as they now are, then the poor quality of programs offered needs to be improved. This is the responsibility of John Doe, citizen, who needs to let advertisers know that he wants more thoughtful and challenging programs and that he will not tolerate deceit.

We, the people, have it within our power to build an educational system which will truly challenge our gifted youth. We have the resources, both material and human, to accomplish this task. Will we do so, or will we be content to lose our place of leadership in the world by default? Our gifted youths are our greatest national asset. They are also our most neglected national asset.

*   *   *

Note: A number of people in both the United States and Germany helped in the preparation of this chapter through correspondence and by supplying special information. I hereby gratefully acknowledge the assistance of Hans Arnold, Goethe Gymnasium, Königstein im Taunus; Hans Arnsberg, visiting teacher in the United States from Germany; Dr. Fritzmartin Ascher, *Oberstudiendirektor,* Albert Schweitzer Gymnasium, Crailsheim, Baden-Württemberg; Bernard A. Bearer, Indiana University, Bloomington, Indiana; Claus Blome, German Gymnasium student now at George School, Pennsylvania; Herman M. Campsen, Jr., Chairman, Department of Physical Science, Bronx High School of Science, Bronx, New York; D. Ernst Christ, *Oberstudiendirektor,* Stuttgart; Dr. Paul Didinger, Schulrat, Bonn; Dr. Alfred Ehrentreich, *Oberstudiendirektor,* Alte Landesschule, Korbach; Luise Gassner, Berlin; Goethe Haus, Library, 120 East 56 Street, New York 22, New York; Dr. Herbert Hahn, Die Freie Waldorfschule, Stuttgart; Richard Hauff, Georgii-Gymnasium, Esslingen am Neckar; Alois Hafner, Public Schools of Tarrytown, New York; Dr. Theodore Huebener, Director of Foreign Languages, Schools of the City of New York; Professor Erich Hylla, Frankfurt am/Main; Dr. Franz Hilker, Pädagogische Arbeitsstelle, Bonn; Barbara Jacobsen, *Studienassessorin,* Helene Lange Schule, Hamburg; Dr. Alexander Kallos, Assistant Professor, College of William and Mary, Williamsburg, Virginia; Dr. W. Kroelle, UNESCO–Institüt fur Pädogogic, Hamburg; Professor

Günther Keil, Hunter College, New York; Gilbert Manalli, Ripon Senior High School, Ripon, Wisconsin; Warren T. Peace, Rivera, California; Dr. Pesch, *Oberstudiendirektor,* Sophia-Charlotte-Schule, Berlin; Dean John O. Riedl, Graduate School, Marquette University, Milwaukee, Wisconsin; Professor Ernst Rose, New York University, New York, New York; Dr. G. Schuster, *Oberstudiendirektor,* Ernst Moritz Arndt-Schule, Bonn; Josef Schwarz, Bunsen-Gymnasium, Heidelberg; Kurt Zier, *Direktor,* Odenwaldschule, Hessen; Waldorf Schule, Stuttgart.

6

Ideas from English Grammar Schools

Samuel Everett
The City College of New York

In England, as in America, strange contradictions of values and customs are to be found. Medieval class traditions still persist in England in a variety of forms. They are apparent in allegiance to the Crown, the high prestige of the peerage, the social distinctions based upon one's type of work, the purity—or lack of it—of one's speech, and, in education, a hierarchy of secondary schools. People are not thought of or treated as social equals. Yet this is a country whose citizens love freedom and practice it. Over the centuries men, and women, too, have cast off the bonds of arbitrary justice. Trial by one's peers, the common law, and universal suffrage have brought freedom. Today all citizens are guaranteed their rights under law. Political, religious, and social beliefs do not bar one from public life. One finds in this island a proud tradition that if the persecuted in other lands manage to reach English shores, they are henceforth free.

In America the equality of man and the respect for what a person is, rather than for his economic or social position, are principles of our democratic faith. For generations the conditions of frontier life stripped away class distinctions in the hard reality of existence. Millions have sought our shores, and not in vain, for equality of opportunity. "Let the best man win," we say, and mean it. Today visitors from abroad find us a friendly, generous people enjoying a social mobility unrealized in most of the countries of the world. Yet these visitors see also the rights of some American citizens being arbitrarily limited by differences of race and religion. Millions are denied an equal opportunity for an education because of race and geographic location. Visitors find lists of subversive organizations and special loyalty oaths for teachers, which threaten the right of freedom of thought and action.

It is naive to believe, as many American educators do, that American schools and the American people are democratic and that the English are not. Realism would seem to require a more discriminating judgment.

THE GRAMMAR SCHOOL AS AN INSTITUTION

The grammar school is one of three distinctive units of publicly provided secondary education in England. At the age of eleven, the majority of elementary, or "primary," school children take examinations. The results largely determine in which secondary unit a child shall be placed. Primary school records are also used in making this decision. A small number of children do not take examinations but go directly to one of the privately owned preparatory schools, from which some will go to the famous public schools at the age of thirteen.

Students scoring in the highest 20 to 25 per cent on the examinations are enrolled in grammar schools; those in the next 5 per cent go to technical schools; and approximately the lowest 60 per cent, or the "nonscholars," attend secondary modern schools. The remaining students go to a variety of secondary institutions. Some are enrolled in schools for the handicapped. A few remain in primary or "all age" schools in communities where secondary institutions have not yet been made available. A small but slowly increasing number go to comprehensive schools which enroll pupils of all abilities.

The still predominant three unit, or three track, system definitely represents a class conception. Parents, citizens, and educators give their highest respect to the grammar school attended by the most able students. Next in prestige are the technical schools. These are followed, at a considerable social distance, by the secondary modern institutions.

State supported elementary and secondary schools are financed jointly by the central Ministry of Education and the local county and borough councils. The Ministry does not dictate what is to be taught in the schools, nor do the Local Educational Authorities of the county and borough councils. In accordance with the English conception of freedom educational authorities give professional advice but do not dictate to administrators and teachers in the individual schools.

The distinguishing characteristics of state supported grammar schools, which provide for the ablest youth, have been largely influenced by practices originating in the famous independent English public schools of the nineteenth century. These include small size, compared to American schools; segregation of the majority of students by sex; distinctive uniforms for both boys and girls; formal relations between teacher and pupil as compared to American high schools; a lecture-notetaking procedure which, however, has been loosening up in recent years; student leaders, or prefects, chosen by "heads" and faculties, not elected by their peers; a curriculum limited to the liberal arts, now in the process of expansion to provide for some practical electives; religious education in each year of school life; small classes, again compared to American classes; few study periods through the first five years; plenty of homework; and the usual requirement of games for everyone, which emphasize character building quite as much as competition.

EVALUATION IN AMERICAN TERMS

American democratic traditions, both in society and in the educational profession, preclude acceptance of a class system of secondary education.

In England grammar school youth are surrounded by an aura of superiority. In a very real sense they have already achieved a lasting superior social status. This is accepted by a majority of citizens. Sixth form work is conducted almost entirely by university graduates with high honors degrees, and a majority of grammar school teachers are university graduates.

American exchange teachers, almost without exception, condemn the examinations at the age of eleven which determine the educational and social status of the majority of English youth. Early examinations do not always determine intellectual ability. Moreover, the academic orientation of standardized tests does not differentiate other types of giftedness.

But no American can be more condemning of the various discriminatory educational practices than are many Englishmen themselves. Local Education Authorities with the encouragement of parents and the Ministry of Education, are "busting out all over" with constructive changes in the operation of the three track system, which will better meet the needs of youth without changing the basic social character of these institutions.[1] As has been indicated, some L.E.A.'s are developing comprehensive schools. The Labour Party is devoted to the revolutionary change of establishing the comprehensive secondary school throughout England and Wales.[2]

Purpose and Orientation of this Survey

We are not exploring English grammar school curriculums for desirable social orientation. Rather, we wish to examine the *quality* of their education for students of superior ability.

Let us not be misled by the prevalence of many practices we would not like to copy. It is not in our tradition to segregate children by sex in our publicly supported secondary schools; nor to make them wear uniforms; nor to maintain considerable formality in teacher-pupil relations; nor to teach religious doctrine; nor to have adults choose student leaders.

We may, however, learn something about the advantages of the small school unit, which might lead us to break up many huge metropolitan high schools into several administrative units within each school; or something of the educational quality of games, which might result in more intramural sports; or, on the national

---

1 *Secondary Education for All: A New Drive* (Ministry of Education [London: Her Majesty's Office, December, 1958]).

2 *Learning To Live* (The Labour Party [London: Transport House, 1958]).

educational front, that even major national financial support of local schools does not necessarily lead to central control.

In the exploration of English grammar programs, *curriculum* is used in the sense in which it is broadly interpreted in the United States. This includes the content of the various subjects, teaching methods, and, indeed, all experiences under the guidance of the school.

Only *best practice* will be reported. The purpose is to record specific school curriculums which give most promise for American secondary school programs for our more gifted students.

Data were obtained in two ways. First, numerous statements of purpose, syllabuses, student notebooks, and examinations were procured from correspondents at a number of grammar schools which send a good proportion of their students to English universities. Second, data were obtained in a firsthand study of 55 of the "best" English secondary schools of all types.[3]

THE CURRICULUM AND TEACHING

Students are commonly divided into three "streams," which correspond to ability grouping in American high schools. The A stream includes those who have the highest potential for future university work. The B stream is made up of the middle group in ability, some of whom may attend a university. The majority of C stream students will not go on to universities but may go to technical schools of various types. All three streams are given a liberal education in the English university tradition.

From the beginning all grammar school programs emphasize a degree of study in depth not commonly found in American high schools. For the first five forms there are few elective academic subjects, with the exception of a foreign language. Throughout this five year period there are few, if any, study periods, and homework is regularly assigned. The two sixth forms which follow are made up of students who aspire to attend a higher educational institution. For these, further specialization is required.

Sixth-form students major in from two to four subjects, depend-

3 Samuel Everett, *Growing Up in English Secondary Schools: Significance for American Practice,* University of Pittsburgh Press, 1959.

ing upon their interest and ability. They take university examinations at Advanced Level. A very select few stay on for one additional year to prepare for Open Scholarships to the universities.

A curriculum program submitted by a London school illustrates the nature of grammar school subjects:

1. *Art Courses:* Languages (English, Latin, French, German, and, for some individuals, Greek) and History.

2. *Mathematics and Science Courses:* Pure Mathematics, Applied Mathematics, Physics, Chemistry, Biology (Botany and Geology), Engineering Workshop, and Drawing Office available for those proposing Technology.

3. *Economics Course:* Economics, Economic History, Political Science, British Constitution, Geography.

In addition there are religious education, physical training, and games (all required), as well as art, music, crafts, and domestic science (electives).

In striking contrast to the American elective system, even for students in our college entrance programs, English youth must take an extensive central core of subjects.

A typical required program for Forms I-V includes English, French, history, geography, mathematics, and science (general science, biology, physics, chemistry).

Students do not take all subjects every day. History, geography, the sciences, and even foreign language may be taken two or three periods a week. This makes possible the development of sustained programs in each subject.

The rigidity of the requirements is based on the assumption that educators know better than children, or their parents, what a sound basic education requires. The thorough secondary education possible under this system has led many experts to believe that graduates of English grammar schools are approximately two years in advance of those from American high schools in both specialized preparation and intellectual maturity.

Class size is also a factor in the recognized excellence of the product. In the first five forms classes are somewhat smaller than those in American public high schools. And in the two sixth forms the typical class has 15 students. I have visited sixth forms of only four to six students. Statements to the effect that we cannot seem to afford this low pupil-teacher ratio in the United States commonly called forth the reply: "You have a large country and you can lose some of your gifted pupils. In England we cannot afford to lose any of them."

In order that very few grammar school boys and girls shall be lost, the L.E.A.'s grant scholarships to needy students. This practice is continued and extended at the university level.

The teaching staffs of grammar schools are an unusually able group. They are university graduates, which means not only that they are people of high intelligence but that they belong to the upper 5 per cent in education as well. The more mature and brilliant members of a faculty are commonly chosen to teach sixth-form students.

Examples of programs in a number of academic subjects will now be presented to give a more detailed picture of secondary education for the upper 20 per cent of students of ability. At the request of the Ministry of Education, the names of contributing schools have been omitted.

English

A major effort is made in state and public grammar schools to teach all students the purity of speech emphasized at English universities.

Writing and building a literary background are the special concern of English departments. The ability to speak pure English has as its concomitant the development of a clear and forceful written style. Both are made distinctive through the unassuming use of literary allusion. All three—speech, writing, and literary background—are perfected through intensive practice and study.

One purpose predominates in the education of English youth in the mother tongue and in literature, as it does in all other departments of these schools for the ablest youth. It is independence of thought. The right, indeed the obligation, to be a person—to stand alone against one's fellows if need be—is of paramount worth. Conversation, writing, and the study of English classics are illuminated by this pre-eminent value.

For the first five years English programs typically include formal training in English expression; the classical tradition in English literature, which is intended to develop literary background and standards of behavior; and more poetry, verse, and drama than is common in the United States.

The scope and depth of sixth form study is illustrated in a report from one school.

This year we have read and discussed the following plays:
Translations of:
  Aeschylus, *Agamemnon*
  Sophocles, *The Theban Plays*
  Euripides, *Medea*
  Marlowe, *Dr. Faustus*
  Shakespeare, *King Lear, Othello, Antony and Cleopatra*
  Webster, *The Duchess of Malfi*
  Ibsen, *The Doll's House, Ghosts, The Wild Duck*
  Eliot, *Murder in the Cathedral*
We have read some Early English lyrics; ballads; Chaucer's "Prologue to the Canterbury Tales" (in the original); parts of Spenser's "Faerie Queene" Book 1; some Elizabethan lyrics; some of the works of the Cavalier Poets; a selection of poems by John Donne; Milton, "Paradise Lost," Books 1 and 2, and the minor poems; Keats' Odes and "Hyperion"; parts of "The Prelude" by Wordsworth and a selection of his other poetry, including "Tintern Abbey" and the "Ode on the Intimations of Immortality"; some poems from Browning's "Men and Women"; and a few poems by G. M. Hopkins, T. S. Eliot, and Dylan Thomas.

In the two years of the sixth form and in a third year of preparation for Open Scholarship examinations, which are taken by a select few, there is less formality than in the earlier years. The fact that the upper sixth classes average 15 students in size undoubtedly makes for informality of teaching and learning.

Geography

In the post-World War II period the average American discovered the outside world for the first time. He began to believe that the interests of many different peoples were not totally unrelated to the future welfare of the United States. Because of our long insularity world geography in many American high schools remained almost a closed book. Only now are we coming to realize the necessity of geographical knowledge if we are to survive and prosper in an interdependent, though currently fragmented, world.

Long ago close proximity to the Continent led the English to an appreciation of the significance of geography. The building and maintenance of an empire demanded a knowledge of many lands and peoples, as does the developing British Commonwealth today. It is therefore no accident that the study of geography is required through each of the early secondary school years. The quality of individual research is commonly high. National necessity has made geography a required subject, and that necessity, coupled with a predilection for the development of excellence, has made for superior work in this subject.

Geography can be quite different from the cloistered academic experience sometimes ascribed to English grammar school education. Eleven- and twelve-year-olds observe and record the tides and water traffic. They use topographical maps in studying their local communities. At thirteen and fourteen they go farther afield. Visits to the chalk country encourage records of rock formations, the effects of erosion, and river bank phenomena. Older students often spend a "Geography Week" in field centers for advanced study. Here they work on problems set by their teachers or by the director in charge of the center. In the summer, sixth form students may do field work on the Continent.

The study of geography becomes real in many classrooms through an abundance of models, charts, diagrams, and even paintings. Here is a sample of such materials in one school:

1. THE EARTH'S ORIGIN, COOLING, AND ULTIMATE FATE. Paintings by an imaginative artist to illustrate one hypothesis put forward at the present time.

2. THE EARTH'S ATMOSPHERE. Diagrams and photographs in color of its phenomena—upper "lays"; aurora; air circulation; depressions; clouds; thunderstorms; nitrogen cycle.

3. MOVEMENTS OF WATER. Models to demonstrate ocean currents and wave motions—including an exhibit to illustrate the Kon-Tiki expedition.

4. WORLD DISCOVERY MAPS. A frieze illustrating the pushing back of the fringe of outer darkness by the adventures of men and the spread of knowledge. These explorations are the growing tips of human history.

5. EXPEDITIONS OF GEOGRAPHERS ABROAD. In recent years illustrated by a relief map of Europe and showings (on request) of films and slides in color taken each year. Showings included Lapland, Corsica, Stromboli, the Sahara, the Azores, and the coast of Asia Minor.

6. LAND FORMS AND LIFE. Map studies of a series of actual examples

(mainly from the British Isles) of the work of rivers, ice, wind, and waves; and their influence on scenery and human settlement. (Geography VIth)

7. THE EFFECT OF SEASONS. Charts showing the yearly calendar of human occupations dependent upon the seasonal rhythm of selected typical regions of the world.

The systematic and creative nature of classroom study and field work in geography can be realized probably only when one has the opportunity to observe the teaching and to examine the numerous texts and reference books, maps, work sheets, models, student notebooks, and research reports which characterize a geography program in a good English grammar school.

History

History is a major subject for the same reasons that geography is. The development of the British Empire makes it necessary for all secondary school youth to learn about many lands. Long-time ties with the Continent necessitate the study of European history. The use of the Royal Family as a symbol of unity, accompanied as it is by medieval pageantry, requires a detailed knowledge of the early customs and traditions of England itself.

History, like geography, also has an integrating function in the curriculum. In addition to combining elements of geography, anthropology, government, economics, and sociology, the history curriculum is related closely to English literature. Many dramatic performances make history come alive. The art of the past is studied in costume design, architecture, and medieval pageantry. History notebooks, kept religiously in all classes, are commonly enriched by careful drawings and artistic designs.

Nor is history always oriented only to the past and to the acquisition of knowledge. A brief list of purposes from one school indicates the range of interests among the many teachers of this subject.

The major problems of the history curriculum as a whole:

1. To help pupils to understand the world in which they live, putting problems of 20th century into perspective and, at the same time, introducing the girls to their heritage of European world civilization.

2. The study of evidence and development of judgment.

3. To develop certain attitudes of mind, especially tolerance and the art of seeing the other point of view.

4. To develop habits of independent work, powers of selection, and of lucid expression.

5. To develop observation of pictures, place names, architecture, etc.

6. To give pleasure, wider interests, and to increase the enjoyment of travel, literature, art, and to increase the pleasure of understanding of other subjects by emphasis of history.

Items from one syllabus illustrate the extent of history study in many grammar schools. Europe, with which the English people have been so closely related for centuries, and England are the chief subjects for study. In the early years historical personalities are used to make the subject more meaningful. Later, history becomes a specialized study of chosen periods in preparation for university examinations.

Form I   3 lessons and 1 homework.

Age 11+   *Introductory background followed by selected topics from ancient and medieval history.* (The final selection of topics will depend to some extent on the previous background of girls entering the school.)

1. Time.

2. Brief outline of Pre-History and of the history of early empires linked with work done in writing lessons.

3. Fifth century Greece with some background of early stories of Homeric stories (linked with work done in English) and stories of the Persian wars.

4. Alexander the Great.

5. Some stories from Roman History, Julius Caesar, Rome in the time of Augustus.

6. The Roman Empire. Britain as part of the Roman Empire.

7. Breakdown of the Roman Empire and coming of the Barbarians (mainly from point of view of British History).

8. The Conversion. Anglo-Saxon Britain. Stories from Bede.

9. Charlemagne.

10. The Vikings and Alfred.

11. The Norman Conquest and its results as shown in the County.

12. Social life in the 12th and 13th centuries with reference to local examples.

13. The medieval church taken mainly through biographical stories— St. Benedict, St. Bernard, St. Thomas à Becket. Stories of the Crusades. St. Francis.

14. Trade. The Story of Marco Polo.

15. 14th Century. Black Death; Peasant's Revolt with reference to Froissart; Hundred Years' War; The Church (linked with work done in English).

16. Chief changes in government during the Middle Ages leading to the breakdown of strong government and the England of the Pastons.

It is hoped that each form will do two pieces of individual work during the year.

Form II   2 lessons and 1 homework.

Age 12+ *English History with European Background 1485–1660.*

Form III   2 lessons for half the year, 3 lessons for half the year.

Age 13+ *English History with European Background 1660–1850,* including reference to relevant topics from American history. Individual work on social life in 17th or 18th century.

Form IV   2 lessons and 2 homeworks each of 30 minutes.

Age 14+ *English History from 1850 to the present day with special reference to the period 1871–1939,* to be taken in the General Certificate Examination (Cambridge) at ordinary level.

Form V   3 lessons and 3 homeworks.

Age 15+ Syllabus based on requirements for Cambridge General Certificate Examination at ordinary level. *Outlines of European History 1815 to the present day with special reference to the period 1878–1939.*

VI B   Lower Form   2 lessons.

Age 16+ The present-day working of the Constitution. The fundamental characteristics of the Constitution.

1. Central government.

2. Local government.

3. Finance—rules and grants in aid.

4. The development of the social services. Relations of the United Kingdom with the other members of the Commonwealth. Legal and constitutional problems of intercommonwealth relations. Difference between dominions, colonies, dependencies, and trust territories.

VI A   Lower Form   6 lessons.

Age 16+ Beginning of the two year course for Cambridge General Certificate Examination. At advanced level in English and European History.

VI   Alpha   Lower Form   6 lessons.

Age 16+ Beginning of Advanced Course in Economic and Public Affairs, following syllabus for the Cambridge examinations. (Upper Form Syllabus for Cambridge General Certificate Examination at advanced and scholarship levels.)

VI Alpha Upper Form 6 lessons.
Age 17+ Syllabus for Advanced Level—Economic and Public Affairs Papers. I and V. (Upper Form Syllabus for Cambridge General Certificate Examination at advanced and scholarship levels.)

VI A English History 1485–1714.
Age 17+ European History 1494–1715.
        Special subject—The Reign of Elizabeth I.

VI Alpha Upper Form 6 lessons.
Age 17+ Syllabus for Advanced Level—Economic and Public Affairs Papers. I and V.
Senior Form Preparation for University Entrance.

Foreign Language

The liberal arts tradition, which has dominated English state grammar schools since their organization in 1902 and independent grammar schools for several centuries, puts a high value on the study of language. Language is viewed as a key to the understanding of other cultures. Those who travel and trade on the Continent find linguistic ability of practical use.

Several years of foreign language are obligatory. French is commonly required for five years, with a second language offered, and sometimes required, for four years. Those who continue into the sixth form may further extend their language study.

Initially foreign languages were rarely offered in English secondary modern schools, which are attended by some 60 per cent of adolescent youth. The difficulty of language study of grammar and literature was recognized, as was the fact that the large group of nonscholars will not be in vocations in which another language is an asset. More language study is now provided as a result of the belated realization that there are able boys and girls in these schools, as well as in grammar and technical schools.

In recent years the Ministry of Education has instituted a scheme in which foreign assistants are made available to grammar schools.

The assistants, who come from various countries on the Continent, themselves wish in turn to perfect their English. Such helpers have proved to be of major value in improving pronunciation and in guiding language study by small groups of students, particularly at the upper levels.

In a typical language course of study in a relatively large (650 pupils) grammar school, French is taken by all pupils through the fifth form, and all take the ordinary level of the General Certificate Examination in this subject. It is continued for a further two or three years in the sixth form by those pupils who choose French as one of the advanced and scholarship level subjects. In the same school German and Spanish are started in the second form.

The foreign language is generally employed in the classroom but English is used if comprehension is not assured. Grammar is usually taught in English. In French the sounds are taught phonetically. Free composition of the "guided" type is developed gradually throughout the school, but "theme" and "version" as formal exercises are not introduced until the Vth Form. Suitable Readers of graded difficulty are in use from the IIIrd Form upwards. The study of literature and the critical study of foreign texts is not begun before the VIth Form.

The foreign assistants are used with groups of pupils from the IIIrd Form upwards to afford practice in conversation and pronunciation. In the VIth Form the services of these assistants are particularly valuable in stimulating and guiding discussions on more serious topics and also in promulgating a deeper knowledge of the culture and way of life of their country.

Private reading in the foreign language is encouraged early in the course and in the VIth form a fairly wide selection of classics and suitable modern novels and plays in the foreign language are read in the pupils' leisure hours.

The more gifted pupils take, in addition to the Advanced Level papers of the General Certificate of Education, a Scholarship paper in the foreign language. For the latter, tutorial classes are held in which the critical faculty is more intensively developed by means of literacy commentaries based largely on the well-known "Lecture Expliquée."

Selected pupils remain in the VIth Form a third year to take competitive Open Scholarship examinations for Oxford and Cambridge universities. These pupils are obliged to work largely on their own under the guidance of an experienced teacher, owing to exigencies of staffing.

Interest in foreign languages is stimulated in most grammar schools by the systematic exchange of students with European secondary schools, correspondence with pupils abroad, and regularly scheduled group visits to foreign schools during holiday periods.

Mathematics[4]

The demand for mathematicians and scientists in the United States has served to focus attention on the programs of elementary and secondary schools, colleges, and universities.

In their early formative years children are taught by elementary school teachers, many of whom have little knowledge of the nature of mathematics and inwardly abhor the subject. It is impossible to estimate how much of this attitude is communicated to young children. As pupils progress into algebra, the situation is not likely to improve. Too often here the instruction aims at the memorization of rules in order to manipulate symbols in such a way as to arrive at an author's answer. The logical development of geometry and the meaning of such terms as "proof," "hypothesis," and "conclusion" are no longer a part of the mathematical training which a student brings to college. Too few secondary schools carefully select the really able mathematics students and instruct them in special classes of reasonable size under competent teachers.

At the college level, corners are cut in order to advance the student in the study of calculus—the integrated analytic geometry—calculus texts give a minimum amount of training in analytic geometry, a subject in which each exercise can be a test of mathematical ingenuity.

In evaluating the quality of mathematical instruction in selected English grammar schools, examples have been taken from examinations administered in these schools at the age levels of thirteen to fourteen and fifteen to sixteen.

Age 13–14

1. A hollow trough made of sheet metal 1 yard wide has the cross-section shown in the diagram.

[4] This section was prepared by Sherburne F. Barber, Professor of Mathematics, The City College of New York.

If the height of the trough is x inches, what is the area of the cross-section? What would be the value of x in order that the trough have a maximum capacity?

To solve this problem a student must understand intermediate algebra, a simple geometric formula for area, and differential calculus.

2. P is the point (3, 4) and Q is the point (a, b). The line x + y = 10 bisects PQ perpendicularly. Calculate the co-ordinates of Q.

To solve this problem a student must know basic formulas (slope and mid-point) of analytic geometry and be able to translate geometric situations into algebraic equations.

3. Arrange in descending order of magnitude:

$$\sqrt{3} \qquad \sqrt[3]{4} \qquad \sqrt[4]{8} \qquad \sqrt[6]{18}$$

To solve this problem, a student must be thoroughly familiar with the theory of exponents—a topic of intermediate algebra.

4. Draw a line ABC such that AB = 2″ and BC = 1″. Using ruler and compass only, construct:

   a) The circle on AB as diameter.

   b) A perpendicular PCQ to AC through C.

   c) The circle touching the first circle externally, touching PQ and such that the common tangent to the two circles at their point of contact passes through C.

State which theorems about tangents to circles you use in your construction.

(Leave all construction lines clearly visible.)

To solve this problem a student must have extensive knowledge of the theorems of plane geometry relating to circles.

Age 15–16

1. Resolve the function $\dfrac{7 - 8x}{(1 - x)(2 - x)}$ into partial fractions and hence, or otherwise, expand the function in a series of ascending powers of x to four terms. State for what range of values of x this expansion is valid and prove that from the 4th term onwards the coefficients are all negative.

The first part of this problem on resolving the fraction into partial fractions depends upon ideas usually presented in advanced algebra (or college algebra). The second part on expanding the function into a series of ascending powers of x depends upon fundamental notions of calculus.

2. Show that the lines $3x - 4y - 3 = 0$, $5x - 12y - 13 = 0$ are tangents to the circle with centre $(-3, 2)$ and radius 4. Also find the equations of the angle bisectors of the given lines. Which of the two represents the equation of one diameter of the given circle?

   This problem from analytic geometry is more than just a routine problem in the use of the normal form of the straight line.

3. Integrate: $\int_0^2 (1 + \sin x)^2 dx$.

   This problem involves a knowledge not only of integral calculus but also differential calculus and the application of analytic trigonometry in integral calculus.

By comparison, the levels in the American system at which the topics covered in these questions would normally be met are the following:

Plane Geometry	10th year—age 15–16
Intermediate Algebra	11th year—age 16–17
Trigonometry	11th year—age 16–18
Advanced or College Algebra	12th year
Analytic Geometry	12th year (Advanced placement or special classes), freshman year in college or possibly even later
Differential Calculus	12th year (Advanced placement or special classes) freshman year in college or possibly even later
Integral Calculus	usually college

In addition to the examinations, notebooks, carefully prepared by the students who took these examinations, were examined. These notebooks indicated that the students had received intensive instruction in topics normally included in algebra, trigonometry, and advanced algebra and were able to handle problems in analytic geometry and calculus. The following examples are taken from the notebooks of a student aged thirteen plus:

1. A point P whose x co-ordinate is a, is taken on the line $y = 3x - 7$. If Q is the point $(4, 1)$, prove that $(PQ)^2 = 10a^2 - 56a + 80$. Find the value of a for which this expression is a minimum. Hence deduce

the co-ordinates of the foot of the perpendicular from Q to the line $y = 3x - 7$.

This problem requires for its solution a knowledge and understanding of analytic geometry and a simple differential calculus as well as a familiarity with algebra sufficient to express the problem in algebraic symbols and carry out the operations of the calculus.

2. What are the co-ordinates of the points of intersection of the straight line $y = 4x$ and the curve $x^2 = 2y$? Determine the area of the segment cut off from the curve by the straight line.

This problem involves not too difficult algebra and integral calculus applied to the problem of finding area.

3. If a and b are the roots of the equation $3x^2 - 2x - 3 = 0$ find $a + b$, ab, $(1/a) + (1/b)$, $a - b$.

This problem was solved by using theorems pertaining to the sum and product of the roots of a quadratic equation without actually finding what a and b are.

4. If $3 \sec^2 x + \tan^2 x = 5$, find $\tan x$.

This not too difficult problem in trigonometry was solved by using the basic identity $1 + \tan^2 x = \sec^2 x$.

At the age of thirteen plus the student is familiar not only with many of the topics of algebra, both intermediate and advanced, and trigonometry, but also with their application in the solution of problems in analytic geometry and calculus. With good training in arithmetic, a youngster, gifted in mathematics, could move ahead well into algebra by this age. The work in calculus is amazing, however. While the techniques of calculus can be formally taught, the examples illustrate that the student must know how to apply the calculus and use analytic geometry.

Without dwelling longer on specific examples, it seems that the following circumstances must exist in order to teach calculus and its applications understandingly to students in the thirteen to sixteen year group:

1. Careful selection of students—homogeneous grouping and classes of reasonable size.

2. Careful preparation of teachers. The teacher of arithmetic must understand the basic ideas of algebra. There must be actual teaching rather than reliance on workbooks where students may fill

in correct answers without understanding what basic principles are at stake.

3. Emphasis on careful training in other subjects—especially reading, writing, and the use of English. Too often our students are handicapped by not even understanding the correct and careful English in which ideas, definitions, and problems in mathematics are expressed.

4. With good students and good teachers, mathematics taught painstakingly and understandingly.

Biology[5]

Students entering English grammar schools at the age of eleven are required to take science for five years, which leads to examinations at Ordinary Level. At the beginning of the sixth form, and in some cases earlier, advanced work begins for those planning to take university examinations at Advanced and Scholarship levels. There are two major aims of science teaching. The first is to present basic scientific material, hoping that an aptitude for science will develop spontaneously. "It is better caught than taught" writes one science specialist. The second aim is to fulfill requirements for specific professions.

The study of biology in the early years in English schools includes, first, a "principles" survey of general physiological and physico-chemical activities in plants and animals: metabolism, respiration, digestion, circulation, excretion, reproduction. This is followed by a survey of the plant and animal kingdoms, emphasizing taxonomy, morphology, physiology of typical organisms in the phyletic groups, life histories, cytology, histology, ecology. American schools, on the other hand, emphasize practical biology, especially human biology.

Pedagogical devices in American schools include much classroom discussion, individual laboratory work, demonstrations of dissections and other processes, field trips, projects, and plentiful audiovisual aids. American laboratory resources, as well as trained laboratory assistants, are superior to those in English schools, where, for instance, a student often does not use his own microscopes until

5 Prepared by P. L. Bailey, Jr., Professor of Biology, The City College of New York.

his final years. English schools do more laboratory work in the form of dissections and slide preparations, whereas American schools use the project method (group as well as individual) to a greater degree.

Three-hour *essay* examinations are used almost exclusively in English science education, along with practical examinations of similar length. Tests occur throughout the term, with questions often taken from, or patterned after, old General Certificate Examinations. Answering these obviously requires enormous knowledge of theoretical and factual material and also the ability to integrate this material, to organize it, and to *think* about it. Questions on these papers indicate that the quality of the material and the requirements for understanding are often on a level with advanced college material in the United States.

Any student in an English school who has passed examinations at the Advanced or the Scholarship level has had biology certainly of the quality of our elementary college courses and possibly of certain of our advanced courses. At these specialized levels the essay answers on the individual papers examined indicate a very high standard of grading. In addition to actual subject material, great emphasis is placed by both student and instructor on literacy, spelling, and grammar.

American methods involve chiefly *objective* testing: i.e., multiple choice, association tests, filling in blanks, as well as notebook examinations; laboratory reports, oral questioning, laboratory co-operation in "squad" work, development of scientific hobbies, project excellence, et cetera. The regard for literacy, spelling, grammar, and penmanship observed in the English papers seems almost entirely lacking in the American system. In fact, the type of testing in the United States makes but little, if any, demand upon such skills.

American schools have a much broader pragmatic ideal and approach than do the English grammar schools. Our courses do not emphasize academic biology. On the contrary, they give an elementary introduction to a few fundamentals with little attention to abstractions, theories, or other philosophical implications. There is little attention here to basic taxonomy, phylogeny, growth, and evolution. Students working toward a professional career in biology will have to take an elementary college course to get much of this.

American students appear in general to be restless and impatient with work as undramatic as that characteristic of English advanced biology courses. We want to see results and progress. Our students are not interested in gaining a good idea of experimental design nor an understanding of accuracy and expertness in precise communication. These are elements of worth-while importance in English science education.

The British student, by the time he gets to the university, will have been well grounded in theory and abstraction and have had considerable practice in reasoning. In addition, the more gifted students will already have been sorted out in high school. The British student, whether scholar or nonscholar, will be far better versed in communication skills and the ability to express himself, although the American may be a more sophisticated citizen of the modern world and may feel more personally secure in dealing with his own environment.

Chemistry[6]

In studying the teaching of chemistry in English secondary schools, I was impressed, first, by the age at which it is begun and, second, by the number of years such study is continued.

In the sequence of topics I studied, the emphasis does not seem to be on the logic of chemistry as a science. Few, if any, theoretical considerations are introduced. Avogadro's Hypothesis is mentioned, but there is no reference to an atomic theory on which to base the hypothesis. Again, Gay-Lussac's Law of combining volumes of gases is mentioned before the study of the behavior of gases.

I was impressed not so much by the amount of material covered for the Ordinary Level examinations as by the extension of study over a period of several years. One suspects that in a good high school chemistry course in America all of these topics could be covered in one year. In our high schools, however, there is very little laboratory experience compared with English practice. In both countries there seems to be an emphasis on qualitative, rather than quantitative, treatment of subject matter. Apparently at the non-

6 Prepared by A. G. Anderson, Associate Professor of Chemistry, The City College of New York.

specialized level both systems hesitate to ask students to think in exact mathematical terms.

In a syllabus for the Advanced Level, the first topic listed is "Deduction of laws of chemical combination from experimental data." One can infer only that during the first four years the approach in this case was dogmatic rather than logical. As further illustration of this point there is the topic, "The periodic classification of the elements." This appears also to be a first exposure, in the fifth or sixth year of science study. A third topic deals with a *simple* treatment of the phenomena of oxidation and reduction involving simple electron transfers." One wonders how this subject was covered in earlier years. In the total of 27 topics covered on the advanced level (two sixth form years) considerable emphasis is placed on methods of preparation and the properties of various elements and compounds. A fair amount of organic chemistry is also included. There is rather extensive laboratory work.

At the Scholarship Level the content corresponds closely to college courses in elementary analytical, physical, and organic chemistry. This is now the eighth year of science study in the grammar school, the last several of them in chemistry. Scholarship boys are about eighteen, or roughly three to four years younger than our college seniors at graduation.

During four years of college most American students majoring in chemistry are subjected to at least those courses prescribed by the American Chemical Society. After this exposure the top group of American students should fare well on the university entrance examinations at the Scholarship Level taken by the top group of English grammar school graduates.

Physics[7]

Data for this brief analysis come from descriptions of grammar school syllabuses, a number of student notebooks, and university examinations at Advanced and Scholarship Levels.

Topics tested in the physics examinations consulted include mechanics, thermodynamics, some kinetic theory, electricity and magnetism, waves, and geometric optics. These are all "bread

[7] Prepared by Harry Soodak, Assistant Professor of Physics, The City College of New York.

and butter" topics in classical physics. The glamorous subjects—
such as quantum theory, relativity theory, atomic and nuclear
physics, and elementary particles—are not mentioned, except for
some elementary coverage in atomic and nuclear physics. But the
"bread and butter" topics are covered thoroughly and well, both
theoretically and experimentally. Similar comments, except for the
experimental aspects, hold true for the applied mathematics curriculum.

Advanced Level examinations in physics test for theoretical and
experimental knowledge, as well as for understanding of the
standard contents of the course of study. Thus, the instruction in
one examination contains the two sentences:

1. Candidates should wherever possible show by their answers that
they have seen or themselves performed experiments on the subjects they
are discussing.

2. For full credit it is not sufficient to obtain the correct results to
numerical questions; the principles involved and their bearing on the
question must be clearly stated.

The mathematics required is mostly algebra, plus a small amount
of elementary calculus. Finally, the examinations do not truly test
a student's ability to answer nonstandard questions.

Scholarship Level examinations in physics and applied mathematics cover essentially similar topics but require more calculus
and some differential equations. Apart from the mathematical considerations, the questions are less standard, more searching, and
occasionally demand that the student put together ideas from different branches of physics.

The English student is given the opportunity to learn a large
amount of basic physics by the age of seventeen or eighteen. Indeed,
he may have had elements of physics in required science work for
six or seven years. His training places him about two years ahead
of his American counterpart in topic coverage. More important,
however, is the fact that he already has had a number of years of
deep research and hard serious study. In contrast, an American
student of the same age and the same innate ability has usually
had a single course in high school or the first year of college, without deep research and hard study.

It seems appropriate to raise the question of whether the more relaxed atmosphere in American schools, which allows the student a great choice of courses and activities and gives him more room and more time to decide on a future career, balances this two year lead in knowledge and systematic investigation. Or has this leisurely approach wasted the time of student and teacher by spoiling the student for concentrated work, possibly resulting in a negative attitude toward scholarship?

The choice of an intense or relaxed attitude is largely a matter of taste, but a relaxation that leads to superficial coverage and shallow understanding is clearly an educational crime.

GENERAL EDUCATION ACTIVITIES

Academic courses in grammar schools are highly specialized. This has the advantage of promoting knowledge in depth, but it has the disadvantage that the relationship between specialized subjects may not be understood. Insofar as this is the case, a major purpose of a liberal education—to see life and knowledge in its wholeness— is circumscribed.

The English attempt to guard against the dangers of specialization in a number of ways. In scholarship university examinations a three hour General Paper must be written, and searching questions in the fields of specialization must be answered. Topics for the General Paper cover a wide variety of subjects. They include philosophy, aesthetics, ethics, literature, architecture, political theory, social and international affairs.

Because they are aware that scholarship students must be prepared to deal with questions of broad scope, and because of their own educational convictions, the administrators and teachers in grammar schools have developed a wide variety of courses which stress general rather than highly specialized knowledge. Many aspects of these enrichment programs could well be adapted to American needs.

A well-known combined grammar and technical school offers a "General Studies Scheme."

This course aims at fostering in the Sixth Former an awareness of the world around him and its problems; at humanizing the specialist courses by consideration of general issues; at increasing in these boys the power of thought and the power of expression. It seeks not so much to impart knowledge as to stimulate the ability and the desire to acquire knowledge, to weigh evidence, to criticize and evaluate, to judge, to argue, and to speculate.

All items in the syllabus for this scheme do not have to be covered. Masters make choices on the basis of the subjects most pertinent at the moment. The course deals with three major areas: (1) current affairs and politics, (2) science and its application to life, and (3) the fine arts.

A London grammar school schedules a series of lectures for sixth-formers on philosophy and ethics once a week throughout the year. Discussions follow presentations by faculty members. A second London school requires that all arts majors in the two sixth form years write a weekly essay on previously assigned topics such as "Religious Revivals," "The English Are Free Only at Election Time," or "The Art of Biography." A third grammar school features a specialized course in economics. Students from this class have furnished the leadership for a program on economic problems in which the entire upper school has participated.

Various enrichment devices are used in teaching these general courses. Experts from the local community as well as foreign visitors, may be invited to address the classes. Masters from different subject fields participate. Research work may be done in museums, and community institutions may be visited. Films and recordings are often used.

STUDENT CULTURAL ACTIVITIES

The term *cultural* is peculiarly appropriate to describe the activities engaged in by grammar school youth. These are the boys and girls who enjoy intellectual fare and naturally engage in pursuits which stimulate and broaden their understanding. Numerous clubs and activities continue the intellectual emphasis of the classroom.

One major play a year is as much as many grammar schools can manage while concentrating on examination subjects. Outstanding music and art activities in these schools are distinctly the exception rather than the rule, and for the same reason.

Students delight in controversy. Formal debating teams in many grammar schools are now, however, distinctly in second place compared to the new modern affairs societies and the councils for education for world citizenship.

The Modern Affairs Society has the distinct educational advantage of enrolling all those in a school who are interested, not just a few debaters. These new organizations bring in outside speakers on many controversial subjects. Question periods are always in order. The arguments that begin in such sessions spill over into conversation at luncheon breaks, as well as into history, geography, and English classrooms.

Many grammar schools belong to regional organizations, which in turn are affiliated with the Council for Education in World Citizenship, a national student group. I attended a Central Council meeting devoted to Latin America and later, when visiting schools, asked about its influence on participants. The students were "impressed by the nonprevalence of a 'color bar' in Latin America." They contrasted this with South Africa where they felt conditions were "absolutely shocking." Some had become increasingly disturbed about discrimination on the basis of race in their own country. Others were concerned that "textbooks often promote ill feeling between countries."

Trips and excursions are educational devices which are much more widely and effectively promoted in England than in the United States. Hostels are used in trips in the British Isles, while private homes are favored in excursions abroad. These journeys are financed in considerable part by L.E.A.'s, for they are regarded as an integral part of school programs. When visiting France or Germany, English students may spend part of each day in going to school with their new acquaintances. Living in private homes gives an opportunity for observation of personal life and customs in an intimate family setting. Community agencies are investigated. A foreign language is practiced. English schools and families are in turn the hosts for groups of secondary school youth from the Continent; the exchange results in new knowledge, new perspectives, and new friends. Intellectual maturity, so characteristically a product of grammar school preparation, is thus furthered by both local excursions and intimate contact with foreign cultures.

PROMISING IDEAS FOR AMERICAN HIGH SCHOOLS

We can learn much from the ways in which the ablest English youth are educated. In considering the practices which might be adapted, however, two important limitations should be kept in mind.

First, many English practices are not appropriate for American high schools. They do not fit a democratically oriented education. Included in this category are examinations at the age of eleven, which still largely determine a child's future school program; the teaching of religion in all schools; and the institution of separate schools for academic, technical, and nonacademic pupil.

Second, qualifying examinations to grammar schools at the age of eleven test abstract intelligence and not potential ability in the arts. The programs in English grammar schools continue the intellectual and traditional academic emphasis. One does not find in English grammar schools numerous examples of creative work in music and art.

Promising Ideas in General Education

1. *Purity and facility of speech are emphasized in all grammar school courses.* School activities such as drama, debating, and discussion groups on current affairs supplement regular course work. The result is that educated Englishmen are everywhere recognized by the effectiveness of their oral expression.

2. *Essay writing is a major activity.* Fluency and style in writing are characteristic of educated Englishmen. In one instance reported, sixth-formers are required to write one essay a week for a period of two years—in addition to written assignments in the academic subjects.

3. *A sense of history is developed.* Years of required courses in both history and geography get results. The speech and the writing of educated Englishmen are rich in historical allusion. Geography has developed an awareness of the problems of many different peoples. Literature as taught and drama as acted also contribute to a sense of history.

4. *Independent thinking is sought in all subjects.* The English prize personal liberty. The long struggle of nobles and commoners

for freedom is stressed in English history. Freedom is a necessary concomitant of intellectual excellence.

5. *A sense of personal responsibility pervades school programs.* This is a value inherent in the aristocratic tradition which grammar schools have inherited and now perpetuate. Clear lines are drawn between what "gentlemen" and "ladies" will and will not do. Probity in personal conduct, in trade, in government, and in sports is a central emphasis in all school activities.

Promising Curricular Practices

1. *A number of basic academic subjects are required in the lower forms of grammar schools (ages 11–15+).* These include English, one foreign language, history, geography, science, and mathematics. Other subjects, such as art, music, and domestic science, are also studied. Electives include a second foreign language. In total, this program is believed to provide the groundwork for a sound liberal arts education.

2. *The large number of required subjects in the first five years is made possible by scheduling various subjects only two or three periods a week.* A developmental program in each area is thus made possible. The thoroughness of preparation for which grammar schools are noted is due in no small measure to many years of continuous work in required subjects. Even though most students do not go to a university, they may thus have four or five years of one or more foreign languages and the same number of years in other academic subjects.

3. *A high degree of specialization is carried on in the last two years of the secondary school.* A certain number of subjects are still required in the lower and upper sixth forms, but the work load is lessened to allow more time for specialization. Students major in two to four subjects, depending upon their interest and ability. Those qualifying for a university may have studied one or more languages for seven years or one of the specialized sciences for four or more years.

4. *Special intellectual activities broaden understanding.* Many grammar schools require all sixth-formers to participate in various types of intellectual activity in addition to the regular course work. Regularly scheduled sessions of from two to five periods a

week are devoted to various themes—intellectual history, modern social problems, art in its various forms, the writing and evaluation of an essay a week. Such intellectual fare supplements study in depth. It raises the intellectual quality of grammar school experience.

5. *Homework is required in all regular academic subjects.* The nightly load is not so heavy as it first seems, since not all subjects are taken every day. Care is exercised to limit specific homework assignments. Concentration is stressed. In the words of one master, "It is surprising how much can be accomplished by a talented eleven-year-old in twenty minutes of concentrated study in each of his subjects."

6. *Classes in the last two years of grammar school average around 15 students.* In the earlier secondary years the average is somewhat, but not materially, below the American equivalent. There is little doubt that small classes account in part for the high quality of grammar school work. Building individual reading lists, individual research, and an approach to the tutorial relationships between student and teacher are thus possible. In the United States the present increase of interest in education conducted in unusually large groups does not controvert the continuing need for intimate personal guidance in the education of youth.

7. *Both internal and external examinations are taken at different levels.* This testing is a vital factor in keeping grammar school standards high. English masters take a dim view of new types of tests. They are convinced that real learning can be tested only when the student is required to relate knowledge, concepts, and principles in meaningful ways. Reliance is therefore placed on essay examinations, given at periodic intervals.

8. *The wide use of travel, both in the British Isles and on the Continent, is a civilizing influence.* Whether the major purpose is recreation or study, a change in one's environment brings stimulus and perspective. L.E.A.'s promote and partially finance educational journeys of grammar school youth.

In general, the graduates of English grammar schools are considerably more advanced in academic knowledge and ability to deal with ideas than are graduates of equal ability from American high schools. The evidence presented in this chapter indicates just how far, particularly in subject matter, this advantage extends.

I wish again to make it quite clear, that we should not go to English grammar schools for social value orientation. Our comprehensive schools are democratic in orientation, while the English grammar schools are aristocratic and class conscious. Nor, with notable exceptions, should we go to grammar schools for especially effective programs in the fine and graphic arts, beyond that of writing. English grammar school programs, moreover, do not furnish significant leads as to how emotional and social maturity may be developed. For a variety of reasons, including the wearing of uniforms which mark their adolescent status, grammar school boys and girls seem young in nonintellectual aspects of maturity when compared with their American counterparts.

It is in the traditional academic, or "solid," subjects that one expects to find, and does find, special excellence. Finally, and significantly, freedom of thought and individuality, so necessary in the development of gifted youth, find unique expression in English grammar schools.

PART III

PROGRAMS
IN OPERATION IN THE
UNITED STATES

7

Enrichment for Talented Rural Youth

Howard G. Sackett and Glyn Morris
Board of Co-operative Educational Services
Lewis County, New York

HALF a dozen cars and station wagons pull up before a former electrical appliance shop in the small village of Lyons Falls, New York, and high school boys and girls go into the remodeled store, now an improvised classroom. These are members of the Lewis County Youth Seminar arriving from schools 40 miles apart. Even though the county is in the snow belt of New York State, with an average snowfall of 124 inches a year, these young people gather once a week for a stimulating intellectual experience. Seated around a large table, the group develops the implications and problems in the relationship between communication and civilization, a problem formulated at the beginning of the year. They read extensively, take field trips, view drama, listen to music—all with one purpose in mind: the discovery of the meanings in these experiences which throw light on the central problem.

This experiment will be the basis for this chapter, which will describe a seminar for talented pupils from its beginning in 1955. The methods used, some of the many problems encountered, and, finally, the implications of this program for dealing with talented young people will be appraised.

A description of the rural setting in which the Lewis County

Youth Seminar operates is essential to an understanding of the problems faced in undertaking the experiment. The 22,000 people of the county are widely scattered on farms and in small villages. Except for the county seat, with a population of about 3,500, all the villages have populations of less than 900 each. Approximately 34 per cent of the labor force is engaged in agriculture, mostly dairying, and another 25 per cent is employed in the paper industry. This indicates an economy closely tied to the land through its farms and timber. Except for the school in the county seat, with an enrollment of 1,800 from kindergarten through the twelfth grade, all the others are under 800, and the majority have less than 600 students.

The project is frankly experimental and cuts across nearly every issue involved in developing a program of education. Many divergent points of view have had to be reconciled. A faculty had to be trained. There were problems of curriculum and administration to be surmounted. Consequently this report may not convey all the nuances, positive and negative, with which the project is flavored.

The Lewis County Youth Seminar was officially started in June 1955, when the principals of seven Lewis County schools decided to set aside time and resources for this purpose. The decision resulted from the fusion of several concerns. In the first place, the nine supervising principals had a lively and continuing interest in the awards given pupils who participated in the annual State Scholarship Examinations. Second, the question of how to challenge superior pupils in rural areas had been frequently discussed by the district superintendent and his staff.

There was general agreement that some further experience was needed for talented pupils, although it was not clear what form this enrichment should take. Therefore, the administrators selected seven teachers, together with the director of guidance as coordinator, to serve as a committee to explore a possible course of action and to make recommendations. A teacher was selected from each of the seven schools participating and from as wide a representation of disciplines as possible. The final committee included teachers of English, homemaking, commercial education, social studies, foreign languages, and science. This group was briefed by the superintendent and principals on the need for providing adequate experiences for the talented students through a program which, among other things, would help in the following ways:

1. Provide more adequate competition and stimulation.
2. Integrate knowledge.
3. Fill in gaps, if any, in skills and knowledge.
4. Reduce boredom.
5. Provide experience of a kind which pupils might find in college, i.e., research, intensive study, more rapid reading.
6. Provide the opportunity to follow special interests.

The committee presented the administrators with the broad outline of a suggested plan, the immediate point of which was a proposal to explore ways and means of establishing a specific program for the academically talented youth.

GETTING UNDER WAY

Early in September 1955 the teachers met who had made the preliminary recommendations to the administrators. Meanwhile, the district superintendent had made arrangements with Teachers College, Columbia University, to provide technical assistance in developing the project.[1] The term "Talented Youth" was adopted, and the group decided to call the project "The Lewis County Youth Seminar."

Determining Purposes

Although the teachers seemed close together in their aspirations for talented youth, clarifications on many points were necessary. But agreement was quickly and easily reached on this point—that the project should not get under way with the pupils until the faculty had reached an understanding on aims and procedures. It was, therefore, in this spirit that deliberations were carried on.

It is one thing to state in broad terms what should be done for talented youth, but quite another to spell these generalities out in detail. It is one thing to wish for fewer restrictions in the day-to-day, highly organized school program, but quite another to organize a program of a less structured kind when the opportunity is avail-

1 Talented Youth Project of the Horace Mann-Lincoln Institute of Experimentation, Teachers College, Columbia University.

able. Here there was absolutely no requirement to be met save the best development of each of about 20 high school seniors. Hence, it is not difficult to believe that the first few meetings of the faculty were not always "on the beam," although the faculty never faltered in its zeal nor lost sight of its ultimate goal.

Many questions were raised, always variants of the major one: "What are we going to do?" As the variety of needs of talented youth became known—each need with its own appeal—it was difficult to be inclusive yet restrictive, to carve out an area which would be adequate yet not get out of hand. For this reason the group decided it must formulate its own statement of aims.

Since the faculty could assume that all the students of the group were candidates for college, most of the objectives were keyed to the needs of college students. Everyone agreed that each student is entitled to all the education he can and will absorb, that he should have at his disposal all of the available resources and personnel to help him gain all of the experiences in critical thinking and planning which he needs and desires.

Following each of the first few sessions, the chairman asked each teacher to write a summary of the discussion, together with his view of the progress made and problems to be solved. The appraisals were forthright and useful in clarifying thinking; they also served to point up a semantic problem. To help solve this problem it was decided to discuss concretely the program for the first day of the seminar, thus reducing every issue to a tangible form. For most of the group this procedure proved to be the first experience in reducing general aims to a specific program. From this standpoint alone the time spent was worth-while for the individuals involved.

Eventually a statement of aims and principles was produced which served as a guide during the succeeding years. One group of statements described the aim of the project for the pupils. Another group of statements had to do with guiding principles for those who would serve as teachers. Abstracts from the long document developed by the teachers read as follows:

I. We believe that this group of pupils will tend to have special capacities for living. For instance, they may be more sensitive to environment than many other pupils their age; they may have deeper insights; have more power of concentration; greater ability to abstract principles from concrete situations. Because of this, we think this experience should help them to:

1. "Know themselves" and find an adequate role which challenges them enough yet does not demand more than they have to give; and, to the extent of their desire, to discover and use all potentials for a full life of service and happiness.

2. See life as a whole, with its contradictions and paradoxes, relationships and interdependencies, and learn to accept the unchangeable.

3. Ask and try to answer more serious and involved questions than may be possible in the ordinary classroom.

4. See the "means" as "integral" with the "ends" of all living—hence, to respect and support democracy as a way of life.

5. Seek the truth.

6. Recognize and grow in the ability to accept their societal responsibilities.

In order to effect these general aims, the group will focus on experiences which will provide opportunity for:

1. Clear thinking and communication, oral and written, and wherever necessary, to give help on the basic skills involved, e.g., reading, spelling, computation, research, and study habits.

2. Judicial consideration of debatable positions, theories, and viewpoints, with the disciplines involved for protecting man against bias and for discovering truth.

3. Helping pupils to state a problem and develop an idea or concept via art, words, and other symbols.

4. Probing deeper into history, literature, and science to the end that motives and relationships and concepts are considered and clarified.

5. Filling in gaps in knowledge and experience whenever possible.

6. Consideration of those aesthetic experiences which contribute to man's sense of beauty and order.

II. Guideposts for the Faculty.

1. This is a new experience for which it may be necessary to learn techniques and methods of procedure in transit.

2. Leadership responsibility will be rotated and mutually shared.

3. The faculty will not hesitate to stop at any time during class to appraise a puzzling situation and make appropriate plans in the light of it.

4. Much group planning will be required.

5. The faculty recognizes its responsibility to challenge the pupils to come to grips with new and more difficult experiences.

Although these statements are general, they seemed inclusive enough and broad enough, and yet sufficiently specific, to satisfy the faculty. The faculty was also gradually moving toward the concept of enrichment for the talented rather than "more of the same" classroom experience. The *esprit de corps* was high at all times and served to pull the group through this new and creative experience.

Selecting the Pupils

Obviously considerable attention was focused on the criteria for selection. The procedure has undergone several changes since its inception. It was early recognized that the group faced a typical rural problem in finding young people with the high I.Q. usually associated with the gifted. The median I.Q. in large areas of rural America is approximately ten points lower than in urban areas, as measured by standardized group tests. The median in Lewis County, though slightly above that of many rural areas, still made it necessary to accept more than a high I.Q. as criteria. An arbitrary minimum of 110 was decided upon, but other factors were considered which might be indications of giftedness. It seemed to those working on the project that giftedness may well be a relative thing. Hence they sought ways of selecting the most able students regardless of how they compared with students in another section of the country.

Criteria for selections the first year were finally based upon the following: approval by school faculty; I.Q. of 110 or above; ability to profit by the experiences provided; potential scholarship examination candidate; and rank in class.

The experiences gained the first year indicated several weaknesses in the method of selecting students. Because of the nature of the seminar a student needed to have a rather high ability to verbalize. The individual with high mental ability, who was otherwise shy and withdrawn, sat and listened but made no real contribution. In fact, this type of person was likely to be uncomfortable in the group. The person who was able to talk and take an active part in the discussion tended to be most enthusiastic and responsive to the opportunities available. On the other hand, several pupils who were initially handicapped by reticence were helped to overcome this through seminar experience.

The factors involved in selecting a student are now more clearly understood. Experience has shown that success in a group of this nature is dependent upon a combination of abilities, not solely upon high intellectual ability. In addition to a better understanding of the qualities needed for success in the seminar, it has become advisable to add some of the most able ninth- and tenth-graders to the group. The following procedure is now being used for selection of students:

1. The principal asks individual members of his faculty to submit the names of students whom they consider eligible, together with reasons for the selection.

2. Each school submits the names of eight candidates, four of whom are considered as alternates.

3. The criteria for selection are intellectual ability, reading ability, ability to verbalize, ability to participate in group discussion and to share in group thinking.

4. Where pupils in grades ten and eleven have high intellectual ability —that is, higher than a pupil in grade twelve—and all other factors are equal, such pupils are selected for membership in the seminar.

5. Each pupil selected by the school is asked to write a composition on a topic chosen by the seminar faculty to determine his ability to express himself, organize his thinking, and show originality. Here is a sample problem: Assume you are to be sent to a lonely government outpost, equipped with the usual D.C. electric generator, where you will remain for one year. There will be several other persons assigned to the post, and you will be permitted to take 100 pounds of luggage in addition to the necessary equipment and clothing for subsistence. What would you take with you and why?

6. If further screening seems necessary, the seminar faculty interviews the candidates.

INITIAL GROUP PROCEDURE

After 12 planning sessions the faculty felt reasonably ready to begin, and the first seminar was scheduled. The 20 students who had been selected met for lunch in the homemaking department of the Lyons Falls School. The strategic importance of a first meeting cannot be overemphasized. The teachers were keyed up in anticipation of working with talented young people in an unstructured situation. The pupils were curious and excited to see what was in store for them.

After considerable exploration, in the first attempt, the students were divided into four groups to suggest and then discuss areas of interest which they might like to explore. Each group came up with many suggestions, some of which were: the history of music, music appreciation, classical literature, some economic and technical aspects of industry, and developments in science.

Although the faculty made a strong attempt to formulate a problem which would include the variety of interests suggested by the pupils, this effort had to be abandoned. Four areas were finally selected: science and industry, music and art, classics, and human behavior. Each group then went to an assigned meeting place and made plans for their work. Finally, all came together for a half-hour during which each group reported on what it hoped to accomplish.

Since this experience modifications have been made in the first day's program. The members of previous seminars now meet to plan orientation for new members. They assume the responsibility of explaining the seminar to new pupils. They demonstrate a typical seminar. Furthermore, at the outset the faculty takes time to explain points of procedure and seminar aims which were previously left to the student to discover for himself.

Generally the program now follows this schedule: All meet at 1:00 P.M. in the homemaking room; students immediately disperse in groups or to take exploratory trips; and a summary session is held at 3:00 or 3:30 P.M.

During the first year there were many individual and group activities. Various kinds of impromptu panel discussions were arranged. Occasionally the co-ordinator visited each group and chose a theme which seemed appropriate to all, and then asked selected pupils to react to it. For instance, one group was discussing Hemingway's *The Old Man and the Sea*. The main character's persistence against the onslaught of nature raised the question of why he continued to do this. Here was a starting point for the discussion of motivation. The group studying psychology was familiar with the problem, as was the group discussing science and industry. Interestingly enough, the music and art group could raise the same question regarding the persistence of an artist in the face of material and psychological obstacles. Obviously the questions raised by Hemingway's masterpiece could stimulate almost endless discussion and development.

Throughout the remainder of the year some groups took field trips. At times all were brought together for an entire afternoon of listening to classical music, reading poetry aloud, and discussion. The discussion was mostly spontaneous, growing out of such topics as: "What is happiness?", "What is evil?", "What are the criteria for goodness?" Pupils gave reports on special projects covering a wide range of topics. On one occasion the faculty experimented with assigning a wide variety of topics related to one theme. Pupils were guided in their investigations of this overarching theme.

An evaluation of the seminar at the end of the first year gave some rather significant findings, which are detailed later in this chapter. As a result of the first year's work, however, it was the opinion of the faculty that in the future a more structured program would be desirable.

A More Structured Program

In planning the subsequent seminar, the group selected a theme. The seminar was not broken into set groups but worked as a unit, with provisions for grouping when necessary. The theme selected was "Communication." The seminar devoted several meetings to setting up problems on which to work. Eventually nine questions were formulated:

1. What makes communication difficult?
2. What is the place of symbolism in communication?
3. What part do feelings have in communication?
4. What does the recipient's background, etc., have to do with communication?
5. What is the effect of culture on communication?
6. What is the function of government in communication?
7. Is there communication between creatures without overt symbols?

8. How are learning and communication interdependent?
9. Can more effective communication improve living?

As these questions were raised, the group saw that there were discrete areas and concepts around which a study of communication might be localized, such as: the senses; semantics; music; art; relativity; science; and emotions.

As soon as the questions were formulated, the group visited a small Roman Catholic church. Here religious symbols were described and to some extent their meaning was explained. Many other questions were raised by the pupils as a result of this experience. Hence, from this time on, communication took on new and larger dimensions for them.

Discussions were further enriched by visiting the Munson-Williams-Proctor Art Institute, the Supreme Court at Utica, and several other churches and by hearing recitals on a baroque pipe organ and watching television programs selected for their mature quality.

An example of significant thinking occurred in the discussion of issues involved in the conflict between church, state, and individual conscience raised by *The Lark.* In another case the entire group viewed the film *Friendly Persuasion* and thoroughly discussed the value conflict arising among the several members of a family regarding the obligation to take up arms in defense of country. Other films viewed were *Life in Bali Today, The History of Printing, The Major Religions of the World,* and *Making Yourself Understood.* All were tremendously valuable.

In addition to the more obvious audio-visual experiences, the group did considerable selected reading. *Patterns of Culture* by Ruth Benedict, *Essays* by Emerson, the *Saturday Review,* and *Language in Action* by Hayakawa, proved most stimulating. Each member was provided with a dictionary, and it became routine to investigate new words and develop vocabulary.

Considerable time was given to the study of semantics. In some respects this may have been the area in which insight was most rapidly acquired. On one occasion opportunity was given for a cursory examination of two foreign languages, and some significant differences in syntax were noted.

The experience gained by the faculty during the first two years of work with the seminar made them confident about initiating activities in the third year. The time usually required for initiating the year's work was shortened considerably; by the end of the third session the problem for the year had been formulated.

At the beginning of the third year the opening session was more structured, the faculty being motivated by a desire to move faster through the exploratory experiences and to arrive more quickly at a concrete study topic based on "Communication." They had agreed that "Communication" was broad enough to embrace many approaches and had by no means been exhausted by previous seminars.

The students began with a 20 minute essay elaborating the theme "An educated person is . . ." This was followed by a ten minute essay on the subject "Communication is . . ." This written work gave the faculty greater insight into each student's concept of himself, his view of his relations to the world, and his pattern of values.

After some veterans of the preceding year's seminar had talked to the group on the nature of seminar work and the role of the participant in such a study, the film *Life in Bali* was shown. Any film on any people could have served, since the basic ingredients of all civilizations are present in any single one.

A great number of questions followed the showing of the film, a few of which follow:

How do these people communicate with God?
Is dancing like watching a play?
Does good always triumph over evil?
Does evil have relative meaning for different people?
What communicative media do these people lack? Are they worse off for it?
Do better and increased communications add up to higher civilization? If so, is the reverse true?

From these and numerous other questions the following tentative hypotheses were agreed upon by the seminar for investigation:

1. Civilization is contingent on communication.
2. Civilization results in happiness. (Happiness is relative, conditional, and continuing.)

3. Happiness is the greatest good.
4. Television is a mark of progress.

Within the framework of these hypotheses the group reduced and developed a few possibilities with a view to an over-all question which would constitute the study problem for the year. At the third session the following question was agreed upon; it had already been raised at the second session and needed only to be restated and accepted: "What effect does communication or lack of communication have upon civilization, progress, and happiness, assuming that happiness is the greatest good?"

Following acceptance of the problem came structure. After a cursory blocking out into segments—(1) things to discuss, (2) information needed, (3) things to do, and (4) uncertain—the group probed possible solutions to the main problem and subproblems. The big step ahead was the construction of a chart, diagramming somewhat the approaches to the major problem.

This chart adorned the wall of a former electrical appliance shop in Lyons Falls, now the new meeting room for the seminar. It outlined the program in three major steps, which followed this order:

I. Development of the major topic, "Communication," into a problem. (This had been done by now.)

II. Establishment of criteria for tackling the problem inductively. (A tentative approach listed art, education, entertainment, religion, economic life, science, social structure, government, and home life as facets of civilization.)

III. Approach to the study by correlation and contrast—i.e., the study of our civilization versus another—and testing hypotheses.

The time element required a delimitation of the study, and the group agreed to begin with one facet of civilization. They settled for art. Each member then selected for study one phase of art based on interest—drama, music, architecture, sculpture, fashions, artifacts. For each group an assignment sheet was constructed. The one for the music group, typical of those for other groups, follows:

Suggested outline for seminar members: Music
NOTE: Follow the framework of the seminar and relate your project to this wherever possible.

1. Listen regularly to following programs:
   a) WBRV—Sunday 1:00–2:30
   b) WBIX—Sunday 3:00–4:30
2. Listen to recordings—at least one of each major composer
3. Become acquainted with—(Note and write on distinctions)
   a) Greek or ancient modal forms
   b) Counterpart in Elizabethan music, i.e., Ballads in Early American music
   c) Modern composers—Strauss, Richard; Stravinsky; Copeland; Rogers; Ravel; Debussy.
4. Read a review of a musical performance.
5. Read at least one book—complete—on music interpretation.
6. Read at least one biography or autobiography of a composer.
7. Keep a log of music heard: name of piece, composer, date heard, comments.

By the end of the year these study groups had worked hard, both outside the seminar and at sessions, and had achieved more profound contributions toward the over-all problem than had earlier seminars. Yet they had followed individual interests. Among the noteworthy products was a huge scrapbook of designs made by a ninth grade student.

The third year the faculty faced a real problem in preventing compartmental study by groups straying from the central question. To avoid this, reports of progress by individuals and groups were referred to the wall chart. The faculty needed to help each group to (1) structure its study, (2) obtain materials, (3) set up field trips, and (4) plan activities related to group studies and the central theme.

There have been times when the faculty has had to deal with unforeseen and bewildering problems. They found somewhat early in the third year that this seminar seemed disputatious and unable to discuss anything in depth. The faculty at one time wondered if the age and grade spread were factors. Meeting more often for more detailed study of this problem resulted in some rewarding changes. The long single row of tables gave way to a quadrangle table arrangement where all could see and be seen.

A major discovery also was that the group needed more common reading assignments to provide nucleuses for more group discussion.

The faculty felt rewarded when its plans to dispel vagueness and lend clarity and movement to the project were successful.

The third year seminar visited the *Watertown Daily Times* and interviewed the editor and the publisher. They saw the Crane Symphony Orchestra in rehearsal. They visited the new St. Mary's Cathedral in Ogdensburg and studied its art. They heard the pipe organ in the Gunnison Memorial Chapel of St. Lawrence University in Canton, and later enjoyed a more varied concert in the Forest Presbyterian Church of Lyons Falls, New York. They visited the television station and observed the assembly line techniques in the General Electric radio plant in Utica. They listened to hi-fi recordings in a private home in Lyons Falls. While discussing values, the group went to Utica by school bus to see *The Bridge on the River Kwai.* Usually one of the participating schools furnished a school bus for transportation. As in the previous year, the faculty met for 23 sessions, usually after school and in the evening.

At this writing the seminar begins its fourth year. The theme is "Change in the Life of Man." With experience gained over more than three years, the task of structuring an over-all problem for the year now seems relatively easy. The older members lend support and guidance to the new.

What of the Future?

Initially the seminar was viewed as a way to round out experience or fill in the gaps in programs of twelfth grade pupils. The program itself has suggested some revisions, however, in the over-all content of the regular school program. Perhaps this is what they meant when, at the closing session of the first year, several pupils said, "Why can't all pupils have this kind of experience?" In any case, it was clear that if pupils were to gain maximum benefits from the seminar, they should come to it better equipped to participate in group discussion and to structure a problem of some complexity; they should also feel secure about discussing questions to which answers may not be immediately forthcoming, or for that matter, which admit of no final answer.

With such learnings in mind, the superintendent and local administrators are now considering the following programs:

*The Development of Projects for Talented Pupils in the
    Elementary Schools*

In one central school a group of eight boys in grades five and six have been identified as talented. Plans are under way to develop a program for them. This will involve the cooperation of several teachers, including elementary supervisor and the high school science teacher. Each pupil's major interests will be identified and utilized for motivation. The essential characteristics of the seminar method will be followed whenever possible, i.e., the development of major questions, together with their implications, coupled with the use of the problem-solving method and discussion skills.

At a pace compatible with the resources and circumstances of the local situation prevailing in the nine schools, as many such groups as possible will be organized. If groups cut across grade lines, at least one group can be established for as few as six potentially gifted pupils in even the smallest school.[2]

*The Development of Selected Aspects of the Seminar Program
    Within Each High School*

The seminar is essentially designed to open up horizons and stimulate pupils to do independent study to a degree not prevalent in the typical classroom. Some of the potentiality of this experience is lost, however, because attention has not been given to relating seminar experience to the potentialities of the local school. It is planned that this will be remedied. Currently, for example, seminar students are asked to write a 20 to 50 page paper during the year —the most extensive writing project they have done so far. English teachers will be brought together to discuss implications of the major theme in order to assist the seminar students in each school.

Consideration will be given to such experiences as creative writing, music appreciation, and the development of groups to carry on seminar-related projects with a team of interested teachers. Here again the scope and nature of each project will depend upon the characteristics and potentialities of each school. Some variety can therefore be expected. For instance, in one school the English,

---

[2] Glyn Morris, "Helping the Mentally Superior Child in Rural Areas," *Journal of Exceptional Children,* January, 1956, p. 161.

social studies, and homemaking teachers plan to work with the principal on the development of a seminar-related project for a small number of pupils. This group may include several pupils who are not attending the seminar but are considered as alternates. In this small school also, the English teacher is interested in developing a small group in creative writing. In another school the guidance counselor and the English teacher will help develop the implications of the major seminar theme. And in another school two counselors and the music and art teachers will combine forces.

The Training of Teachers to Function in an Unstructured Situation

The next step is to introduce an increasing number of teachers to the seminar by rotating the staff. First, they will sit in on a number of sessions, and then they will be invited to participate in training sessions designed to develop the understanding and skills necessary to exploit the potentialities of talented pupils.

Briefly stated, this program will include five major concerns:

1. Study of the nature of giftedness, the multidimensional character of intelligence, the place of motivation, and quality education. Attention will be given to understanding the meaning of conceptualization, generalization, developing implications, and thinking abstractly.

2. Developing skill in identifying and avoiding bottlenecks in discussion. This skill is particularly important in exploring value systems and in extending the boundaries of discussion among intellectually gifted pupils. Most teachers are familiar only with a "closed system" of education, i.e., answers around which the teacher frames questions and situations which will lead inevitably to right responses. This limitation is particularly apparent where value judgments are involved; often the teacher's question precludes any answer but one. Long years of such experience, together with current schemes of evaluating pupils, make both pupils and teachers uncomfortable in any other setting. Only rarely does a pupil challenge this situation.

Members of the seminar have been emphatic in their belief that they should have been trained in group discussion. One of the most fruitful sessions was the one in which the faculty demonstrated how mature people carry on a discussion by asking questions of each other which help develop the other person's point of view. Techniques include the courteous presentation of facts which may have been overlooked but which qualify another's opinion and the separation of facts from opinion. Discussion can thus become inquiry rather than argument, but the ability to take an effective part in group work must be taught.

3. Developing skill in defining worth-while problems. Essentially this skill is of a piece with the classical problem-solving method developed by John Dewey, Harrison Elliot, and others. It requires the ability to state a problem in terms which provide for developing and testing solutions. In developing a large scale problem which a group may investigate for an entire school term, however, skill in both developing implications and in limiting the investigation without impairing it is necessary.

4. Developing the feeling of "being at home" without knowing all the answers. Much is implied in this point, particularly with respect to the ability of a teacher to withstand the threat of the unknown. It is obvious that this problem is related to the preceding one. Some teachers are more capable of fostering such security than others, but most teachers need help. Often both pupils and teachers seek "closure."

5. Helping teachers capitalize on the educational possibilities of any segment of life by recognizing the universals implicit in it. Repeatedly the seminar staff has found itself capable of initiating a fruitful intellectual experience by permitting pupils to develop a considerable number of questions about a simple artifact. Placing a chair on a table and saying, "Let's talk about this chair," raises questions pertaining to utility, form, culture, art, and eventually a value system. Sooner or later the query "Why?" emerges, and a group is off on a discussion of ultimate meaning.

Persistent Problems

A creative project does not emerge without displacement and strain at some points. In the Lewis County Youth Seminar the most obvious strain is the occasional absence of the seminar students from the regular class held one afternoon each week. Other difficulties include the following:

1. Relating the seminar experience to the outgoing program of the local school. Some efforts to solve this have been made through bulletins sent to each school which briefly describe the seminar experience, for interested teachers to use in motivating a more extensive study of their own subject matter. This procedure will be extended as more teachers are involved for short periods in the seminar activities.

2. Overcoming initial teacher resentment at having able pupils removed from their classes. It is not known to what extent this resentment prevails, but there is reasonable certainty that it does.

3. Synchronizing the seminar program with all the contingencies of bringing together pupils from six schools. This problem is aggravated where long winters and distance make transportation precarious. This is not a major problem, but a persisting one which the seminar staff must learn to accept gracefully.

4. Identifying and training teachers to work with gifted pupils at all levels.

EVALUATION

Does the current program make any difference? This is a practical question which administrators, teachers, and parents ask. The staff, therefore, together with the personnel of the Talented Youth Project of the Horace Mann-Lincoln Institute of School Experimentation, have been concerned with developing methods of evaluation.

A number of procedures have been followed, but no adequate method of objective appraisal has thus far proved acceptable. For instance, there has been some experimentation with "before and after" inventories and questionnaires given to pupils, teachers, and parents. Inadequacies in both number and response preclude an accurate analysis of these data. There is considerable evidence of a subjective kind, however, to indicate that the program is worth while.

Other evaluative procedures include the following:

1. Detailed opinion questionnaires given to pupils at the end of the seminar year

2. Informal evaluation by two pupils, recorded on tape at the close of each session

3. Comparison of essays on open-end topics given at the beginning and close of essays of the seminar year

4. Evaluation by the seminar group at the end of each year, recorded on tape and analyzed.

A follow-up study of former seminar members now is in progress. There is no doubt that a majority of the participants found the experience worth while. A number of them have written letters to teachers, extolling the value of the seminar in their college experience. From the mass of comments by pupils, the following are typical:

We don't stop at "yes" or "no" answers. We try to find out "Why?"
We speak our thoughts freely.
Learn more—School is more enjoyable. We're not restricted or embarrassed. We are helped in other school work.
It's like a treasure hunt.
Helped to accept other people's opinions and ideas; no one is always right or wrong.
Timeless questions are now occurring that we can come to no definite conclusions about.
Discussion is on a higher level now that the faculty has shown us how to discuss.
We had to use our minds, something which one very seldom does. This has been the first time I believe my mind has been exercised in such deep thought which I had believed was nearly impossible for me.
On field tours, I was able to find out how industries operate, how they get along with labor, and how they differ from each other. I have also come in contact with many new terms and have come to understand them.
I'm glad I had the opportunity to meet and to become friends with the others in this way.
Developed the ability to think beyond the surface of a problem or question.
I was scared stiff at first but later in the afternoon I was so interested I forgot to be afraid.

There were negative responses as well, and from these, as they were sorted out of the transcribed tape recordings and questionnaires, the faculty discovered what procedures were most effective. The continuous evaluation served as a feedback, and adjustments were made accordingly.

As stated earlier in this chapter, coming to grips with new experiences was one of the seminar goals, a goal which implies helping pupils develop independence of thought and action. On the basis of the pupil responses, the seminar appears to be doing this. If the talented are to take their place as leaders in society, they must be helped to develop the will to stand alone for what they believe to be right. They must learn to champion new ideas, new causes, new ways of doing things. Frontier thinkers need to learn to expect and accept the criticism and unpopularity that so often go with creativity. The talented must be encouraged to experiment, create, and break barriers.

Taken as a whole, there is no doubt of the value of this program. Parents are asking questions about it, indicating both their interest in its progress as well as their desire that their children be participants. Pupils, too, are showing an increasing eagerness to become members of the seminar. It seems reasonably sure that the seminar procedures will be extended.

8

An Enrichment Program in a Small High School

Henry Scattergood
Germantown Friends School

GERMANTOWN Friends School, founded in 1845, is an independent Quaker School under the care of Germantown Monthly Meeting of the Society of Friends. It accepts children in kindergarten at the age of five and provides both an elementary and a secondary course. There are about 700 students in all. Of this number only approximately 25 per cent are the children of members of the Society of Friends.

Since this is a religiously based school, it carries a special responsibility to educate the children of Friends, and this group is given preference in determining who shall be admitted. The school is coeducational and tries to keep a fairly even balance of boys and girls in each grade. There are a maximum of 45 children in kindergarten and never more than 50 children in two sections in grades one through six. In the seventh grade 10 to 15 students are added, and the total is divided into 3 teaching sections. There is little change in size or composition of the class group after the seventh grade. Few students withdraw and only a few are added. This means, of course, a relatively stable school population, with at least half of most twelfth grades composed of those who have been enrolled for 12 or 13 years. Most of the others have been enrolled for six years. Upon graduation virtually all continue their formal education, 95 per cent in four year liberal arts colleges, a few in junior colleges, and the others in special art, music, or business schools.

ADMINISTRATIVE PROVISIONS

Attention here will be centered primarily on the senior high school—tenth, eleventh, and twelfth grades. Since there is a great deal of overlapping of faculty, of curriculum planning, and of activities between junior and senior high school grades, it is impossible to separate these areas completely. There are, however, two men designated, respectively, Head of the Junior High School and Head of the Senior High School. Both also teach English, one to the seventh grade and the other to the twelfth grade. There are two assemblies per week for the entire upper school—composed of grades seven through twelve—a brief religious assembly at the beginning of the school day on Monday, and a 40 minute assembly on Friday. In addition, the junior high school grades have their own assembly every Wednesday.

Each Thursday the upper school students and teachers gather in the Friends Meeting House, next door to the school, for a Quaker Meeting for Worship which lasts about 45 minutes. A few adult members of the Meeting also attend.[1] In these activities there is a six year age range, but experience leads the faculty to believe that they help to stretch the younger students and prepare them to take greater responsibility in assemblies and Meeting in their senior high school years than if the junior and senior high schools were completely separate.

When the Advanced Placement Program was started in 1953, Germantown Friends School became one of the pilot schools. It was soon discovered, however, that a senior high school of 190 did not have enough sections and ranges of ability to warrant starting separate "honors" sections in every subject area. The attempt was made, therefore, to enrich the academic program in a number of areas. Germantown Friends for many years has offered a rather rich course for all students, with considerable individual choice of

---

[1] This Thursday Meeting for Worship is the regularly appointed midweek Meeting of Germantown Monthly Meeting and it is held throughout the year regardless of whether or not the school is in session.

strictly academic subjects and strong programs in music, art, drama, and student activities. The actual program of classes and activities now in operation will be described later.

The teachers are almost without exception graduates of liberal arts colleges or universities. Most hold master's degrees either in their special fields or in education. The school has been fortunate in having a low turnover of its faculty, especially of those teaching senior high school grades. This situation results in a considerable age range as well as wealth of experience. With one exception every teacher has taught in at least one other school before coming to Germantown Friends.

It is extremely difficult to enumerate and evaluate the qualities, motivation, character, and personality that every school seeks in its teachers. Suffice it to say, that as a Friends school expressly concerned with communicating religious and spiritual as well as purely academic values, Germantown has made the effort to select individuals who represent the best in mind, character, spirit, and potentiality for continuing growth. More specifically, with a student body of high average intelligence, plus a friendly, informal faculty-student relationship, teachers need not only to know their subject, but also to have intellectual depth, humility, humor, and a real liking for, and faith in, adolescents.

INDIVIDUAL GUIDANCE

The school is organized on a homeroom basis, which means that every student sits in a homeroom with about 20 other boys and girls of his own grade. The homeroom teacher is directly responsible for guiding each student's daily school life. In addition, the head of the senior high school and the principal supervise and supplement this guidance with special attention to selection of courses. College guidance is carried on by the eleventh and twelfth grade teachers. In the senior year each student is assigned to one of the senior teachers or to the principal, with the result that each guiding faculty member is responsible for about a dozen students.

Some of the most valuable guidance comes from "personnel meetings" in which all those teaching in a given grade spend an afternoon or evening, at least twice during the school year, carefully considering the strengths and weaknesses of each individual student in that grade. Not only academic aptitude and achievement are considered but any aspect of a student's life that merits attention. In the spring, for example, each student's course of study for the following year is considered and must be approved by the majority of his current teachers. Often many faculty members are unaware of special problems of health, social adjustment, or family background that affect a student's class work and behavior. Just the sharing of several teachers' observations, plus the use of all the records available, nearly always increases understanding and frequently leads toward a solution of an individual's school problems.

One other form of guidance is systematically used, that of parent conferences. Since this is a twelve year school, the faculty has the advantage of getting to know parents thoroughly. By senior high school a number of conferences have been held, a considerable body of information about the student and his family has been collected, and usually a close, friendly relationship between school and home exists.

All factors contribute to close individual guidance. In addition to the systematic procedures noted above, there is also a good deal of flexibility and informality in the guidance program, so that students feel free to seek out any member of the faculty for counseling on school work, personal problems, summer jobs—in short, on a great variety of subjects.

COURSES OF STUDY

The faculty of Germantown Friends School expects to prepare students for college but is equally interested in their total development. In common with good teachers everywhere, it seeks to stimulate students to think independently and to help them develop into good citizens with high purposes and some concept of unselfish service. Therefore, the course of study attempts to go beyond the purely academic. Older students are encouraged to take part in worth-while community and service activities. The faculty believes this can be done, with wise guidance, without sacrificing academic values, and indeed considers this "plus element" in college preparation as one of the most valuable parts of the curriculum.

Senior High School Courses

10th year	11th year	12th year
English*	English*	English*
History*	History*	History, U.S.*
Biology or Geology	Chemistry or Mass and Energy	Physics, Adv. Biology
French—2nd year	French—3rd year	French—4th year
Latin—2nd year	Latin—3rd year	German—2nd year
	German—1st year	Mathematics
Mathematics*	Mathematics	Public Speaking (½ course)
Choir	Choir	Choir
Art—Shop	Art—Shop	Art—Shop
Physical Education*	Physical Education*	Physical Education*

* Required.

The senior high school course of study is designed primarily to meet the needs of better than average students who are preparing for four year colleges. In addition to those courses marked with an asterisk, other requirements are at least one laboratory science, religious instruction, and mathematics through the eleventh grade for those planning to enter a four year college. Normally students select five courses in the tenth and eleventh grades and four and one-half courses in their senior year.

There is considerable individual choice in a student's course of study. In a class of 60 seniors there are likely to be at least 50 different schedules. This makes it possible for students to concentrate fairly heavily in languages, science, mathematics, or the arts, according to individual interests and abilities.

The following course and departmental descriptions were written by the teachers most directly concerned and give in some detail the chief objectives, as well as an idea of the methods, content, and results, of some of the senior high school work.

History

History is required of every student in the tenth, eleventh, and twelfth grades. This requirement reflects the school's conviction that a study of man's past is essential to an understanding of man's present. We try to lead the student to see that his times are unique, but that they are an outgrowth of the problems and challenges and insights that men essentially like himself have experienced.

We recognize the impossibility of covering everything, and we are coming more and more to the conviction that history must be presented as real problems that real people wrestled with. Course titles are misleading, primarily because we are in the process of making serious revisions in our courses of study. The title of the tenth grade course is now "Ancient and Medieval History"; of the eleventh, "Modern European History"; and of the twelfth, "American History." At present the tenth grade course highlights certain segments of ancient and medieval history within the framework of a comprehensive textbook. We are in the process of developing a course that builds on the anthropology course in the ninth grade. It will take a close look at how men organized their societies—how they lived and what they believed—in five or six key periods of Western history. There will be no basic text but rather a series of central readings augmented by a great many primary and secondary sources of varying difficulty.

In the eleventh grade course three emphases are developing. There is a focus on the roots of present-day problems as they appear from the seventeenth century on. A six week detailed study of the United Nations—its purpose, its functioning, its achievement, and its potential—is included. There is also an extended look at one non-European country—its history and its relations with the West. Obviously the title "Modern European History" does not really fit any longer.

Teaching methods vary considerably, but some observations can be made that have relevance to the problems of the gifted student. We try to get away from separate nightly assignments. In all three grades assignments are made a week or two in advance. There is provision for individual ability, for self-set goals, and for student planning of class work. Text reading, extra reading, and written interpretations are expected on most assignments. There is a great deal of emphasis on written work. The history teacher is as much concerned about how something is said as about what is said.

Discussion and interpretation take up most of the class time. The student is expected to be a question raiser as well as a question answerer, with the questions and answers directed toward his classmates as much as possible.

Often the classroom becomes the scene of some major controversy of the past. The students try to defend proposed courses of action without the benefit of hindsight. For instance, a twelfth grade classroom may become the House of Commons for a few days, while the Government and the Opposition debate the wisdom of passing the Coercive Acts. Those with key roles to play, usually the more gifted, will spend a good deal of time in research, trying to determine from what premises and convictions a particular man might have argued.

There is a textbook for each course, but it serves almost as a reference book. Much of the material used is in the form of pamphlets, paperbacks, private and government publications, along with duplicated excerpts from various sources. Students are encouraged to buy paperbacks for their own libraries. There is an extensive classroom library in the American history room. We are now concentrating on building up classroom libraries for the tenth and eleventh grade courses.

During the school year a number of foreign visitors come to the school. The eleventh and twelfth grade history class schedules have been arranged so that the two grades can meet together with any particular visitor. The more interested and more able students also have frequent opportunities during the year for attendance at seminars and workshops, as well as at conferences sponsored by the American Friends Service Committee. These affairs are anywhere from two or three days to a week in length.

There are no advanced courses or advanced sections within a course. We believe the real problem of individual differences is being met by greatly differentiated assignments and the growing use of small group work. Students know that much of the work of the class is dependent on their initiative and preparation.

Foreign Language

The foreign language program begins in the eighth grade where every student takes a course in beginning Latin. This is designed to be an exploratory course whose purpose is not only the learning of Latin but, more important, to discover the student's ability to master another language. On the basis of an individual's achievement he plans his high school foreign language program. Those most able and interested continue Latin and start French in the ninth grade and continue with both languages at least through the tenth year. Many are encouraged to study Latin or French at least through the eleventh grade. Those few who have serious reading problems take no foreign language for two years and usually study German in their final two high school years.

Since the majority study French for at least three years, it might be well to describe the school's basic philosophy relative to language as presented by the French department.

One of the more important developments in the teaching of French at Germantown Friends School has been the shifting emphases from foreign language as a purely cultural ornament to direct communication.

We begin speaking the language in the earliest stages when teacher and pupils, or pupil and pupil, form the simplest questions and answers. Learning is at first empirical and later analytical. It progresses through exercise in original written and oral expression until a certain amount of spontaneity has been acquired. Ability to converse with native Frenchmen is sought. A few students each year have occasion to exercise this ability as they go on work camp missions to England, visiting en route their French friends in the community of Falaise, seat of College Louis Liard, a school affiliated since 1945.

We have tried to foster communication with our friends in Falaise through the exchange of letters; written articles designed to interest or provoke discussion on each side of the ocean; and the exchange of gifts, books, paintings, music records, tape recordings, and other art objects chosen to reflect the culture of our respective countries. This affiliation has led to an exchange of students. Some 25 from foreign countries (including 9 from Falaise) have visited our school, and 4 of our students have spent terms of study and residence in France during their high school years.

We choose, even at the elementary stages, stories and descriptive or historical accounts which reflect the enduring cultural aspects of the French people. While the ninth- and tenth-graders are primarily busy acquiring skill in handling the spoken and written language, material of the type described above is introduced through selected texts, pictorial illustration, maps, photographs, and phonograph records. In the eleventh grade a more advanced study of civilization is made through textbook material, supplementary teacher-provided lectures, oral or written dissertations resulting from individual research, and illustrative magazine or other pictorial materials. French student visitors from Falaise give talks on regions of France with which they are familiar. One student from Alsace wore her regional costume when she addressed the group. At the senior level, students can be expected to handle more advanced reading on French thought and culture. Discussions at this level are carried on in French with very little attempt at translation.

Mathematics

The mathematics curriculum is currently being revised in the light of studies made at the University of Illinois, Yale, and elsewhere. The so-called "new mathematics" affects the teaching of this subject throughout the school.

We are little interested in finding only the right answer but, rather, in having our pupils analyze a problem for the relationships involved and then develop a logical and reasonable formula for the solution. Too often mathematics students (and, indeed, teachers) are inclined to want to find a rule that will apply to all problems.

There are certain absolute and cardinal relationships, however, which must be understood even in rather elementary mathematics if a pupil is to develop an understanding of and some appreciation for proper mathematical procedures. In short, we feel that mathematics should be taught today so as to help pupils properly to analyze situation problems and then set up the solution with an understanding of the terms and structure of present-day patterns. In other words, mathematics should be taught creatively.

Elementary and intermediate algebra have been continued without any great change in actual content. There is a change of emphasis, however. Manipulative skill is continued but not as the sole end. We are attempting to get a broader view of a wider structure. The equation is given emphasis as the basis of all mathematical calculation in whatever form. Variables, relations, and functions are given considerable emphasis.

In the seventh and eighth grades pupils are given an opportunity to become acquainted in an intuitive and informal way with geometric measurements and concepts generally. Geometry is continued in a formal way in the tenth and eleventh grades, one half-year in each grade. First the emphasis is upon a sound understanding of the nature of proof and deductive reasoning. We have reduced the number of required theorems but have tried to keep a good sequence of proofs to sustain the idea of sound proof to the relationships which we use.

Many exercises, both formal proof and arithmetical, are used. We find that these contribute in fine measure to the work in trigonometry. The basic ideas of trigonometry, with some computation, are included in second year alegbra. Some extension of this approach is used in trigonometry. Solution of triangles with a limited number of examples is included. The emphasis is generally upon analytical trigonometry and a treatment of identities and equations, et cetera. Trigonometry is presented so as to make a contribution to the general flow and philosophy of mathematics.

Currently we have created a "fast" mathematics section in the ninth grade. This group will presumably be able to do three years work in two years. Its members will complete elementary algebra and plane geometry by the end of the tenth grade. Following this acceleration, they will complete the regular senior course in trigonometry and advanced algebra and will be ready in the twelfth grade for the Advanced Placement course in calculus and analytic geometry. The present plan is to provide this opportunity for approximately the top quarter of each class in mathematics.

Advanced Biology

Candidates for the advanced biology course in senior year are selected carefully on a basis of ability and sincerity of purpose. First year biology in the tenth grade is a prerequisite, and every effort is made to limit the size of the class to 12. The course is designed to meet the requirements of the Advanced Placement Program of the C.I.E.B.; it must contain zoology and botany. The students have had an opportunity in their first year to learn something about handling dissections, apparatus, laboratory materials, and stains. They can now settle down to some real laboratory work, which is featured in the advanced course. They make quality studies of animals and plants which represent the principal phyla. Living material is used whenever possible and is supplemented by audio-visual materials such as films, recordings, and demonstrations.

Some class periods are devoted to straight lectures, demanding notetaking, with one period a week held open for discussion or reports from students on recent publications and projects which have been conducted outside of class. Often the latter are carried on under the guidance of professional biologists not directly associated with the school.

Each student has his own microscope, dissecting kit, and specimens. Standard reference books are always at hand. The first term text, Elliot's *Zoology,* is designed for an introductory college level course. The entire second term is devoted to botany, using Wilson's *Botany,* also a college text. In the spring there are two or more field trips. At least one trip is devoted to conservation and applied principles. Other trips to horticultural schools, the Zoological Gardens, hospitals, medical schools, the Pennsylvania Farm Show, and good collecting sites occur at intervals, but it is not possible to cover all of these in any one year.

Two goals are of major importance in the advanced biology course. The first is the study of life functions as they are accomplished by animals of increasing complexity, with special attention to the evolution and development of the structures involved. The second is the exploration of the principles of modern biology. In working toward these goals, each year the course grows, develops, mellows. For every class a few things are left out in favor of something else which appears to be more valuable. In this way a stereotype is easily avoided.

In a few cases this course has been terminal. Other students have taken the Advanced Placement examinations and have gone on in college to major courses and honor work. The number who have done this each year is small, which is probably to be expected. In addition, it has been found that advanced work has created a climate favorable to all work in biology in the school.

Historical Geology

The general public thinks of geology chiefly in terms of its recreational and economic aspects and concludes that it is therefore of interest to relatively few people. What is needed to arouse more general interest in the subject is the great middle ground of geology—its influence on the political, social, and cultural life of man and its relationships with other school subjects.

This course includes field trips and the study of fossils, as might be expected in any work in historical geology. A college textbook is used only for selected readings. A distinguishing feature of this course is the extensive reading required. During the year the students will read about 20 books. In addition to *The Sea Around Us* by Rachel Carson, we also use as text materials selections from *The Biography of the Earth* by George Gamow; *Man in the Modern World* by Julian Huxley; and *The Meaning of Evolution* by G. G. Simpson.[2] Wide and varied readings reveal possibilities for correlation and points of contact with other fields. They demonstrate that geology is a part of the very fabric of life itself.

The Sea Around Us is read as a textbook after a consideration of the Ordovician period. It brings to life the whole problem of relationships of the sea and cosmopolitan climates.

Silurian aridity is considered in general as well as in certain specific places, such as Australia. Students are encouraged to read a travel book on Australia at this point.

The Pennsylvanian, Permian, and Cretaceous periods offer a host of areas for collateral study, extending from the Carboniferous mountains of Central Europe to our own Alleghenies. The influence of geology in history is stressed at this point. As an illustration, the Ardennes form a natural boundary between France and Germany but for some reason founder in Belgium, helping to make that country the battleground of Europe. A great deal more is done here to show the influence of topography upon the whole way of life of a people. The lack of physical boundaries in Poland, the lack of navigable rivers in Spain, the effects of the central massifs of France and Spain, the fjords of Norway, and the highlands of Brittany—all are used as examples.

[2] The complete list of references will be furnished on request.

A great teaching opportunity comes with the study of Pleistocene glaciation. Our own Great Lakes, as well as the large numbers of lakes in the North Central states, New York, and New England, affect transportation, flood control, agriculture, and the tourist trade. Many other influences of glaciation can be included—the Canadian wheatfields, New England's soil, New England's drowned shoreline. A curious footnote to history, incidentally, is the direct relation between that drowned shoreline and New England's early mercantile interests, interests that were of paramount concern in the War of 1812.

As thought-provoking as some of this physical material may be, the chief interest of secondary school students centers around the evolution of life. They are intrigued with the staying power of life forms. We still have the evergreens. For that matter, we still have lung fish.

In considering the Devonian period, we find Homer Smith's *Kamongo* helps to bring this period alive. There is an absorbing tie-in here with religion and philosophy. It is gratifying, as well as pleasantly surprising, to see how well secondary school students take to problems involving conceptual thought.

The study of geology and its inherent implications, moreover, offers tremendous opportunities for significant creative writing. For examples of such possibilities, every teacher of English should investigate the works of Rachel Carson, Jacquetta Hawkes, Homer Smith, Marston Bates, and Stuart Collis.

Anyone concerned with having the study of the earth receive its proper recognition realizes that the examples cited from the historical geology course touch only the surface of the great middle ground of geology—that middle ground of appreciations that may give new meaning to a host of things we read, think about, and do.

English

The progression in the Upper School English program is from how to read to what to read. In the tenth grade, where the emphasis is on how to read, the organization of the curriculum is by types of literature. Books read by the whole class include *Ethan Frome, A Single Pebble, Macbeth, The Bridge of San Luis Rey,* and collections of essays, short stories, and poems.

In the eleventh grade the work becomes more individualized. English classes meet only three times a week, with the emphasis mainly on writing. Once a week, in addition, students meet in small groups (7 to 12 in size) for close analysis and discussion of such literary works as *Crime and Punishment, The Plague, Lord Jim, The Tempest, The Sea and the Mirror, All the King's Men, The Cocktail Party, To the Lighthouse, Moby Dick,* and *Tiger at the Gates.* The student's individualized reading is an extension of the ideas raised in these groups.

Each senior has four regular English periods a week and may join, if he chooses, one of many voluntary reading groups, each of which meets once a week. These voluntary classes are offered during what would otherwise be free periods for the teacher. Although classes are not homogeneously grouped, the small groups are set up according to ability.

The advantage of this organization is that during the regular class periods the teacher can set a level of accomplishment which he may expect from almost everyone. Then in smaller groups the more talented or more interested do supplementary reading. The result is that the whole class will read certain key books and the conference groups will, in addition, discuss books that illustrate the ideas raised in class. For example, all students read *Walden,* in which some American standards of success are questioned. A voluntary reading group might find a more contemporary and concrete illustration of this idea in *The Great Gatsby.* The small groups try to cover a book a week.

Readings fall into three large groups. The first concerns man's values: *The Heart of Darkness,* "The Hollow Men," *Walden, Patterns of Culture, Babbitt, Huckleberry Finn, The Late George Apley, The Man of Property, Gulliver's Travels, A Passage to India, A Portrait of the Artist as a Young Man, The Great Gatsby, 1984, Brave New World,* and the Sermon on the Mount.

The second group centers on freedom and responsibility: The Trial and Death of Socrates, *On the Duty of Civil Disobedience, Saint Joan, Barefoot in Athens, Darkness at Noon, Bread and Wine, The God That Failed, Two Cheers for Democracy, On Liberty,* the Declaration of Independence, the Bill of Rights, and *The Prince.*

Finally, we study the nature of tragedy, man's answers to the question of suffering: Job, Ecclesiastes, *Antigone, Oedipus Rex, Hamlet, Othello* or *Lear, A Farewell to Arms, Hedda Gabler, Beyond the Horizon, Winterset, Death of a Salesman,* and *Billy Budd.*

Obviously not all the books are read by all students. The reason for having small homogeneous reading groups, meeting once weekly, is that students can select books suited to their abilities. The abler groups tend to read most of the books listed. The slower groups read those more adapted to their abilities. Easier books—*The Fountainhead* or *The Caine Mutiny,* for example—can be subtly substituted where necessary.

The Arts

Despite the fact that until a generation or two ago Quakers paid little attention to the arts, this important area is now, and has been for some time, an important and rich part of the curriculum at Germantown Friends. All students from kindergarten through the ninth grade take music and art. Shop is required through the eighth grade. In addition, there is choir for the fifth and sixth grades and also choir and orchestral groups in junior high school on an elective basis. For the past two years eighth-graders have had a required music course (11 weeks, 4 periods per week, with outside assignments). Therefore, by senior high school, students have had a great deal of experience in the arts through singing, instrumental work, listening to music, dancing, painting, crafts, and dramatizations of various kinds.

In the tenth, eleventh, and twelfth grades the arts are offered on an elective basis, but student interest runs high. Many continue to take studio art and music theory for credit. A few play in the orchestra, and approximately half of the three upper grades sing in the choir, which is in two parts: the chorus, a group of 90, and a special choir of about 35 boys and girls. It is worth noting that both art and choir periods are scheduled within the regular school day so that they do not conflict with athletics and social activities for student time.

The words of the teachers of art and music explain clearly the philosophy underlying their teaching. They believe that "art is a language; it is an important means of expression involving skills and imagination; music and art are not the handmaidens of social studies and other departments; history can be taught through the arts."

What happens to students who participate either actively or as viewers and listeners cannot be measured with any accuracy, but some of the experiences that the choir has had in the past few years will perhaps indicate the depth and scope of the work undertaken.

1953 Performance with Temple University Choir of Brahms' *Requiem* with the Philadelphia Orchestra.
1956 European Tour—24 students sang in 32 concerts (summer) in Germany, France, and England.

Work performed:
1957, 1958 Bach's Christmas Oratorio
1954, 1958 Honegger's *Roi David*
1954   Bach's *Magnificat*
1955   Kodaly's *Missa Brevis*
1956   Buxthude's *Missa Brevis*
1956   Mozart's *Requiem*
1958   Crawford's *Magnificat*

Again, in the words of the teachers: "Good music creditably performed is an important part in the education of everyone; and the musically talented need to be challenged beyond this point."

No description of the arts program at Germantown Friends would be complete without at least a brief account of the place of dramatics in the curriculum. All through the school, classes put on plays, informally in the classroom and more formally in school assembly programs.

The culmination of dramatic activity comes in the senior year through the public speaking course. Though not required, this course is taken by virtually every senior and deserves a special word. It meets twice a week all year. During the first semester there are experiences in such techniques of public speaking as making simple announcements clearly, reading poetry aloud, extemporaneous and prepared speeches, and pantomimes. In addition, seniors gain further practice by taking turns presiding at school assemblies. In the second half-year the class prepares and presents seven or eight plays in school assemblies. These presentations are called "The Malvern Festival."[3] Every member of the class takes part in at least one play, the emphasis being on interpretation rather than on elaborate costuming and scenery. In 1957–1958 the following plays were given as a whole or in part: Noel Coward's *Hands Across the Sea;* Shakespeare's *A Midsummer Night's Dream;* Reynold Rose's *Twelve Angry Men;* Terence Rattigan's *Table Number Seven;* Giraudoux's *The Madwoman of Chaillot;* T. S. Eliot's *The Cocktail Party;* R. B. Sheridan's *The Rivals;* and Lewis Carroll's *Alice in Wonderland.* It is hard to evaluate the effect of this course, but experience has convinced the faculty that these plays provide a marvelous opportunity for growth, understanding, and appreciation, especially to the actors but also to the school audience.

CLASSROOM

The aims of classroom teaching at Germantown Friends School are not unusual. Each faculty member tries through his teaching to arouse in his students an enthusiasm for his subject, and hopes that, in addition to a thorough mastery of subject matter, they will gain important long-range understandings, appreciations, and attitudes. Every good teacher is concerned with both subject matter and the application of learning to behavior. Perhaps it is sufficient to say that thorough preparation for the next stage of learning (usually college) is an important aim. Teachers should be even more concerned, however, to stimulate intellectual curiosity and a keen critical sense and to develop individual and group responsibility.

Teachers bring their own individual enthusiasms, likes, dislikes, prejudices, and idiosyncrasies into the classroom. In fact, often these qualities add tremendous zest to their teaching. In general, however, the methods used are an informal combination of presentation of material by the teacher and recitation by the students, coupled with a great deal of discussion in which strong efforts are made to achieve a maximum amount of student participation.

3 Irvin C. Poley, "More Chances for Growth," "The Value of a Malvern Festival," *The English Journal,* October, 1951. "We Like What We Know," "The Value of a Masefield Poetry Reading Contest," *The English Journal,* February, 1950.

In many classrooms desks and chairs are arranged in a square or rectangle so that students face each other. Such an arrangement seems to stimulate good discussions. Obviously in subjects like science and mathematics, where demonstrations are frequently given, seating arrangements are more traditional, with the whole class facing the blackboard or the teacher's desk.

Most major subjects meet five times a week, never less than four. In languages and mathematics, assignments are usually made on a daily basis, whereas in English and history they often extend over a period of several days.

It is fair to say that most teachers employ a variety of methods, but because of relatively small classes—rarely more than 22 students —an informal atmosphere prevails, with a good deal of teacher attention given individuals.

One of the most important aspects of classroom climate, which relates to both aims and methods, is the de-emphasis on competition for marks. Plenty of competition exists in any group learning situation, be it football, algebra, or French, but the faculty of the school believes that the best teaching and learning exist in a cooperative, not a competitive, climate.

If teachers are to find time to prepare for and carry through first rate teaching successfully, especially the kind called for in small conference groups, their total teaching load must be revised. At Germantown Friends, English teachers of the eleventh and twelfth grades are responsible for three teaching sections, or roughly 60 to 65 students. This load seems fair considering the amount of reading and correcting of papers that they do, in addition to the time spent in conferences with individual students about their writing. The average load is 4 teaching sections of 20 to 23 students each. In some elective courses, however, classes may have somewhat fewer than 20.

EVALUATION

The courses and the teaching are evaluated through department meetings. There is also a standing faculty committee on the curriculum which periodically reviews the courses offered and recommends changes to the school administration. The judging of students' work is shown on report cards which are mailed to parents five times during the school year, with three reports in the first semester and two in the second. The grading system adopted a few years ago is far from perfect, but the faculty feels that it is more satisfactory than the former system which used the traditional "A," "B," "C," "D," and "E" symbols. A brief enumeration of the ratings, which is printed on the report cards and is attached to all college and transfer records, follows:

"1" Outstanding achievement in every area of the course
"2" Highly competent performance
"3" Good achievement
"4" Work clearly better than just passing
"5" Work just passing
"6" Failure

In addition, space is provided on the report for comments by teachers. When carefully thought out, these can be extremely helpful to both students and their parents in interpreting an individual's achievement. For example, John Doe's history teacher might mark him "3" and comment as follows: "John shows a clear knowledge and understanding of the material; he is competent in class discussions and his tests have been strong but he has not completed his written assignments this month." Richard Roe's mathematics teacher might turn in a "4" with this statement: "Richard is a persistent student; mathematics is not easy for him, and he finds written problems especially difficult, but his willingness to struggle and to come and ask for help should enable him to improve this record." The faculty of the school believes in conferring systematically with parents as well as with students. Naturally there is a great opportunity in these conferences to evaluate a student's academic progress as well as his achievements in other areas of school life.

STUDENT, SCHOOL, AND COMMUNITY RELATIONS

Quaker education in the past has emphasized four qualities: community, harmony, equality, and simplicity.[4] Friends have been

4 Howard H. Brinton, *Quaker Education in Theory and Practice* (Pendle Hill Pamphlet No. 9, 1949), pp. 41–42.

deeply concerned with putting principles into practice, with equality of opportunity for all races and groups, and especially with the means by which a given objective is accomplished. These concepts are, of course, found in many schools, but Friends schools have perhaps been especially concerned with practical service and with the development of social responsibility. Therefore, it is not surprising that the school committee and faculty have sought ways by which students could learn to take responsibility through appropriate activities and thus not only gain valuable experience but also perform useful work which would help both the school and the larger community.

Germantown Friends School offers many opportunities for students beyond the Meeting House, classroom, library, and athletic fields. These opportunities begin with younger students in their homerooms, merely in the simple tasks of daily school living such as cleaning blackboards, putting away materials and tools in the art room and the shop, taking care of the bulletin board, and tidying up one's desk. In addition, younger pupils become accustomed to serving on the Student Council, the Assembly Committee, and groups chosen to organize various social functions.

By senior high school age, therefore, students are ready to undertake more ambitious projects within the school and also to participate in a variety of activities outside its walls. In the following list of committees special attention is given to those that may be less often found in other secondary schools.

Chief Committees

Pastorian (literary)
Blue & White (yearbook)
Clothing collection
Money collection
School store
Dance
Work camp
School affiliation
Advisory

Poster
Parking
Ushering
Costume closet
Stage crew
Choir council
School-community council
Assembly
Faculty-student selection

All committees have a faculty adviser and a student chairman who is elected by the committee members and approved by the

Student Council. Each committee reports at least annually to the Student Council. In most cases a student volunteers for a committee and the Student Council approves the membership. Thus, some groups, like the board of the literary magazine and the Stage Crew, are self-perpetuating and students try out for the available places. A few, like the Student and Athletic Councils, are elected by fellow students.

Assembly Committee

This group decides and arranges for the high school assemblies which occur every Friday and occasionally on Wednesday. Students preside at assembly, making announcements and introducing faculty members, other students, and guests. The presider nearly always selects a reading, usually from the Bible.

The school is justly proud of its assembly programs, which involve a high degree of student participation. In addition to the presentation of plays, choir, and orchestra concerts, students frequently report in assembly after attending conferences and work camps. Last year most of the academic departments prepared assembly programs based on material being currently studied in the classroom. The science department, for example, staged an exciting program on the Geophysical Year, involving more than 20 students. In other words, assemblies contribute heavily to the life of the school and clearly strengthen and enrich the educational program.

School-Community Council

Since the school is fortunate to be located near several independent and public secondary schools, the local Germantown Community Adult Council has sponsored a "Schools Council" with representatives from ten schools. This interschool group's activities include editing a newsletter, promoting Saturday work camps, attending conferences, and arranging for interschool visiting. It has provided valuable experiences for its members, not the least of which are working with the Adult Council and greatly improving relations among the students of the member schools. Heretofore the chief point of contact with other schools was through athletic competition.

Advisory Committee

This group has no faculty advisor. Its membership consists of about a dozen students elected by their classmates for their maturity and understanding. Its purpose is to guide and help individuals or groups of students who are in difficulties, usually of a social nature. The Advisory Committee may ask for faculty advice but is not obligated to make any report to the teachers. When its membership is strong and concerned, it has rendered great service.

Faculty-Student Selection Committee

This joint committee of teachers and students (the latter chosen by the Student Council) has been operating for about eight years. It came into being because of the increasing opportunities for students to attend conferences and work camps. Formerly teachers selected the candidates, but many teachers came to feel that students should have a voice in the selection. The committee works in this way. When the school is invited to send representatives to a conference or a work camp, students are notified and asked to volunteer. The committee then meets behind closed doors and discusses the qualifications of each candidate very thoroughly. Decisions are made in most cases through discussion and "a sense of the meeting" rather than by ballot. Both teachers and students have grown in understanding as a result of these sessions. There is no doubt that students know one another far better than do their teachers, so that the resulting selections have been fairer and better than if they had been made by the teachers alone.

Community Activities

Since 1951 the school has annually participated in an International Work Camp project organized by British Quakers. For the past several years three girls and three boys have been sent to Europe, usually with a leader from the faculty. The group has visited our affiliated Falaise school, traveled in France, and then attended work camps in Great Britain. Since students from the eleventh grade have participated, the entire school has benefited vicariously on their return.

Students from Germantown Friends School regularly join a group of students, usually 15 or 20, from several independent and public schools who spend a week in the city of Philadelphia. During this time they visit various state and municipal social institutions, such as mental hospitals, prisons, courts, and the City Council. They have opportunities to talk with officials of these institutions as well as with individuals connected with labor and management. The group usually lives in a settlement house and under good leadership discusses, during the evenings, its experiences during the day. The entire week is almost always a tremendous eyeopener and, as in the case of work camps, a great deal is brought back to the school by the participants.

Though definitely a part of the curriculum, the choir also has extracurricular features, since it gives several concerts during the year. At Christmastime and again in the spring, the choir gives evening concerts and is frequently invited to sing at churches and with other schools. In 1956 a picked group of 25 students spent five weeks in France, Germany, and England, where they gave concerts, mostly in secondary schools which were still in session.

During summer vacations Germantown Friends students do service work in hospitals, playgrounds, and settlement houses. These experiences supplement the school program and contribute to student growth and to school-community relations.

SOCIAL RESPONSIBILITY

One of the major aims of the Society of Friends, and of all Quaker education, is the development of a strong sense of social responsibility. Because considerable space has been given to the place of student activities both within the school and in the outside community, it should not be assumed that the school is content to have students simply accept the *status quo* in learning about social and other issues. Any thoughtful, critical, and sensitive adult is aware that serious injustice exists in the world around him. A teacher of adolescents has a special opportunity and responsibility to try to strike a healthy balance between preparing students to meet the world as it is, recognizing present strengths and weaknesses, and at the same time teaching them to care enough to want to do something about the weaknesses.

It is relatively easy to develop in bright people a critical spirit.

Too often, however, this spirit is not translated into action; and the result is cynicism. One of the most important functions of a school fortunate enough to have a high proportion of gifted students is to try to develop in these privileged individuals both a critical spirit and the feeling of obligation to serve their fellow man.

The Society of Friends has from its beginnings felt this concern, and their schools especially should make every effort to teach social responsibility. How this can best be done is of course not simple, but it can be suggested that in every area of a student's school life—in the classroom, in the lunchroom, in the gymnasium—there are opportunities to be socially responsible. This quality, however, usually does not just happen but needs to be taught through adult example, through activities, through discussion in the classroom (especially when an issue comes up within regular course work), through assembly programs, and wherever or whenever an alert teacher sees an opportunity. Students will respond to real situations, and though they will make mistakes, it is clear from the experiences of many teachers that they are eager to be trusted and to show what they can do on their own.

It is the responsibility of every faculty to keep searching for ways and means to increase the growth of social responsibility among its students. At Germantown Friends there is a great deal of concern on this point, and it is hoped that the course content, the teaching methods, as well as the many student activities described above, illustrate specifically the kind of effort the school is currently making to try to help students grow into socially responsible citizens.

This brief description was not written to suggest that the Germantown Friends School program is unique. Many schools do as much and more. Our school has always attempted to challenge its students intellectually. In the last couple of decades it has paid much more attention than formerly to individual capacities and interests, resulting in the creation of new courses and, more recently, in a modified Advanced Placement Program. Just as important as the wider and deeper academic challenge are the extension of student activities and the resulting outreach into the community. The effect of all this appears to be a program that offers a wide variety of opportunity that should stretch all students with the intelligence, energy, and motivation to take advantage of them. Some students, however, are not challenged, and it is the constant task of the faculty to rethink, to re-assess, and when necessary, to remodel the program in order to involve more students more deeply. If this is done successfully, perhaps the school can make a small contribution in preparing students not just for the world as it is, but for the world as it ought to be.

9

Learning in a Core-Centered Program

Margaret Willis and Herbert L. Coon
The University High School, The Ohio State University

THE University School serves as a laboratory in education for The Ohio State University. Housed under one roof is a student population of about 400, who range in age from four-year-old kindergarten children to high school seniors. The senior high school comprises some 120 students. This is a tuition school, whose population tends to show high academic ability.

Although the student group tends to be drawn primarily from upper middle class homes, with a heavy concentration of children from the homes of college professors, an effort is made to get a wide representation of socio-economic backgrounds. Every graduating class of 35 to 45 students will contain several who have spent 12 or more years in the school. Every class contains several children with a Stanford Binet of 140 or more, although each group has some students of less than average ability. The median I.Q. for the school is in the range of 115 to 120.

Parents who send their children to the school have far above average expectations for them. About 90 per cent of a graduating class will attend college. The high school program is therefore oriented toward work of high academic quality for those talented in this direction. Continuous exposure to the creative arts, however, is a requirement for every student.

The school has no printed set of standards to determine which applicants should be admitted. Decision rests in the answer to such questions as: Will this child add to the "spread" of abilities, interests, or backgrounds of the student body in his grade group? Will the school program release potential which might have been undeveloped up to this point? Will the student be able to work effectively with staff and other students? Will the student and his parents be happy with a program which differs substantially from that found in most public schools? Will the student profit from a program which places much attention on individual freedom and responsibility?

EARLY YEARS OF PREPARATION

From the earliest grades the school culture recognizes talent, sometimes unique talent, as something to be prized and cultivated. This cultural approval encourages the development of ability, and thus a cycle of identification, development, approval, and more identification is inherent in the total school operation.

The elementary school curriculum is organized around units of work, or group studies, which are defined by teacher-pupil planning. In this planning, as well as from many other sources, the special talents and interests of children become apparent. As group study develops, many opportunities arise for the pupils to work at the growing edge of their learning. A third grade study of pioneer life, for example, draws on a great range of material. The child at that level who is able to read sixth or seventh grade material which is pertinent to the third grade study is urged to do so as far as his ability and time permit.

While the elementary school program provides for departmentalized instruction in art, music, and physical education, every effort is made to provide children with an opportunity to integrate their total learning experiences around major centers of significance. The study of pioneer life is enriched and deepened by the music department which presents the songs, dances, and instrumental music which the pioneers enjoyed. Recreational activities of pioneer days are experienced in physical education classes. Typical arts projects associated with a study of this earlier life are similarly developed.

In each area a broad and balanced program offers the scope and sequence of learning deemed appropriate, regardless of its involvement in the integrating or enriching activities related to unit work.

The junior high school core program is basically an upward extension of the unit of work approach used in the elementary school. It does, however, have more structure in the sense that a list of 14 problem areas of study, which the faculty has accepted as important to general education, has been developed. The list is used during the planning involved in selecting a core unit, and an attempt is made to spread the units over the suggested list of problem areas.

The broad topics studied and the definition of learning experience by teacher-pupil planning provide many opportunities for gifted students to work at the full level of their capacity. The reading program for each individual is developed by the student, the core teacher, and the librarian. The reading record of the child since his earliest enrollment in the school is here utilized. It is not unusual for gifted junior high school students to be reading materials normally considered appropriate for senior high school students or even college freshmen.

The general procedure of providing outlets for talented youth in the elementary school group study, and in the junior high school core classes, continues in operation in the senior high school.

Senior High School Program
Required courses and periods per week

CORE 9: Content is drawn primarily from English and social studies but not confined to these areas.

Physical Education 4
Arts and Music 4
American History 5   May be taken either the junior or senior year.

Elective courses and periods per week

Mathematics 5	Science 5
Intermediate High School math	Biology
Nature of proof (Geometry)	Chemistry
Advanced High School math	Physics
General math	Advanced High School science

Foreign Language 5
  French I
  French II
  French III
  Spanish I
  Spanish II
  Spanish III

English 5
  English workshop
  English seminar

Social Studies 5
  World cultures and geography
  World history

Arts 5
  Fine and/or industrial arts
  Home arts
  Music (by arrangement)

Superior students, by special arrangement, have taken university courses in mathematics, science, foreign language, history, music.

During the past several years a number of highly talented senior high school students have attended regular university classes. Permission to take college work has been requested for only the most productive and gifted high school students. All round competence is regarded as necessary before the school seeks the opportunity for a student to push ahead in one major field of interest. The student should have done superior work in his major area of interest in all courses available in the high school program. Frequently he will have been on an accelerated program of specialization and will have run out of possible things to study in an organized class situation.

Students who have done all the work required by a course are given a grade, even though they cannot yet be officially enrolled for credit. A student who subsequently enrolls in the university always receives full credit then. Without exception these high school students have done good or excellent work in their college classes. Currently the university is extending the opportunity to do college work to any high school student in the metropolitan Columbus area who has been recommended by his principal as ready for this type of experience.

THE CORE PROGRAM

The content of the core in grades ten, eleven, and twelve, as in the lower grades, is usually described as consisting of the common problems of young people growing up in our society. This definition is useful for some purposes, but if accepted literally it tends to be misleading in at least two directions. First, many other courses are concerned with the common problems of young people in our society. Basic mathematics, American history, and physical education might be cited as examples. The core is thus not the whole general education program. Second, the definition seems to imply that the problems of young people have a common level, or that the core is concerned with the lowest common denominator of problems. Such an interpretation overlooks the fact that every common problem is common only in the sense that most young people are involved in it. But it is essentially an individual problem, as it varies according to each student's perceptions, the nature of his involvement, and the solutions which he can work out or accept. Anyone who attempts to help a group understand and meet its common problems must be highly sensitive to and skilled in meeting special intellectual, social, and psychological needs.

Problem Areas

In many work sessions faculty committees in 1946–1948 identified the following areas of experience as those in which learning units might be sought.

1. School living
2. Healthful living
3. Communication
4. Government
5. Producer-consumer economics
6. Conservation of resources
7. Values and beliefs
8. Human behavior (understanding self and others)
9. Conflicting ideologies
10. Education
11. Occupations (selection and preparation)
12. A developing cultural heritage
13. Social relationships in a rapidly changing society
14. Living in the Atomic Age

This list has been used in various ways. It gives assurance and a starting point for planning to new teachers, as well as to experienced ones. Units previously studied by a class can also be checked to see how diversified or concentrated earlier study has been. Teachers who have a great deal of confidence in their ability to help groups discover common problems in the process of planning, and who enjoy working in that way, find that they can always fit the unit which emerges into one of the problem areas, even though it may be a theme which has never appeared before.

Teacher–Pupil Planning

Whatever use is made of the problem areas, all core groups involve the students in planning to some degree, depending upon the group, the circumstances, and the teacher. A legitimate field for student planning and decision is one where students are concerned enough about the result to be thoughtful in their judgments and informed enough to make a reasonably sound judgment, and where the teacher is willing to live and work with the student decision whatever it is. Probably one of the common mistakes of a beginning teacher is to permit students to vote on a question which he has already in his own mind decided for them. He then finds himself completely blocked when the students do not decide his way.

In planning sessions the teacher does much to set the atmosphere. First of all, he insists on consideration for the interests and point of view of every individual. Planning usually begins with the listing of all the suggestions which anyone, including the teacher, wishes to make. These initial suggestions are then discussed briefly, one by one.

In the first stage of discussion the emphasis is on the positive reasons why, in the opinion of one or more members of the class, each suggested topic would be a good unit. It is important to value creativity and originality and to honor its expression. Negative comments are discouraged at this stage, though they are accepted and weighed before a final choice is made. The teacher quickly learns which students are likely to condemn a novel suggestion merely because it is new. He also learns to recognize those who are apt to embrace some novelty without considering such realities of the situation as the availability of materials and experts who can give special help.

After the preliminary discussion and narrowing of the list to three or four of the most promising suggestions, the teacher's role becomes one of insisting that the class develop a practicable unit in that it can be handled in the class, that it takes account of the school situation, and that it considers the desires of all class members. A plan for a unit, adopted by even a two thirds majority, which makes no provision for the legitimate interests of the minority, whether it is a minority of the gifted or of slow students, is not satisfactory. On the other hand, when every effort has been made by both the majority and the minority and they still fail to reach a consensus, it is time for everyone to recognize that if work is to go ahead, the minority must learn to live with the majority decision for a certain period of time. The exact point at which this stage is reached varies with the maturity and experience of the students, but a sensitive teacher will recognize it at least as quickly as the students.

The unit frequently begins with a general survey or organization of background information. But at some stage the unit will be broken down into group and individual studies, requiring research, notetaking, and reporting. As students choose the parts on which they wish to work, there is a strong tendency for the gifted to select the more mature and complex phases, though this does not mean that they prefer to deal only with abstractions. Indeed they are more likely than others to spend many hours building models of atoms or suspension bridges, drawing diagrams to illustrate their points, and making working models.

In the development of learning experiences, many opportunities are found for a talented student to go farther in his special area of interest or ability while he is making a contribution to the general problem being studied by the group. Special science interests can be pushed farther while studying the unit "Problems of Living in the Atomic Age." Unusual interest in language can be developed while studying some aspects of "Problems of Communication." Students gifted in understanding and explaining social relationships can be expected to make a substantial contribution to a study of labor-management questions found in the larger study of "Producer-Consumer Economics."

Guiding Individual Work

Reporting individual studies becomes a problem at the upper grade level. In the elementary grades and through much of the junior high school, most children can tell in a few minutes all that they have learned from fairly extended research. By senior high school the sheer bulk of information acquired by an individual makes complete reporting exhausting and futile, since listeners cannot absorb it. Students and teachers search together for ways to select the relevant and present it in interesting and challenging form. It is normal for the gifted, in their own field of interest, to go far beyond specific commitments into material which cannot and should not be reported to the class except in a much simplified form. The core unit often offers a student the opportunity to carry a deep interest into broader fields and see its relation to other areas.

Where a student chooses a phase which the teacher believes is too hard or too easy in terms of his skills, maturity, and intelligence, he needs guidance. The function of this guidance is not necessarily to thrust a student immediately into an appropriate activity, but rather to find out what causes him to err in estimating his ability. Only then can he be helped to form a more satisfactory self-picture. A student who seems to overestimate his ability may be eager to improve his record and may need only a few specific suggestions as to practical steps leading toward dramatic academic gains. The one who is satisfied with minimum performance may be insecure or emotionally disturbed. While he needs to raise his achievement standards, he is unlikely to do so until the cause of his under-achievement is removed.

The core work period is central to the core way of operating. When students are engaged in individual studies chosen by them and approved by the teacher, there can be long periods of productive, self-directed activity. The teacher may respond to calls for advice or may circulate through the group, discussing work with individuals. Help or advice sought by the student or offered by the teacher in a concrete situation, is several times more effective than that of a conference removed from the situation. The guidance can also be directed at the level of each individual, so that the gifted, for example, receive the specific help they need and are not compelled to listen to instruction of others who are not so advanced. Students may need help in checking corrections on their written papers. They may need explanations of difficulties in usage or sentence structures. They may need suggestions about ways to work on their spelling problems. Checking leisure reading records and offering reading guidance may be better in a special period reserved for the purpose, but individuals frequently bring up such problems during ordinary work periods. Guidance in work habits comes naturally at this time. A word of commendation to a student about the way in which he has helped the group toward a wise decision or a suggestion of how he might have helped someone else is very easy to offer in this context. If a longer conference is needed, it can easily be set up without the traumatic effects of the summons to stay after school.

Communication Skills

One of the needs of young people in our society is for steadily increasing competence in communication—reading, writing, speaking, and listening. The work on core units, already described, provides for functional guided experiences in tool writing, research reading, speaking, listening, and seeing in both planning and reporting. Field trips are planned by either faculty or students, with faculty approval, in order to gather information or to see illustrations of facts, situations, or processes already studied. Interviews, either in or out of school, and television programs, assigned and unassigned, are other experiences which sharpen observation and help to integrate school and community. Other language experiences not directly related to the unit are provided for in core time. Most important are guidance in leisure reading and regular experience in creative writing.

Standardized reading tests are given in the fall of every school year. The sequence of these scores, by grade levels and percentiles over a period of years, gives a picture of the individual student's growth in reading skill. The important question, however, is what he is doing with the skill, whether there is evidence that he is developing a reading habit and whether his choice of reading material shows growth in taste and discrimination. The student himself supplies the data by keeping a record of the books he reads on a printed form which allows room for ten titles and a brief comment on each. One of these sheets is due when school opens in the fall, as a report on summer reading. Another record sheet is handed in for each quarter during the school year. The very fact of making the record serves to focus student attention on reading. The records themselves offer a sound basis for guidance by the core teacher, the librarian, or the English teacher.

The reading records of four seniors for their last quarter in school follow. It should be noted that students' comments are quoted exactly as they appeared on the reading record which was submitted to the senior class core teacher. It should also be remembered that the last three months of a high school senior's year are quite hectic and are not normally quite so productive as previous quarters have been.

Boy, taking English seminar

Hodier, André. *Jazz: Its Evolution and Essence.* Extremely interesting to read a Frenchman's views on an American commodity.

Gide, André. *The Immoralist.* Novel. Slow in some places but fun to contemplate it taking place.

Andreyev. *The Seven Who Were Hanged.* Novel. My first encounter with Russian literature and very enjoyable.

Anderson, Sherwood. *Winesburg, Ohio.* Novel. I enjoyed the means Anderson employed in holding these "sketches" together.

Boy, no English outside core

LaFarge, Oliver. *As Long As The Grass Shall Grow.* Biography of ethnic group. Excellent combination of prose, photos, and facts.

Sartre, Jean. *Les Jeux Sont Faits.* Novel. Existentialist—interesting.

Scott, Sir Walter. *Lady of the Lake.* Poetry. Easy to follow; well written.

Kerouac, Jack. *The Subterraneans.* Novel. "Beat generation"—disjointed and incoherent.

Miscellaneous. Science fiction—3 paperbacks. Science fiction. Clever—good way to kill a short period of leisure time.

Girl, two years of English including English seminar

Cozzens. *The S. S. San Pedro.* Novel. Very good.

Michener, J. *Sayonara.* Novel. Wonderful.

Djilas, M. *The New Class.* Analysis of communism. One of the most interesting books I've read.

Shellabarger. *Captain From Castile.* Novel. Very good.

Huxley, A. *Brave New World.* Novel. Exceptionally good.

Girl, one year of English in tenth grade

Cather, Willa. *A Lost Lady.* Novel. A very interesting and moving treatment of social and moral problems of the changing late 19th century west.

Riordan, William L. *Plunkitt of Tammany Hall.* A collection of Plunkitt's speeches with a biographical introduction by Roy V. Peel. An extremely interesting collection of a very interesting man's thoughts.

Wilder, Thornton. *The Bridge of San Luis Rey.* Novel. A well-written story about some very interesting people.

O'Connor, Edwin. *The Last Hurrah.* Novel. An interesting character study, and excellent story of the old time politician.

Michener, James A. *The Fires of Spring.* Novel. A very interesting and perceptive character study.

Creative writing is an important and regular part of the core program for a number of reasons. Facility in the use of written language develops only through experience. Many short papers over a period of time give more practice in writing than the same number of words in one long paper. The long paper, however, demands organization, which itself is an important writing and thinking skill. In searching for subjects for creative writing, students learn to look at their world with greater attention. In sharing their interests and thoughts, they learn an identification, a common humanity, and an acceptance of self and of others.

Occasionally the class will ask for an assignment of subject or form, but usually the writing is free, and it is due every other week. A student who seems at home in only one form—a boy who writes nothing but political essays for three months, for example—may be urged or early required to try other kinds of writing. Every paper is read carefully by the teacher and commented on in writing. Comments may deal with what the student is trying to say, how effectively he is saying it, and how grammatically and mechanically correct the paper is. Students are required to correct or revise papers which fail to meet acceptable standards, before they are considered complete.

There are periods when papers are read in class, though any student who marks his paper "Please do not read in class" will have his wishes respected. Papers which will interest the class and which they can discuss critically are selected for reading. Rarely is a paper chosen whose weaknesses are so serious that there is nothing kind to say about it. Students prefer to give favorable comments and are encouraged in this, though it is not too hard for them to learn to say, "It would have been more effective if he had done . . ." Thus the reading period offers an opportunity for the teacher to raise the critical level of the class. An appreciative audience for one's writing is stimulating, and constructive criticisms are usually easy to accept in such an atmosphere.

Students who are high in their reading and writing skills, habits, and tastes and who are ready to profit from more challenging advanced language work, are encouraged to elect the English seminar. Students who are fairly proficient but wish to work harder and more consistently than time allows in the core may elect English workshop. Most students take at least one year of English outside the core during the senior high school years.

The core provides a wide range of activities to which all students are able to contribute according to their particular abilities. To the gifted student the core offers the opportunity to contribute according to his special abilities and to learn to accept his gifts as a social responsibility, while recognizing that in other desirable characteristics some of his classmates excel him. In a group situation where the success of the whole undertaking—a core unit, a dance, a trip—depends upon the effectiveness with which each individual carries out his responsibilities, the group values the special abilities of its members and appreciates excellence of performance.

Individual Counseling

Evaluation and guidance are continuous and are the two sides of the same sheet of paper. A core teacher is counselor for the students in his section. Reading records and reading test results are passed on to him by the previous counselor. These plus many other records are kept in the student's permanent folder in the office. Records of parent conferences, individual Binet or Wechsler I.Q.'s, and various achievement test scores help identify those students who present guidance problems. They are usually students who have an inadequate self-picture, who think of themselves as academic failures, "clowns," the stupid one in a clever group, the one that everybody ignores, or the person who can get by without really trying.

A student makes his own schedule and, if necessary, changes it with the approval of his counselor, who tries to see that his reasons for elections are sound and his choices consistent with long-term goals. The long-term plans themselves may become the subject of a unit on "Vocations and Colleges," or they may be the subject of an assigned paper and subsequent discussion between the student and his counselor. Test results in reading, mathematics, vocational preferences, scholastic aptitude—all are used by the counselor and the student together. Though I.Q.'s are not revealed to the student, the counselor does indicate his general level. Moreover, the recent decision of the Educational Testing Service to permit schools to tell students their scores on College Board Examinations will soon add another dimension to the data which can be used.

The guidance problems presented by the gifted are as individual as their special gifts. Sometimes it is a problem of persuading a modest person and his parents that fine colleges and universities are likely to welcome him and give him a big enough scholarship to permit him to attend one. One brilliant boy with rapidly expanding cultural and intellectual interests, which he was approaching for the first time at a mature level, needed help in learning how to overcome his ignorance of the fundamentals in each area. His immediate tendency was to bluff in order to cover up, but when he learned to accept his ignorance and began doing something about it, his rapid learning enabled him to fill in quickly the background for each new interest. Another boy was almost belligerently intellectual, negative to the ideas of others, and uninterested in beauty and all emotional and aesthetic experiences. There was evidence that he really had a strongly emotional nature. The school worked in many ways to release it through writing, dramatics, the core unit, physical education, student affairs. Which of the experiences, or how many of them together, brought about a change no one knows, but by the time he graduated he had learned to accept his own emotions and to show increasing warmth and sympathy toward others.

The senior high school block of time provides unusual opportunities for students to use resources available in the school or on the university campus. A student talented in art, who chooses its media through which to report his findings or feelings to a class, can arrange to get help and materials for his presentation. If the high school library proves inadequate, he may arrange to spend two or more hours in the university library. College professors in areas such as science, medicine, and agriculture can often offer the gifted challenges of a high level.

The Faculty

The teaching staff of the University High School is unusually competent in both training and experience. Several members of the teaching faculty have earned the Ph.D. degree and all have studied beyond the M.A. degree. Almost all of the teachers have had public school experience in more than one system, and many of the staff have had more than 15 years of such experience. Without exception the faculty enjoys teaching and working with high school students. All full-time staff members of the University High School have academic rank in the College of Education, and their salary scale is similar to that of instructors of equal rank in other departments of the university faculty.

Since core teaching is regarded as one of the most difficult assignments, an effort is made to staff the core program with competent and experienced teachers. None of the core teachers, however, were prepared specifically as core teachers. They were educated, rather, to be special area teachers in science, social studies, or English. In addition to their core assignment, they normally teach at least one elective class in their major academic area. Thus, they may be regarded as having assignments in both general and special classes.

Competence in core teaching is not different from that in any other field. There is, however, some difference in the way in which class time is used, particularly during work periods and in counseling situations. Understanding and skill in these matters are developed in core teachers through a rather extensive inservice education program.

The faculty meets often in various small groups to consider questions related to the school program or to individual students. All core teachers may meet, for example, with English teachers to get ideas about how to improve the creative writing program, which is a part of the core responsibility. Another meeting may be held with the school physician and nurse to discuss how to work most effectively with individuals whose learning problems appear to have a physiological basis. A grade staff meeting may be held to discuss which kind of schedule is best for a highly talented student. At times it appears desirable to consider the possibility of academic acceleration for a student.

School Organization

Core classes serve as the center of school organizations. The Student Council is made up of representatives elected by all the grades, seven through twelve, and meets once a week during core time. The Council has established the Athletic, Assembly, Lunch-room, and Citizenship committees. Each has representatives chosen by all grades and meets at the same time as the Council. Other groups are likely to use this same period for meeting. The remaining members of the core groups have a study period, which offers an opportunity for them to receive individual help from the teacher.

Each grade group has its own officers and class organization. All meet in core time, usually the day after the Council meeting. The first business of this session is hearing the reports from the Council and the committees before going on to whatever class business is current. Such business includes money-making activities, planning a dance or other social affair, preparing for a trip, and considering suggestions for special activities.

THE ELECTIVE PROGRAM

The core program is only one aspect of the University High School program. At the senior high school level the student spends slightly more than one fourth of his time in core. This, however, is far more than that spent in most American high schools, and this uniqueness warrants detailed attention.

Outside of the required core and physical education classes, the school program has two major areas which offer elective possibilities. The first of these is the arts elective field. The second includes the traditional academic disciplines of mathematics, science, foreign language, English, social studies, as well as some elective courses in fine and practical arts.

In order to encourage growth in the fine and practical arts, the school requires that students work, throughout every year of their high school program, in a relatively small number of arts areas. These normally include vocal music, instrumental music, fine and industrial arts, and home arts. Students have no choice of whether they will or will not work in these areas. They do, however, have a choice among them. Students with high aptitude, skill, and interest in instrumental music are permitted to elect exclusively in this area. The quality of the school's performing groups would be much lower if this were not the case. In general, however, the faculty believes students should not limit themselves to a single area of art but should try to have a continuously expanding circle of arts experiences.

A student's elective program in the arts, as well as in the academic areas, is developed through careful guidance which involves the core teacher, the counselor, the special area teacher, himself, and his parents. Careful attention is given to a student's future plans as well as to his past record. For example, the boy who is interested in industrial engineering might be counseled to elect industrial arts, even though he has developed an unusually good singing voice. A girl aspiring to be an elementary school teacher might be urged to join a vocal music group, even though she has shown unusual skill in the fine arts.

The elective program in the academic disciplines is characterized by a great deal of "openness," which permits much flexibility in building the kind of program each student should have. A one year course in American history is required by state law for high school graduation and is the only subject matter course required of everyone. Students may elect to take it as juniors, seniors, or occasionally as sophomores. The school prescribes no combination of majors or minors as prerequisites for graduation. Senior high school core work is entered on college transcripts as work in English and social studies although, as has been made clear earlier, it contains much more than work in these areas.

Plans for college, other vocational preparation, and the aptitudes of a student are the prime determiners of each student's pattern of academic electives. While a broad exposure to the disciplines of science, mathematics, language, and social studies is regarded as desirable for most individuals, some have three years of a foreign language, while others have none. Some students elect four years of mathematics, while others elect only two. Some take no English outside of core, while others take two years.

The Arts

In the related arts area, where the fine and the industrial arts are housed in adjoining rooms connected by the arts office, students plan and carry out a wide variety of projects. They may paint, weave, work in clay, make jewelry, design and reproduce the designs with linoleum blocks or silk screens, print on the power press, or work in wood or metal. Scenery for plays and operettas is designed and built here. The illustrations for the school's literary magazine, *Buckeye Leaves,* are worked out here with either linoleum blocks or silk screens. The actual printing of the magazine is done on the press. Students with special interests in the arts may work out arrangements with the teachers for an individual program, scheduled at some period during the day when the other people using the area come mainly from the elementary or junior high school level. The arts thus provide individual and group outlets for a great variety of creative abilities at all levels.

Because of limitations of space and personnel, choral and instrumental music are limited to group activity. An operetta is presented at from two to four year intervals. *The King and I* was the most recent. Earlier ones were *Brigadoon, The Red Mill,* and *The Desert Song.* All of the arts, including the dance, are integrated in such productions. During other years the vocal and instrumental groups usually work independently of each other.

A problem in the performing arts which is hard to solve, except in the years when productions are being given, is that of providing challenging experiences for very advanced students. Participation in community groups, private lessons and performances, and in one case a class on the university campus are among the expedients adopted.

The home arts class enrolls both boys and girls and provides a variety of experiences in clothing selection and construction, food preparation and entertaining, as well as home and family living. The home arts teacher is frequently called upon as a consultant for the cores. The home arts area is enjoyed and used by students, faculty, and parents for meetings, for making operetta or folk festival costumes, for trying out a cookie recipe before a party. Students with special interests and abilities may plan to do advanced work with the home arts teacher.

The Language Arts

Juniors and seniors who show unusual interest and skill in English are permitted to elect the English seminar, which is basically an advanced class in world literature. Here a few things may be read by everyone in the class for analysis and discussion. As in other English work, the chief aim is to stimulate a mature individual reading program which each student is prepared to understand and find challenging. The level of reading in this group is higher than that found in many freshman English classes in college.

Other students who elect English are enrolled in English workshop, which aims to challenge students in the middle range of language ability to go as far and as fast as they can. It is our experience, however, that students with serious problems in reading or writing are more likely to progress faster by having some kind of individual help than by being in an English class. The nature and extent of the help needed is a matter to be decided for each individual.

Most students elect French or Spanish in either the tenth or the eleventh grade, and the school is now starting to experiment with beginning language at the seventh grade. A foreign language is taught by the direct method. Translation is avoided, and the emphasis is on thinking in a language as the basis for speaking, reading, and writing it. Much attention is given to understanding both a spoken language and its culture. Every other year, always excepting the year when an operetta is given, all the foreign language classes cooperate in preparing and presenting a folk festival of authentic dances from France, Spain, or Latin America. Boys as well as girls make their own costumes. The athletic skills required for the very active folk dances have a great attraction for the boys.

About half of the students who begin a foreign language stop after two years of study, though a few drop out after only one. The third year of a language is usually elected by the most able and serious students who are ready to go into a mature study of literature and linguistics. Thus an advanced class is formed because of the interest and background of the students.

Social Studies

The social studies electives are world geography and cultures and world history, with American history and government being required by law. A problems of democracy course is not offered as an elective because the units studied in the cores cover much the same social studies content in meaningful relationships with other areas. Many aspects of history, government, and geography are also handled functionally in core units.

All the social studies offerings are regarded by the staff as general education courses. The handling of controversial issues is a central feature of these classes, with emphasis upon the critical examination of ideas rather than upon the learning of "right" answers or long catalogs of unrelated facts. Much of the work is organized in such a way that capable students can be challenged to go much farther than their classmates in original research, critical thinking, and organization and interpretation of large amounts of data. Social studies lends itself to this kind of enrichment and to flexible standards which can demand of every student something approximating his own best performance.

Mathematics

Mathematics courses are required for all students in grades seven through nine. All senior high school mathematics courses are elective, and some are open only with the consent of the instructor. While the general mathematics and nature of proof (geometry) classes are open to all students and may be regarded as general education, the intermediate and advanced high school mathematics courses tend to have more of the characteristics of special education. In view of college entrance requirements, most students will elect to take at least one year of senior high school mathematics (generally the nature of proof course), although a high percentage will elect to take two years. Only those who are most able and interested will elect mathematics every year of their senior high school program.

Students with high aptitudes frequently take advantage of an opportunity "to work ahead into algebra" while they are in the eighth grade arithmetic course. Thus they are eligible to enter senior high school mathematics classes when they are ninth-graders and, if their achievement and interest remain high, they may be recommended for college courses during their final high school year.

A brief description of the content of the senior high school mathematics courses follows.[1]

General mathematics may be elected by students in grades ten through twelve. In general the students who choose it (1) have neglected their mathematics in the past, (2) have found previous mathematics courses difficult for them, or (3) wish to study mathematics beyond the ninth grade but do not want to take the more difficult and highly specialized classes in intermediate and advanced high school mathematics. The content of this course has differed widely throughout the years but it has been predominantly arithmetic and informal geometry.

Intermediate high school mathematics is designed for students with special ability, interest, and recognized needs in the field of mathematics. It may be elected in grades ten to twelve. The course is a prerequisite for advanced high school mathematics.

---

[1] This material as well as additional information is available in *A Description of Curricular Experiences, Grades* 7–12 (mimeographed, The Ohio State University School, 1956).

Materials for study are selected from two sources: (1) those basic ideas of mathematics which are most common in everyday life such as the formula, graph, and equation and (2) mathematical concepts basic to the further study of mathematics. Problems are selected from a common textbook, from guide sheets prepared by the instructor of the class, and from field and laboratory situations.

Nature of proof (geometry) remains in essence an experience in education. The course undertakes to develop within the students a growing appreciation of the concepts of "proof" by stressing in both mathematical and nonmathematical contexts the function of undefined terms, the importance of definitions and assumptions, and the source and validity of implications in any logical system. In the belief that one must teach for "transfer," newspaper editorials, school problems, student problems, laws, public addresses, advertisements, sermons, and political documents are analyzed in extending the principles of proof and critical inquiry into the nonmathematical domain. Methods of reasoning are accentuated, so that students learn the characteristics of inductive and deductive proof and of direct, indirect, and analogous reasoning.

No single textbook is used except as an occasional reference. Needed definitions and assumptions are developed through class discussion and are the outgrowth of the student's thinking rather than a basis for it. Each student organizes these materials in his own way in a notebook which is constantly used as a highly important reference. In effect this notebook becomes the basic text.

Advanced high school mathematics is a course for students who have special interest and recognized ability in mathematics and for those who plan to pursue a curriculum at college in mathematics, science, or engineering. The content of the course is composed of materials selected from algebra, plane trigonometry, analytic geometry, and calculus. For the most part, practice materials are selected from textbooks available to the students, although guide sheets written by the teachers are also used.

All of these courses are taught chiefly by the inductive method, and many opportunities are provided for the most able students to work on special assignments and projects which are challenging to them.

Science

All science courses in the senior high school program are elective. More than 90 per cent of the students, however, elect biology. Of the present senior class more than 90 per cent have also had chemistry, physics, or both. Normally students elect biology, chemistry, or physics in the tenth, eleventh, and twelfth grades, respectively. There are exceptions to this sequence, however, so that there is often a three year age spread among students in these classes.

Currently the two physical science courses are structured, quantitative, and basically college preparatory. Much of the work is "open ended," and those students with special interests and capacities are encouraged to carry out experimental projects. A detailed description of the typical work of these courses can be found in *A Description of Curricular Experiences* previously cited.

Since biology is growing rapidly in popularity as a high school science and since the University School course in it deviates markedly from the usual one, it will be described in more detail at this point. It is believed that the general plan described below makes excellent provision for educating the gifted in science.

The program in biology attempts to create the most favorable atmosphere for individual understandings of the life sciences and especially the scientific methodology of biologists. The instructional method simulates the procedures of a research staff of scientists.

During the fall quarter biology is concerned with a survey of the plant and animal kingdoms, with special studies of type organisms, adaptations, and life processes. Emphasis is placed upon the interrelation of classroom, library, laboratory, and field. Firsthand experiences are made available to each student.

At the conclusion of the quarter's work each class member is advised to compose a paper about the phases of biology which interest him most. On the basis of this paper he is assigned special textbook and reference reading, advised to carry out related activities, and tentatively placed in one of several research teams. These teams are organized on the basis of related activities; thus, there are teams designated "Plant Studies," "Invertebrate Studies," et cetera. Each team meets periodically to define each member's project, to share and solve problems, and to intellectualize the quarter's work.

The teacher functions throughout the entire program as the director of research, whose major responsibility is to guide each student so that he continues to work on the frontiers of his knowledge and ability.

Evaluation is largely observational. The instructor keeps a continuous report of each student's progress in the practice of scientific methodology. Weekly progress reports, daily work reports, a final individual examination, and scientific papers written in the style of research compositions serve as written evidence of the success of the student in realizing the objectives of the second quarter's work.

The third quarter involves the development of a concept of evolution following an intense study of reproduction and genetics. Generally much of the research done during the previous quarter is called into play in the inductive formation of an understanding of evolution.

For the future it has been proposed that the science sequence in the upper four grades of high school be so structured that each year of elective science will be presented in an integrated science course. Here students will grow in their over-all understanding of science, rather than study life one year, matter another, and energy a third. Initial steps have been taken to establish a Science I course in the ninth grade. A pilot project is now under way with an advanced science group whose studies are so organized that the internal coherence of science is a central theme.

SUMMARY

The University High School program for the gifted places great emphasis upon the identification of purpose in the mind of the individual learner. The school believes that each student must accept the long-range personal significance of a learning situation before he will commit himself wholeheartedly to it. Teachers work as counselors and "guiders of the learning process" in such a manner as to help students move as rapidly as possible toward desirable long-range as well as short-range goals. This method of working with the gifted is, of course, the same as that used for all students.

When gifted individuals have reached levels of achievement so far above those of most of their classmates that their intellectual development is better served by more advanced classes, they may either accelerate or enroll in college courses.

Giftedness is regarded as something which can be developed as well as identified. The spread of giftedness is a part of the infinite variation found in American youth. Homogeneous grouping, which must be based on some particular criterion of giftedness, frequently violates the variation and range of talent, particularly in a small school, and the University School avoids it as an administrative device. The small number of relatively homogeneous groups found in such senior high school classes as mathematics, science, and a foreign language are largely the result of "self-selection" exercised by students who elect to do advanced work according to their interests and abilities.

Heterogeneous grouping, particularly in core classes, helps gifted students realize that they are not gifted in everything. Students who are gifted academically may find that poorer students are more effective democratic leaders. The gifted sometimes find that others are more able to accept and discharge social responsibilities which develop in groups concerned with living and working together for the common good. The gifted learn that ability to solve abstract problems does not necessarily mean that they have the ability to solve personal social problems.

The art of living easily and emphatically with others is acquired only through practice and experience. As the gifted learn to live in this manner, others' appreciation of their gifts results in their being chosen more often for leadership roles. This process provides an excellent opportunity for the development of good leadership and followership among students of all levels of ability.

The program is organized to provide many opportunities for the student to develop the characteristics of the autonomous person. This person should be developing his talents, or gifts, in a manner which permits him to be honest with himself, to be creative, self-directive, willing to stand for what he believes with a great deal of independence, while at the same time operating within the limits of social responsibility and sensitivity.

The school does not try to turn out a uniform product of "well-adjusted" individuals developed to the mythical level of accomplishment deemed appropriate for the average American. Rather, the individual approach to teaching permits each student, regardless of the nature and quantity of his talent, to move forward as rapidly and purposefully as he can toward becoming a socially useful, unique self.

IO

A High School Program in a Medium-Sized City

Clifford W. Williams and Harold A. Kleiner
Portland, Oregon, Public Schools

ULYSSES S. GRANT High School is one of 11 four year secondary schools in the Portland, Oregon, school system.[1] It was established in 1924 to serve what was then a new and growing neighborhood in the city. Today Grant High School has a student membership of 2,400 boys and girls. It serves a predominantly middle and upper middle socio-economic neighborhood made up largely of professional and semiprofessional families. Consequently the educational expectancy for most students is comparatively high. Between 65 and 70 per cent of Grant's graduates enter colleges and universities. The school does not have separate tracks for college-bound and non-college-bound students but allows for differences in aims and capacities of students through elective courses and course counseling.

All Portland high schools, including Grant, require students to complete successfully 19 units of work in four years. One full year in one course which meets daily constitutes one unit. Eleven units

[1] For further information on the Portland program see: Bulletin No. GC IR, "A Report Summarizing Four Years of Progress in a Program for Advanced Students" (Instructional Materials Department, Portland Public Schools, 1957); *Education for the Gifted* (National Society for the Study of Education [Chicago: University of Chicago Press, 1958]), chapters 8, 9, 18; R. F. DeHaan and R. J. Havighurst, *Educating Gifted Children* (Chicago: University of Chicago Press, 1957).

are required of each student as follows: English, four years; mathematics, one year; social studies, three years; science, one year; physical education and health, two years. All other units are elective.

For a number of years specialized courses have been available to students with deficiencies in preparation or capacity to learn. As an example, about one third of the freshmen entering Grant take general mathematics instead of algebra. Some take remedial reading. A few are placed in special classes for slow learners. Similarly, special courses have long been available to students with special interests. In this category are courses in business education, foreign languages, industrial arts, journalism, and speech. Courses in art, drama, and music are provided for talented students.

It has been the practice at Grant and at the other high schools of the district to avoid ability grouping in required classes. There are some exceptions, as noted previously. Very retarded students are placed in special sections. Those who are not ready for algebra take general mathematics. Another exception occurs in the senior English classes, where the ablest students are enrolled in an English literature course while others take a less demanding course in literature. A third group who are able but deficient in English skills are assigned to still another course which emphasizes a fundamentals review in conjunction with the literature. For the most part, however, students are enrolled in required courses without regard to ability.

In content fields where several years of study are required, such as English and social studies, class membership remains heterogeneous throughout, with the exception of senior English. Mathematics and science courses which are required for only a single year become progressively less heterogeneous in advanced courses, since only successful students are encouraged to enroll. Even in these classes a wide range of ability exists. When two or more sections of senior mathematics, physics, or other advanced courses are established, no attention is given to ability grouping.

Conditions Which Suggest a Special Program

Heterogeneity of groups was probably one factor which contributed to the growing demand for more attention to gifted students. Ungrouped classes undoubtedly have a number of advantages. The strongest claim for heterogeneity of class membership probably lies in the area of human relations. Students of varying capacities and interests should learn to work together. Without question, the understanding and appreciation of differences thus gained is an important part of education in the broader sense. However, ungrouped classes, despite their value in developing some facets of human understanding, have a weakness which must be considered.

Over the past few years appropriate instruction for each individual in a heterogeneous class has become difficult, if not impossible. Four factors have contributed to this condition: (1) the rapid growth in population, combined with school building programs which have been unable to keep pace, has necessitated larger classes; (2) legislation in many states requiring children to remain in school to age sixteen or, in the case of Oregon, eighteen has resulted in wider variations in ability in later high school years; (3) the rapidly changing economic, industrial, and political complexion of America and the world has required more intelligent trained leadership; (4) a shortage of adequately prepared teachers which has existed since the war years.

The first two factors have made it necessary for teachers to plan programs for larger classes with widely varying abilities. Ideally classroom instruction should be characterized by individual rather than group standards of performance. Assignment of reading, research projects, and skill development programs should be geared to individual abilities. As things are, however, even though a teacher wishes to work with individuals, he must spend the greater part of his time with students of near average ability. With well-planned teaching procedures, including homework assignments, a good teacher can provide appropriately for about 80 per cent of his students. Those at either extreme of the ability scale have needs which differ from the rest of the class. Because slow learners' problems are more obvious and seem more pressing, most of the remaining instructional time is devoted to them, for teachers have a strong tendency to be challenged by a student's inability to learn. Traditionally teachers judge themselves and their pedagogical prowess by the absence of low scores in the tests administered to their classes. Too often very able learners are neglected because they are expected to perform comparatively well with a minimum of individual attention.

Furthermore, slow learners are more likely to engage in disruptive practices if left to their own devices. Able students, because of their command of the skills of reading and writing, seem more likely to take care of themselves. To keep peace in the classroom most teachers spend more time preventing disruption than eliminating superficial reading or writing habits.

The third factor contributing to the difficulty of instruction—the rapidly changing world—presents a very real and formidable problem. Throughout history schools have been responsible for interpreting the culture of society to youth in order to assure its continuation and improvement. To be sure, in some periods of history, society's demands that the young be conditioned for subservience to the common will, or the will of the ruling class, have been respected by the schools. Much more rare was the society which taught freedom of the individual spirit, the right to individual investigation, the right to give voice to one's considered opinions.

Whatever the prevailing conditions, appropriate knowledge and skills have been imparted to children for the purpose of preserving the practice of the group. Each group also attempted to inculcate attitudes in youth for the preservation of values which were considered desirable. Because individual initiative, questioning, and doubting have often been discouraged, cultural change has been slow.

World War II stimulated enormous advances in science and technology, with resulting shifts and developments in other fields. The world-wide nature of the change, with its impact on economics, politics, and industry brought new developments at such a rapid rate that schools have been unable to keep pace. This situation plus, moreover, the rapid growth in student population combined to force schools to place inadequately prepared teachers in many classrooms. Consequently, at a time when conditions required better teaching than ever before, it became difficult to keep the present quality of teaching from deteriorating.

This situation exists in Portland, Oregon, as it probably does in every city in America. Grant High School administrators and the heads of other schools in the district knew that adjustments were necessary if the schools were to function as a modern school must.

AIMS OF INSTRUCTION FOR THE GIFTED

The program for advanced or gifted students at Grant is a combination of individual instruction in heterogeneous classes and special courses of study in select classes. Stated in their most general terms, the aims of the Grant program for advanced students are no different from its aims for all students.

Intellectually gifted students are capable of thought at a higher and more complex level than most students; in fact, this is what is implied in the term "intellectually gifted student." The program for the gifted in the high school therefore places greater emphasis on the development of complex thinking skills than does the regular high school program. Gifted students are capable of learning and remembering facts and principles at a rapid pace. At any grade level they are capable of acquiring more advanced knowledge than other students, and thus need special courses. For example, students who are exceptionally talented in art, music, dramatics, or written expression need opportunities for learning advanced principles and skills in these fields.

In regard to the development of social-living skills necessary for satisfactory interaction in a complex society, gifted students require some of the same experiences as other students.[2] Even more, however, they need to learn skills for interacting with their intellectual peers.

An intellectually gifted student who has spent his school years as the brightest one in his class may well find that in college, graduate school, or professional work he will encounter others who are as able or even more able than he. He may find that the skills which

[2] Henry J. Otto, *Social Education in Elementary Schools* (New York: Rinehart and Co., Inc., 1956), pp. 34, 35. "Human relations may be categorized as existing among and between people and people, people and institutions, people and the earth, and people and goods. Social education consists of all the desired social attitudes, skills, knowledges, and behavior which today's society is seeking to engender in its children; it also includes the methods, materials, and situations which are used to promote the desired ends." See also Robert J. Havighurst, *Human Development and Education* (New York: Longmans, Green & Co., Inc., 1953), Chapter 1.

he needs for the discussion of an idea or the cooperative solving of an intellectual problem are different from those he has learned in a heterogeneous classroom. The development of social skills, as discussed briefly here, does not and should not conflict with personal individuality, integrity, initiative, creativeness, or the value of dissent. It seems necessary, then, for the high school to provide a number of small, select classes where the skills of social interaction among intellectual peers may be practiced.

In regard to making wise vocational choices, students with exceptional ability require more technical information about a variety of specialized fields than other students. Because of their capabilities, more fields are open to them, and since the preparation for many of these fields is technical and complex, students need early and complete information about them. This information should include facts about the various colleges and universities specializing in their particular fields.

The faculty and administrators at Grant High School have given considerable thought to the establishment of a program which would meet the specific needs of exceptionally able students. At the same time they have planned so that these students would not lose the benefits from interaction with all types of students.

Administrative Provisions

As is the case with every phase of the educational program, the key person in the development of "Educational Enrichment" at Grant is the principal. Through his guidance his assistants have been able to build a program which fits the needs of able students.

In order to have sufficient teacher time for carrying out special provisions for advanced students, additional teachers are assigned to Grant High School and the other high schools of the district. Additional teachers are assigned according to a formula which takes account of the total enrollment of a school and the number of students of exceptional ability. Grant was assigned two and a half additional faculty members. Part of the additional time is used to release a member of the high school faculty to serve as a co-ordinator of the "EE" (Educational Enrichment) program. The time remaining is used to provide special seminar-size classes for advanced students.

The co-ordinator, released from teaching one period daily, compiles test data and other pertinent information, prepares tentative class lists for seminars and other advanced classes, works with the administrators and department chairmen in planning the appropriate school program, prepares reports as needed, and assists teachers in acquiring necessary books and materials. The importance of the co-ordinator on the faculty, with time to give attention to the specific learning needs of able students, cannot be overstressed.

ELIGIBILITY OF STUDENTS

When students enroll at Grant, after promotion from neighborhood elementary schools, their grade school records are already available. Included in these records may be a special card for those who have shown high capacity and performance. The records include test data, performance records, evidence of their special interests and hobbies, and the elementary school's prediction of their high school success. Test data include group intelligence and achievement test scores given to all elementary school children, special tests of intellectual ability given to particularly able pupils, and talent test records. Performance records include grades from special classes and the results of several years of systematic teacher observation of personality traits.

When these records arrive at the high school, counselors take note of any evidence of unusual ability and make a roster of advanced students. Some entering students are placed in advanced sections of first year courses. All are noted for close observation during the first year, with the intention of placing them in advanced sections and seminars in later years. Early in the first year all students are given a standardized battery of achievement and thinking skills tests. Results are used to verify the roster of advanced students and to add others for whom previous information is lacking. The same battery of tests is administered to all high school juniors so that growth can be noted before final senior advanced classes are organized.

It should be noted that eligibility for advanced classes includes a record of high performance as well as evidence of unusual ability. As a matter of fact, each year some students high in intellectual ability and comparatively mediocre performance are temporarily placed in special sections to see if the advanced study will arouse their enthusiasm. If underachievement has been caused by disciplinary problems or disruptive action, however, it is considered unwise to enroll such students in advanced classes.

At Grant High School the following advanced classes and seminars have been established in the current school year:

Class Title	Year	Number Enrolled
Social Studies—English combined	Freshman	24
American History Seminar	Junior	14
World Problems Seminar	Senior	17
World Literature and Composition Seminar	Sophomore	34 (2 sections)
American Literature and Composition Seminar	Senior	16
First Year Algebra	Freshman	29
Second Year Algebra	Sophomore	26
Geometry Seminar	Junior	19
Mathematics (Modern Math.) Seminar	Senior	(N/A)
Biology	Freshman	29
Biology	Sophomore	25
Chemistry Seminar	Junior	17
Physics Seminar	Senior	10
Art Seminar	Freshman	17
Art	Sophomore-Senior	18

Although the total enrollment in special classes is 339, a few students are in more than one class. Actually the number of students in one or more special classes is slightly less than 13 per cent of the student population of Grant.

Six of the special classes have enrollments comparable to classes of normal size and are referred to as "advanced sections." These are enrichment classes, following the regular Portland course of study. They call for more difficult materials than those usual in

regular classes. Emphasis is also placed on better writing, fundamental research skills, more effective reading habits, more discussion
of critical issues, and other tools of scholarship.

SEMINAR CLASSES

The high point of the program at Grant and at other schools in
the district is the seminar. As the name suggests, these classes are
small in size and generally follow a less strictly prescribed course.
They are, however, sufficiently closely related to general courses
that they may be taken by students in lieu of general courses.

The most typical attributes of the seminars are their small size
and their method. By seminar method is meant a more or less
logical system of finding out how an experience, book, or event
might be interpreted, together with an awareness that interpretations are tentative and subject to modification in the light of new
evidence. It is a method which puts a premium on the pursuit of
truth rather than on its attainment. It requires the participants to
define their own problems, to draw their own conclusions, and to
focus on themselves rather than on the instructor. Wherever possible, primary sources and related authoritative commentaries are
used. The emphasis is on the original personal reaction of the
student to the material he reads, before the intrusion of predigested
interpretations, including those of the teacher.

The preparation of something for the record is one culminating
phase of the seminar process. The précis, the comparison of contradictory propositions, the amplification of a single proposition, and
the definition of the problem without reference to its solution are
examples of techniques which have been introduced to students.

Discussions of a variety of challenging materials make students
aware that mastering the various avenues of approaching a problem,
the necessity for withholding judgment, and the process of gaining
new concepts and expanding and altering old ones are lifelong
tasks. Skillful writing is the result of learning to define a problem,
to interpret material, and to draw conclusions. The creative use of
material can be stressed more satisfactorily in the seminar than in
a general class.

The successful seminar requires an atmosphere of cordial mutual interest. There must be a feeling of freedom and responsibility if students are to develop a concept fully or to pursue an idea at greater length. There must be a growing respect for differences in personality, in modes of expression, and in types of oral contribution. In such an atmosphere the fear of being wrong or appearing ignorant before the group is minimized. The shy or less vocal student is encouraged to participate.

ENGLISH

The Educational Enrichment classes in English have many aims in common with all the Educational Enrichment classes in the high school. In addition, they have certain aims which are specific to the subject. Among these are the following: (1) to produce intelligent and discerning readers through a disciplined examination of literary texts of the highest quality; (2) to improve student writing, by making regular written assignments an integral part of the work, by insisting upon the highest standards of precision, clarity, and grace, by encouraging imaginative writing, and by requiring frequent revision in the interest of these aims; (3) to raise the standards of class discussion by requiring textual substantiation of oral comments.

Accumulation of "facts" as such (When did Chaucer die? Who was the author of "The Three Bears"?) is not a primary aim. But a novel, a poem, or a play is in itself the result of a complex mental process, a "fact" to be possessed and comprehended, and in this sense the mastery of facts *is* all important.

Aims, methods, attitudes, and course materials cannot be separately considered. For instance, literature is distinguished from other kinds of writing by the special concern of the author for style and form. A word in its poetic context demands contemplation. The devices of irony and paradox cannot be absorbed at a glance. Structural patterns carry much of a work's meaning and must be studied with care. Thus, rapid reading, useful though this skill may be in other areas of study, is not a major aim of the English classes. In these classes there is an increase in both range of materials and intensiveness of application. The result is a higher than average proficiency in technical composition skills, greater variety and more experimentation in composition assignments, and increased emphasis on critical thinking. The kind of writing involved in tests, quizzes, and exercises is also emphasized.

The seminar makes special use of the method of comparative study. This is greatly facilitated nowadays by the great wealth of good translations available in cheap editions by Penguin Books, the Doubleday Anchor Series, Mentor, the Beacon Press, Vintage Books, and other publishers. Thus, one unit of the seminar is given over to a comparative study of the *Iliad* and Crane's *The Red Badge of Courage*. The opening week is devoted to the examination of five or six different translations of Homer, drawn from the local libraries. Each student is provided with a copy of the Rieu prose translation. There are always upon the table copies of or selections from Chapman, Pope, Bryant, Rouse, and the Lang, Leaf, and Myers textbooks—an instructive variety of couplets, blank verse, and prose. Attention is focused upon narrative structure, stylistic conventions (epithet, simile, repetition), the intervention of the gods in human affairs, and the Greek religious outlook. For papers, students may choose from a list of such topics as these: Achilles and Paris, a Study in Contrast; Hector as Homer's Most Complex Character; The Legendary Helen as Revealed in the *Iliad;* Home Life and Culture of Greeks and Trojans; Military Techniques; The Women of the *Iliad*. Careful rereading and marshaling of evidence are insisted on as part of the preparation for writing the paper. The application of similar procedures to *The Red Badge of Courage* makes the student more conscious of style and expression and introduces him to the many problems of cultural similarities and differences.

Time Chart for Senior English[3]

(A Guide for Educational Enrichment seminars)

1st Grading Period	2nd Grading Period
EARLY ENGLAND AND THE	CHIVALRY AND
COURAGE THEME	MEDIEVAL LIFE

[3] This chart was prepared by Mrs. Mabel D. Southworth, Miss Dolores Leavens, and Mrs. Janice Schukart (Portland English teachers); with the assistance of Miss Marian Zollinger (Supervisor of Language Arts) and Dr. Donald E. MacRae (Professor of Literature, Reed College).

THE EPIC

English Literature
  Beowulf (portions in text)

Comparative Study
  Iliad and/or
  Odyssey—minimum books 7-12
  Red Badge of Courage
  Moby Dick
Supplementary
  Aeneid
  Song of Roland
  The Cid
  Nibelungenlied
  Other epics like:
    Tales of King Arthur
    Robin Hood

3rd Grading Period

GREAT EXPANSION OF HUMANISM—RENAISSANCE—REFORMATION

DRAMA
  Brief history of drama—library

English Literature
  Macbeth
  King Lear (for an excellent class)
  The Taming of the Shrew

Comparative Study
  Antigone or *Oedipus*
  Arms and the Man
  Pygmalion
  Major Barbara
  Androcles and the Lion
  Caesar and Cleopatra
  Saint Joan

THE TALE

English Literature
  Chaucer, "Prologue" and
    "Nun's Priest's Tale"
Comparative Study
  Tristan and Iseult or
    Aucassin and Nicolette
  Other Chaucer Tales
  Chaucer's "Prayer"
Supplementary
  *A Connecticut Yankee in King
    Arthur's Court*
  Old Testament narratives
  Alice in Wonderland
  Fairy tales:
    Hans Christian Andersen
    Grimm
  Ballads

4th Grading Period

DEEP ROOTED IMPULSE OF POETRY

POETRY
  Introduction to poetic form
    (Material available in book
    rooms and "E.E." circulating
    library)
English Literature
  The Sonnet
    (Use mimeographed collection
    of Milton's sonnets)
  L'Allegro and *Il Penseroso*
  Romantic Poets:
    Wordsworth
    Coleridge
    Byron, Shelley, Keats

  Victorian Poets:
    Tennyson
    Browning

Supplementary
Molière:
Tartufe or
The Misanthrope
Hamlet
Romeo and Juliet
T. S. Eliot:
Murder in the Cathedral (use recordings)
Other Greek drama
Ibsen:
Pillars of Society or
The Wild Duck or
Hedda Gabler

Modern Poetry:
(Selections available in English Masterpieces of Modern Poetry)
Housman
Masefield
Brooke
Francis Thompson
Eliot
Yeats
Auden

Comparative Study
(Use American Poets)

5th Grading Period

THE SCIENTIFIC WAY—
A WORLD OF THOUGHT
THE ESSAY
(Use materials available in high school book rooms and the "E.E." circulating library.)

English Literature	Century
Bacon's *Essays*	16th, 17th, 18th
Johnson	
Addison	
Swift	
Walpole	
Chesterfield	
Boswell	
Lamb	19th
DeQuincey	
Hazlitt	
Arnold	
Macaulay	
Newman	
Modern periodicals:	20th

Atlantic Monthly
Harper's
Saturday Review
The New Yorker
Orwell's essays

6th Grading Period

THE MASSES BEGIN TO
READ
THE NOVEL AND SHORT
STORY
Brief history of the novel
(17th and 18th centuries)

English Literature	Century
Wuthering Heights	19th

Comparative Study
The Sorrows of Young Werther
in *Great German Short Novels and Stories*
The Red Badge of Courage
Huckleberry Finn
Washington Square
The Turn of the Screw
The Old Man and the Sea
Balzac:
Eugénie Grandet
Père Goriot

Comparative Study

Montaigne	16th
Puritanism:	17th
Milton	
Bunyan	
Benjamin Franklin	18th
Emerson and Thoreau	19th
Periodicals	20th

Supplementary

Available essay collections
Modern Periodicals
Pepys' *Diary*
Emerson's *Journals*
Thoreau's journals or
Arnold Bennett's journals

Supplementary

David Copperfield
Hard Times
Vanity Fair
The Virginians
The Mayor of Casterbridge
The Return of the Native
Pride and Prejudice
The Forsyte Saga
*Great German Short Novels and
Stories*
Kafka:
Selected short stories

Time Chart for Senior English

Composition Work

These suggestions for composition work are intended to accompany the regular assignments in descriptive, narrative, expository, and argumentative writing which would normally be expected in a regular class.

Imaginative or creative writing (Stress figurative language.)
The short story (fictional experience with plot development)
The informal essay (humor, irony, satire, caricature)
Poetry (couplet, quatrain, limerick, short lyric, sonnet; attempts at translation from Latin or a modern foreign language; free verse)
Critical writing (A paper in answer to a literary question, e.g., What meaning do you think there is in Pip's use of fairy tale symbols such as "fairy godmother" and "wand" in *Great Expectations?*)
Character sketch (Relate to class reading.)
Re-creation of atmosphere, mood, or tone (e.g., the marshes in *Great Expectations*)
Contrasts (e.g., *Wuthering Heights* and *Thrushcross Grange*)
The book review (Include comments on style and plot manipulation.)
Critical essays (e.g., paradoxes in *Macbeth*)

Kind of writing involved in tests, quizzes and exercises

Tests of fact and memory (e.g., unit, term, and final tests based upon actual subject matter taught)

Tests to provoke organized thinking under the pressure of a time limit (essays)

Minor quizzes designed to check and promote careful reading

Vocabulary tests

The paraphrase

The précis

Documentation from the text (pulling out evidence) to support an idea (e.g., passages from the *Iliad* dealing with the character of Helen, etc.)

The research paper (emphasis on format)

Eventual formulation by students themselves of significant literary questions as bases for literary essays

Standardized English tests for measurement and motivation are recommended at the beginning and toward the end of the year.

A helpful reference for many of the preceding ideas in composition is Brooks and Warren, *Modern Rhetoric*.

Senior Mathematics Seminar

Since many students have been in special mathematics classes during the ninth, tenth, and eleventh years, the gap between their understanding and that of the average student has been widened, so that it is more important than ever that they be in "EE" classes as seniors. Grant and the other high schools now provide such classes.

The usual senior mathematics is an elementary analysis course and includes some work in analytic geometry and calculus but very little advanced work in exponents, solution of equations, and theory of equations and nothing on determinants and mathematical induction.[4]

Senior mathematics at Grant High School has many points of contact with modern mathematics and leads naturally into enrichment topics. In addition to the topics generally covered, the

[4] See W. E. Milne and D. R. Davis, *Introductory College Mathematics* (Revised; Boston: Ginn and Company, 1941).

seminar studies topics of modern mathematics. Here is a teacher's description of one seminar:

The students did research on various topics and had the responsibility for presenting them to the class. Since the time for the presentation of each topic to the class by the students varied from five to twelve days, the seminar by necessity should be limited to approximately ten students. This seminar group had nine students, which seemed an ideal size.

The first five weeks were devoted to a unit on statistics including methods of computing correlation and regression equations. This unit was taught by the teacher during which time students chose and began preparation of their first individual topics. Choice of topic was influenced by the students' interests, mathematical background and by their browsing through a library of mathematical books.

Each student was responsible for:
1. Careful preparation of his topic
2. Presentation of the material to the class
3. Leading all discussion pertinent to the topic
4. Preparation of material for daily assignment to the class
5. Preparation of subject matter evaluation questions to be written by other members of the class
6. Scoring the written question
7. Writing a summary of the completed presentation
8. Suggesting a bibliography useful for reading on the topic
9. Reviewing briefly the material covered by the report after completion of a series of class reports.

At the end of a series of reports the class wrote two-day examinations on the questions prepared by the students for each report. Each student evaluated the questions answered on his topic.

Some of the topics chosen were:
The Duodecimal System—its application and usage
Mathematical Symbolic Logic
Integral Domains
Topology
Rates of Exchange
Mathematical Induction
Theorems on Determinants
Operations on Integers
Mathematical Basis for the Arts
Construction of Nomograms
The Normal Probability Curve

The Mechanics of Computers
Non-Euclidean Geometry
Conic Sections
Infinity—discussion of Lieber's book[5]
Method of Extracting the Nth Roots of Numbers
Permutations and Combinations

SENIOR SOCIAL STUDIES SEMINAR

The seminars and special sections in social studies share certain aims which arise from the nature of the subject. Among these aims are the following: (1) to develop in students an understanding of the concept of culture and the diversity of social patterns and value systems under which men live; (2) to increase students' knowledge of some of man's common problems and his attempted solutions both philosophically and historically; (3) to promote an awareness of the role of "context of the times"—the effects upon an event or a work of its historical setting; (4) to develop discrimination as to relevance and importance according to standards of logical and causal connection; (5) to make students aware that many problems do not have a single right answer and that disparate and even antagonistic points of view must often exist side by side.

Materials for study are generally selected for their interpretative possibilities within a broad social and cultural frame. Class discussions may develop from either the interpretations of common reading or the ideas gained through independent studies. The search for knowledge can, and does, become an exciting adventure, which may, for example, lead a class from an interest in current debates about freedom of thought and expression back along man's rough road to Socrates, the noble "Barefoot in Athens."

Emphasis on these objectives and success in achieving them will vary from teacher to teacher and from class to class. The following is a teacher's account of the procedures followed in his seminar on world problems:

I believe that one can improve the reasoning process of bright students to a greater extent if the student group is small—twelve or less. I believe that it is extremely difficult to determine how or what students are really

5 L. R. Lieber and High Gray, *Infinity* (New York: Rinehart & Company, Inc., 1953).

thinking until an atmosphere is provided in which the students can express themselves fully. I believe that given this opportunity for a full period each day, students soon become aware of a few flaws in their reasoning process. I believe an intense desire to think more soundly can be created. I believe students can be made to become dissatisfied with the security afforded by dutiful re-creation of teacher introductions and/or analyses and materials read. I believe this procedure does not cause students to lose their respect for the facts. Quite to the contrary, students may become aware more acutely of their necessity. However, the challenge is to teach these students how to put to use that which they have acquired. In the regular classroom environment, much time and effort is spent determining that the basic factual material has been acquired. These are my basic assumptions.

The areas to be studied were selected by the students, a number of whom decided it would be sound to start with a study of early viewpoint regarding the relation of man to government, so a study of some of Plato's writings on this subject was chosen. As they plunged into the reading, the students became aware of the need for historical background to give their discussions perspective. They took time to rough in a brief historical framework. At the end of their interest in this topic, they were asked to sketch the basic philosophy and plan of their ideal government. The resulting papers offered an unexpected solution. Almost all students wished for a benevolent despot or a small god-wise council to shoulder the problems of government. This was their honest, personal reaction after becoming aware of the complexities and problems of ruler and ruled which have long plagued mankind. In the course of the year, one of my goals was to help them develop from this point, to a more complete realization of the implications of this innocent-appearing solution.

One of the class members who had traveled to Europe had become aware of his ignorance regarding all things communistic. He sold the class on a study of Karl Marx. We read, studied, discussed, and re-read small excerpts. The students soon realized that they had neither the historical nor economic background for the task selected. We backed and filled for a few weeks. Teacher and students did what they could to remedy the situation and the result was a considerable understanding of the serious unsolved economic problems which gave rise to this doctrine. This experience gave the students an understanding of how a theory is developed, merchandised, accepted, rejected, and altered. Some individuals worked on other aspects of the topic in individual papers such as the *Russian Adaptation* and *An Analysis of Catholic Pamphlets on the Topic*.

The students felt they had acquired background and understanding that would help them all in their next area of study. Each student selected a particular trouble spot which he wished to study carefully. Southeast Asia, Africa, and the Middle East were chosen after which the students decided that they would need to familiarize themselves with the historical background, colonial policies, reorganization of native economy, and the rising spirit of nationalism in order to follow intelligently the current political maneuverings. They each led the discussion and analysis of the problem of their chosen area. Most of them also reported on some aspects of the problem in written reports. The class also looked at the problems of integration faced by the South after one of the students wrote to a Southern newspaper for more complete information expressing some of the Southern viewpoints.

The last unit was teacher selected and centered around a paperback collection of lectures by Carl L. Becker on the topic of freedom and responsibility in the American way of life. Because Sabin's introduction was quite demanding we spent several weeks on it. This was the first taste of historiography for the class. Here again they learned more about using material that required much thinking, re-reading, reflection, and reference work to be able to comprehend the viewpoint expressed. The lectures were considered fun to read after the struggle with the introduction.

Following this, the students began to evaluate their ideal government again. They had come to realize that they had sought the eternally desired, simple formula or easy way out. They had become very much aware of the possible shortcomings of the benevolent despot, but they still wished it could work. They didn't think too highly of man's relation to his government. They felt most people only bother to view the political scene with a "dab of thoughtfulness" when things are not going well personally or when scandal is exposed. They felt they, too, were as lazy as the next fellow. They expressed a desire to spend their time on personal interests, and they wished the government could just flow along smoothly. They did have the decency to be shocked at their own attitudes. I think most felt that our present democratic pattern would be maintained only as long as our general prosperity allowed us to maintain this luxury. We ran out of time, as is the case in most courses.

The following is a list of books read by all students in the senior social studies seminar. The supplementary list of readings by each individual is too long to be included.

Author	Selection
Schlesinger	*Crisis of the Old Order*
Simons	*Economic Policy for a Free Society*
Lippmann	*The Good Society*
Child and Carter	*Ethics in a Business Society*
Soule	*Men, Wages, and Employment*
Allen	*Only Yesterday*
Machiavelli	*The Prince* and *The Discourses*
Lubell	*The Future of American Politics*
Veblen	*The Theory of the Leisure Class*
Kaufmann	*Existentialism from Dostoievsky to Sartre*
Riesman	*The Lonely Crowd*
Plato	*The Works of Plato*
	The Republic
Rossiter	*The American Presidency*
Barnett	*The Universe and Dr. Einstein*
Mills	*The Power Elite*
Chase	*The Proper Study of Mankind*
Crane	*Getting and Spending*

Senior Physics Seminar

Purposes

The purposes of the physics seminar include those of the regular classes, namely, to give a general background of factual information concerning physical laws and to develop skills and techniques useful in the laboratory. It is also the hope of the instructor that, while gathering facts about physics, a student will acquire greater understanding of the methods and philosophy of science and its historical background. It is chiefly on these indirect objectives that special attention is focused in the seminar. It must be understood, however, that the greatest part of the time is spent in gaining a working fund of facts about natural laws and their mathematical relationships, which is the field of physics.

Method

In science depth, rather than speed, is the approach which gives greatest satisfaction to students of exceptional ability. Questions are aimed to make a student penetrate deep into the problem of why things happen (theory) rather than merely describe the way in which they happen. For this reason a seminar will trail behind regular classes so far as pages of a book are concerned.

One of the interesting techniques which work well with a science seminar is the performance of a demonstration with a minimum of comment, after which the instructor asks the students what they have observed and what conclusions are valid in terms of their observations. Then they discuss the various interpretations of the results.

The most successful laboratory project is to assign each individual, or pair of students, to plan and conduct an investigation of their own. The problem is chosen on the basis of the student's interest, unless the instructor considers it unsuitable, too difficult, or too simple.

After approval by the instructor a student is almost entirely on his own. He solves his own dilemmas as best he can. When he has collected his data, he reports to the class and states conclusions based on his findings. Some of these reports, though not indicating any new and remarkable discoveries, show a high degree of ingenuity and imagination.

Another project is the preparation of a research paper. Topics are chosen entirely by the instructor on the basis of their value in teaching something of the history and methods of science and, in some cases, the philosophy behind scientific thought. Samples of these projects have included: "Dowsing—Fact or Fancy," "Spontaneous Generation," "The Caloric Theory." In a recent seminar, topics were assigned by lot with the privilege of exchange. Interestingly enough, each student kept the one he drew. Fairly rigid standards are established for form and content. Each paper must be documented thoroughly. Part of the requirement is that some of the work be done in the high school library where information about the topics is made available.

In addition to other work each grading period, every student is required to read one book selected from the literature of science, although not necessarily from physics. Part of the time students are encouraged to make their own selections, and at other times books are assigned. Oral reports and discussions are an important part of the course.

The following books were found quite useful as references for work in the physics seminar:

Author	Selection
Deming, H. G.	*Fundamental Chemistry*
Hildebrand	*Principles of Chemistry*
Hildebrand and Latimer	*Reference Book of Inorganic Chemistry* (combined volume)
Holton, G.	*Introduction to Concepts and Theories in Physical Science*
Lange	*Handbook of Chemistry*
Mellor	*Inorganic Chemistry*
Stewart	*Introductory Acoustics*
Taylor, L.	*Physics, the Pioneer Science*
Timbie, W. H.	*Elements of Electricity*

The following topics proved stimulating for research papers:

Dowsing—Fact or Fancy
Spontaneous Generation
Perpetual Motion Devices
Alchemy's Contribution to Modern Science
Arguments in the Case of a Heliocentric System vs. a Geocentric System
Rise and Fall of the Phlogiston Theory
The Accuracy of Ancient Scientific Instruments
The Caloric Theory

FOREIGN LANGUAGES

The program for advanced students at Grant High School has indirectly affected the foreign language field. No special classes have been established and no particular emphasis has been given to encouraging more students to enroll in foreign language classes. The program's general stimulation of intellectual endeavor, however, with the resulting swing to respect for academic pursuits, has caused an upsurge in foreign language enrollments. Other influences have been the nation-wide concern for the teaching of foreign languages, the oft-repeated example of Russian children learning English, and the increased number of student exchanges in foreign countries.

For many years a variety of foreign languages has been offered at Grant High School. Latin was until recently the predominant language by a considerable margin. Now, however, the trend away from it has grown so much that its edge over Spanish is very slight. Spanish, French, and German enrollments show an increase while Latin shows a decrease, not only at Grant but also in every high school in the district.

The Portland high schools offer advanced study of languages the third and fourth year if 15 or more students wish to enroll. The recent emphases that two years of foreign language study is of questionable value and that three or four years is necessary for real accomplishment are having their effect.[6] Although the number of students at Grant enrolled in advanced classes is growing, it is still comparatively small, approximately 10 per cent of the total language enrollment.

Russian is a recent addition to the languages offered in Portland high schools. Five of Portland's ten high schools offer such courses, the number being limited only by the availability of qualified teachers.

A recent trend in the Portland school system is to offer foreign languages in elementary schools. One fourth of the schools offer pupils the opportunity to study a language beginning in the sixth grade. A language is taught as an additional subject in special classes, each school offering the language for which a competent teacher can be found. The conversational approach is used, but pupils who remain in a language class for three years are allowed to enter high school at the appropriate advanced level. As more elementary pupils enter high school with a foreign language, it is expected that both total enrollment and advanced language enrollment in the high school will increase.

EXTRACLASS ACTIVITIES

School organizations such as student governments, clubs, societies, publication staffs, and athletic teams are an important part of the

---

[6] James B. Conant, *Conference Report: The Identification and Education of the Academically Talented Student in the American Secondary School* (National Education Association, February, 1958), p. 138.

life of Grant High School students. Participation in these activities provides an outlet for able students which scholarly pursuits in the classroom cannot provide. The typical gifted student at Grant enters into the group life of the school with enthusiasm. Often he tries to do too much, and only careful counseling can show him the necessity of maintaining a balance between academic studies and social pursuits. The occasional advanced student who has a tendency to keep to himself is encouraged to participate in extraclass activities for the advantages which can accrue to him.

No planned procedure exists at Grant for supplementing the education of gifted students through social or extraclass activities. Many societies, clubs, and teams depend on the leadership which able students can give, and generally such leadership is forthcoming without faculty maneuvering. No matter in what capacity the student serves his school organization, he will help others and will himself receive benefits which are as sure as they are difficult to measure.

Gerald Van Pool, in the Fifty-Seventh Yearbook of the National Society for the Study of Education, lists the values to be obtained from student participation in extraclass activities:

1. Participation may help identify the student with a group.
2. Participation can help develop a feeling of social consciousness.
3. Participation can serve as an outlet for his energy and superior abilities.
4. Participation may help him assume a position of leadership.
5. The sports program has much to offer gifted students.
6. Gifted students can help organize activities.
7. Participation helps retain the gifted student's interest in school.
8. He has an opportunity to serve his classmates.[7]

The more than 300 Grant students who are enrolled in advanced academic classes are organizers, leaders, and participants in a large number of extraclass activities. Their influence is felt in such diverse places as the football field, the newspaper office, the debate hall, and the club room. In turn they are influenced by others in the necessary give-and-take of social living.

[7] *Education for the Gifted* (National Society for the Study of Education [Chicago: University of Chicago Press, 1958]), pp. 311–15.

THE TEACHING FACULTY FOR SPECIAL CLASSES

A successful teacher of advanced high school students must possess a combination of the best attributes of a scholar and a teacher. A scholar's approach to his special teaching field includes impressive competence in the knowledge and skills of that field and a drive to increase competence through formal training and informal study. Knowledge of subject matter is the quality able students most value in a teacher. These students, however, do not expect teachers to digest the content and feed them like birds. But the teacher who knows his field is most likely to guide students along the correct route toward learning, recognizing the road signs, allowing exploration of the side paths along which students may get lost, supplying information when necessary, and knowing where other important information may be obtained. This is the teacher for gifted students.

In a program like that at Grant High School, students who have been identified as having exceptional ability have a mixed schedule of advanced classes and regular classes. The student is never a candidate for a complete series of special classes since his identification rests on his abilities, performance, and *interest*.

Since there is no special school of advanced classes within the framework of the general high school, there is also no special class faculty. Teachers are assigned by the principal to assume the teaching of a special class as part of their teaching load. Typically the teacher of the senior mathematics seminar has four regular mathematics classes to teach daily, and the same load applies to teachers of special classes in other fields.

With a knowledge of the students to be taught, the content to be covered, and the teachers available, the principal chooses the instructor who is best suited for the task. At Grant several teachers in some departments possess the scholarly qualities and teaching attributes needed. Consequently it has become the practice to rotate the teaching of special classes every three years. This procedure is not necessarily true in all departments, nor is it true in other high schools of Portland.

The Portland school system, through its district-wide Gifted

Child Program, provides in-service training classes where teachers can more easily refresh their knowledge of course content and can keep abreast of trends and advances in their fields. Each summer, courses are arranged by local colleges or by individual professors. The distinguishing feature of the in-service and summer courses is their emphasis on content, although reference is made to teaching procedures and materials. The reason for this emphasis is very simple: teachers of advanced students need and want to know more.

Public Acceptance of the Program

When the program in Portland began in 1952, experimental funds were obtained from the Fund for the Advancement of Education. Financial assistance from this source continued until 1957, but in decreasing amounts. As this financial aid was gradually withdrawn, it became necessary to evaluate the effects of the program. Numerous tests and questionnaires gave positive evidence that students were developing a new respect for intellectual endeavor, were able to work more independently as required for successful college study, were less inclined to settle for the gentlemanly "C," and were enjoying the advanced work. With such evidence the school district Board of Directors has annually encouraged the program and has provided funds for its operation and expansion.

Recently a well-planned and controlled study was made of the attitudes of parents, pupils, and teachers toward special educational programs for gifted children in general and toward the Portland program in particular.[8] The opinions were not obtained solely from gifted pupils or from their parents or teachers, but from the general population. All groups overwhelmingly supported the idea that schools should provide a special program for the gifted in addition to that offered in the regular classroom. Parents, pupils, and teachers who were involved in the program in the Portland schools, or who were informed about it, had fewer reservations than others.

There is little doubt that the citizens in the neighborhood of Ulysses S. Grant High School and in the neighborhoods of the

[8] Norman K. Hamilton, *Attitudes Toward Special Educational Programs for Gifted Children* (Doctor's dissertation, Stanford University, 1958).

other schools in Portland favor the present program for advanced students. They are aware that schools are an aggregation of individuals and that none should be undereducated. The fear that a highly educated elite may be the result of instruction appropriate to individual capacity seems groundless at Grant. With a concern for intellectual development as well as for skill in social relationships, the school is producing students who have an awareness of the problems of the world and a desire to solve them, combined with the humility necessary for satisfactory living.

I I

Program in a Large
Comprehensive High School

Lloyd S. Michael, Evanston Township High School
and
Jean Fair, Wayne University

EVANSTON Township High School is a four year comprehensive high school. It aims to provide all its students with good opportunities to achieve as much as they can in areas which are individually and socially important. Its standards have been high over a long period of time. To maintain these high standards, the school has had a persisting interest in developing new programs which have promise for better education.

The high school is located in a large and well-established suburb near Chicago. Near by are several institutions of higher learning and the cultural opportunities of a metropolitan area. Homes and churches, parks and other recreational facilities, the city government, and community organizations are all sources of great pride to many who live here. For many years the community has shown a strong and thoughtful interest in its public schools and a real willingness to give them the financial support they need.

The school serves some 3,300 boys and girls, almost all of the youth in the community. Although an influential majority of them come from families in which one or both parents are in the professions or in some sort of managerial position, a sizable proportion are the sons and daughters of other kinds of white collar worker or of skilled and unskilled laborers. A majority of parents have had at least some college education. Some have graduate training, while only a few have not attended high school. Students are of many religious faiths. A majority are white; a small minority, Negro. About three fourths will go to college or some other kind of educational institution, with approximately one fourth going into full-time employment directly after graduation. In so large a student body there are many purposes and interests. The range of ability is great, from those who are educable but mentally handicapped to those with extraordinary ability to learn. In general, however, better than ordinary opportunities in homes, schools, and community have contributed to giving most of the students better than average academic ability.

The physical plant is excellent, with facilities not only for class sessions and quiet study but for sports, fine arts, shop work, meetings, and laboratory and library work. A great variety of instructional materials is available, from printed materials to closed circuit television.

The faculty is especially competent. Salaries have been among the highest in the country, but interest in education as a profession and in the opportunities for individual professional growth are probably as influential in attracting able teachers. Almost all have had postgraduate work; one out of three have two years of graduate study; and some have their doctorate. Since a comprehensive high school needs a diversity of offerings for its students, many teachers have been able to develop their own special competencies in such areas as guidance, the arts, sports, shop work, human relations, student activities, and remedial work.

A large high school should be organized to provide the many advantages that bigness makes possible and still insure the accepted benefits of smallness in a concern for the individual student and his needs. Our school has introduced several innovations to increase the advantages associated with both large and small institutions and to diminish their disadvantages. The school is organized into four divisions, creating four schools within a school. Each subunit has one fourth of the students from each of the four high school grades. Each has its appropriate administrative, counseling, and clerical staff. Many practices have been introduced to develop efficient organization and effective utilization of staff and to extend the functional relationships among guidance, curriculum, and instruction.

A large comprehensive high school can offer a broad, multipurpose curriculum of courses and activities for students of widely varied interests and abilities. At Evanston there are, for example, college level courses in the academic fields for those students who can profit from them. Special opportunities are provided in the program for students who are talented in one or more areas. The educable mentally handicapped pupils are enrolled in basic courses, including vocational experience, which are closely related to their needs.

Evanston has long been interested in its very able students. Special classes, after-school clubs, and extensive individual help on particular projects have been available to them for some 15 years or more. Honors courses have been offered by the mathematics department for the past 20 years. The need for a systematic, coordinated plan for talented students, however, was recognized some five years ago. The present program represents the efforts of the school to recognize its responsibilities to able and ambitious youth and to develop new and improved practices for the identification and education of their talents.

IDENTIFICATION OF THE GIFTED

The first major task is that of identifying the talented pupil. Identification begins early, preferably in the elementary grades. Increasing attention is being given to the screening process and records of the elementary and junior high schools. In the high school, however, the major part of the identification is done in the ninth grade, with some selection by cooperative efforts in the spring semester of the eighth year.

The school relies on clues from many sources in identifying its talented students. An extensive school-wide testing program supplies for the ninth grade at least two I.Q. scores, at least two measures of reading ability, scores of ability in mathematics fundamentals and reasoning, and an indication of early vocational interests.

For the eleventh grade it supplies a measure of academic learning ability, two more reading scores, another in mathematics fundamentals and reasoning, and another of vocational interest. Individual tests of intelligence and personality are administered whenever needed. Student scores on College Entrance Examination Boards, the Scholarship Qualifying Test, the School and College Ability Test, and many such tests as STEP and Iowa ED are also available. The school is improving its school-wide testing program by including more tests of achievement in the basic skills of subject fields and by IBM distribution of an even wider range of information about student achievement. The development of a larger number of school norms helps to distinguish unusual intellectual ability more readily by avoiding a pile-up of scores in the ninetieth percentile. Objective data revealed by such an extensive testing program are essential in the selection procedures.

Major attention in the development of the testing phase of the program was given to definitions of talent. All of the departments and many of the sponsors of extracurricular activities were asked to develop a definition of talent in their own areas. These definitions were likely to include such characteristics as unusual ability and willingness to think through problems; a far better than average store of information in a subject field; strong motivation and capacity for sustained work and effort in some area; great curiosity to know more about something new or already familiar; great sensitivity in human relations expressed either directly in social situations or indirectly in other ways; ability and willingness to exert influence in some way; unusual aptitude for learning quickly or deeply; wide reading, listening, or observation; and even unusual physical co-ordination.

Talent, then, has never been considered as one characteristic or set of characteristics which students either did or did not possess, but as specific characteristics apparent perhaps in only one area of living, perhaps in several. Talent could be found not only in the conventionally academic subject fields, but in the fine arts, the practical arts, sports, and leadership of student affairs. The school has found it useful to define talent not by absolute standards but in terms of some greater degree of ability. Probably no one faculty group has ever been content that its definition is the proper one, but such definitions have given a basis for work.

Using the definitions as criteria for judging, the faculty contributed students' names and descriptive comments to a master file, which was supplemented by lists of students whose I.Q. scores were no lower than 125 or who had very high final marks in subjects. About one fourth of the student body has been so identified as talented in one or more areas. This master field became a device for communicating information about individual students to teachers and counselors. It was also an initial source of data for studying these young people and for examining the adequacy of the curriculum and the guidance program.

Several groups of students were of immediate interest: those who had unusual ability in some academic subject area; those who had undeveloped potential—the underachievers; and those whose school marks were high but whose scholastic ability was either mediocre or had not been recognized by the teacher—the overachievers. In cooperation with the Talented Youth Project of Columbia Teachers College, the school made an extensive and systematic study of these groups. Departments tried out honors classes or made other provisions for them. Counseling focused on the special problems of these groups.

The master list was used less often as the staff singled out problems to study. In its place the school now uses lists for particular purposes. Talented students are identified when and if the school intends to make some special provision for them. The few of extraordinary ability, roughly those whose intelligence tests scores are above 145, have been spotted for counselors and other staff members. The small minority of potentially talented underachievers, defined rather arbitrarily as those who have a minimum I.Q. of 128 but earn only average marks or below, have been identified for special study, classroom help, or individual and group counseling. Small groups of overachievers have twice been selected for study. Other kinds of identification have been made as well.

One of the most important purposes in identification is to make curricular provisions most commonly, but not always, in honors classes. For this purpose multiple sets of criteria of talent are used, although each of the academic departments places in honors classes students who meet some of several criteria. No department has yet found any one desirable pattern of characteristics. The I.Q. score of each student is usually expected to be above the minimum of 130, and eleventh grade percentile ranks from the College Ability Test are expected to fall within the ninetieth percentile. Some departments, such as English and social studies, however, are most interested in verbal subscores; others, such as mathematics and science, in quantitative items, and still others, in general nonlanguage subscores. All of the departments rely heavily upon teacher recommendations based on the departmental definition of talent in its subject area. All use previous school marks in relevant subject fields which represent the achievement of the top quarter of the school population. The English and social studies departments expect their students to be solidly within the ninetieth percentile on standardized tests of reading and language abilities. The mathematics and science departments expect a similar level of achievement in quantitative skills. For placement in some twelfth grade courses departments consider enrollment in the earlier courses in the subject field as promise of success in a difficult course.

At times the highest in ability are selected from the very able for some such purpose as placement in several honors classes or enrollment in more than one college level course.

Obviously these criteria for talent overlap. Objective data are useful in identifying students who might be overlooked either because teachers are unable to recognize their abilities or because students are in situations in which they do not actually display great abilities. There are highly successful students in every honors class, however, whose intelligence scores fall below 130—occasionally far below—or who somehow did not meet many of the other objective criteria. Some students who did meet the criteria seemed improperly identified as talented once they were placed in a really challenging situation. Although the subjective ratings of teachers have ordinarily agreed with objective data, at times they have not. When teacher ratings have been based on identified characteristics of talent, they have been valuable in identifying students who do, or do not, need special provisions.

Flexibility and adaptation are essential elements in the current plan of selection of talented pupils. Neither the master file nor the present lists for specific purposes have ever been fixed. Names are added or removed at all grade levels. Young people develop in different ways, and provisions appropriate for them at one stage may not be at another. Not even the criteria for identification are permanently determined. Each year sees some modification by some group in the light of its experience in working with young people.

THE CURRICULUM

Honors Classes

Honors classes are among the most important school provisions for the intellectually able. Providing for individual differences within heterogeneous classes has been done, and done well, in many instances and over a long period of time. Still it is less likely that teachers who have several classes and a multitude of other professional responsibilities can find the time to do their most effective job for too great a variety of students. Placing the very able students in honors classes has not created homogeneous groups. It has merely reduced the range of ability and interests. Individual instruction is still necessary.

At some place along the line of development, perhaps in high school, it becomes harder to set up a sequence of learning experiences which promotes maximum growth for everyone in one classroom group. Intellectually able boys and girls are often challenged by activities which are not meaningful to other students. Moreover, in classes with less able students, the gifted must sometimes hide their abilities in order to be accepted. They may tolerate boredom or dominate the class to the detriment of others.

Honors classes have been set up by all of the academic departments of the school. The difficulty of identifying talented ninth-graders and doubts about the need for honors classes at this level have meant that only a few such courses are offered to freshmen. Here there are two levels in mathematics, one for those who began algebra in the eighth grade; two kinds of section in social studies, one for those who want a two-year sequence including world history; and two sections in English. The talented in science are encouraged to enroll in biology, usually a sophomore course. Honors classes have been set up in grades ten through twelve, however, in English, social studies, mathematics, science, French, and Spanish. Honors classes are not offered in chemistry, German, or Latin since enrollment rarely includes a really wide range of ability.

Honors classes are intended for students who cannot be fully provided for within regular classes. They are not intended to include all those who expect to go to college. Regular classes also offer opportunities for the quality of education which is preparatory for college. Enrollment in some kind of honors section in a chosen course is ordinarily compulsory for qualified students. Although a student may choose among special classes within a course and among courses, he may not choose a regular section that is not appropriate for him. Nor may he choose an inappropriate honors section.

Because of the policy of identification of talent in specific areas, a student is assigned neither to a program wholly of honors classes nor to one of none at all. Some students, it is true, are identified as talented in all academic areas; others, in only a few or in one only. Moreover, students are transferred in and out of the honors program in any one subject field in all four grades. The schedule provides one or more classes in the regular course during each of the periods that an honors course is offered.

Combined Studies

The Combined Studies Program is a four year elective offering which features pupil participation and planning within defined areas of content, guidance, and accompanying extraclass activities.

Except for the freshman year, the combined studies department has not felt it necessary to establish separate honors classes for the academically able pupil. This condition obtains because of the wider range of subject matter encompassed in the course; the double class period; the emphasis on individual reading and research; and the opportunities in planning, discussing, and class management for the especially talented pupil.

The special feature of the combined studies classes has been the concept of intellectual leadership. Honors pupils are expected to make a significant contribution to creative individual and group progress. In this connection the various areas of leadership in a given class are identified and related to the interests and potentialities of all pupils both regular and honors. Furthermore, in addition to providing intellectual leadership, the honors pupil in combined studies each year does intensive research on a subject related to his own interest and consistent with the areas being studied that year. His work must show qualitative superiority and a grasp of the relation among many areas.

Advanced Placement Program

Ever since its early participation as a pilot school in what has become the Advanced Placement Program, Evanston has offered, in addition to honors courses, college level courses. Presently there are such courses in English; European history; United States history; physics and chemistry, each of which concludes a three year physical science sequence; and mathematics, which combines analytics and calculus following eleventh grade advanced algebra and trigonometry. Whenever enrollment is sufficient, courses will be offered in foreign languages, biology, and chemistry, instead of the tutorial help now available. Unusually able students are invited to enroll, but enrollment is voluntary. Students have as an alternative a challenging honors class, and for some, such a class is a sensible choice.

Other Curriculum Provisions

The intellectually talented are not segregated in all areas but only in those where special provisions are needed. They participate with other students in all kinds of extracurricular activity, in their homerooms and divisions, in physical education classes, and in many special interest courses. Numerous opportunities for the gifted are also available in other school courses which do not have honors sections. The combined studies or core classes, briefly discussed earlier, have long provided well for their gifted students. Physical education classes have leadership programs. Fine arts, business education, and practical arts have all found ways of individualizing instruction without any formal honors structure.

Over four years most of the intellectually able, like their fellow students, enroll in at least two or more special interest courses. Many are available in several areas: playing in the band or orchestra, singing in a chorus, individual voice or instrument lessons, or studying music as a listener; speech arts of some sort; arts and crafts, painting, designing; typing, shorthand, preparatory accounting, or other business education; shop courses such as mechanical drawing, metal-work, electricity, or auto mechanics; home economics classes; or a short driver training course. While some students may have one of these areas as a major field of endeavor, almost all are enrolled in four academic courses. Rather than requiring five academic courses for its able students, the school has offered them depth in aca-demic areas. There are exceptions, however. Students of extraordi-nary intellectual ability occasionally are better off with an unusually large number of courses. The school is currently trying out a pro-gram in which selected ninth-graders take more than the usual num-ber of courses.

Pupil Activities

A large comprehensive high school can offer a wide variety of extracurricular activities in which talented students participate, as do others. In fact, the very able are often the leaders in Student Government, the Boys' Club, the Girls' Club, a cheer section, and division and homeroom activities. Some students even add a lead-ership training course to programs of four academic courses and extracurricular responsibilities.

First-string teams in sports are almost by definition made up of students of unusual athletic ability. Students with intellectual ability are sometimes first-stringers, though they are more likely to be members of some intramural sports team. Publications, and particularly the school newspaper, are staffed by students who have enrolled in an eleventh grade honors English journalism course. Many students of unusual ability are in the orchestra, band, and choruses, which meet as classes during the school day but spend much additional time before and after school in preparation for performances. Dramatics has a loyal band of followers, some of whom have real talent either in performing or in stage design. Many of these also enroll in a class in speech arts as freshmen or sophomores, or as seniors in English speech, or in stagecraft. Other activities appeal primarily but not exclusively to those with an intellectual bent: chess, foreign language club projects and outings, creative writing, discussion of the humanities or international affairs, and musical performances for small groups.

Out-of-school organizations, especially "Y" clubs, church groups, and the Youth Conference, interest both the talented and those not especially talented. Large numbers work for pay at some time, more often during the summer than during the school year.

Satisfying friendships, wholesome interests, social responsibility, and sheer fun have been encouraged, but the extracurricular program does not insist on turning out "well-rounded" individuals.

Typical Courses for the Gifted

As has already been indicated, challenging courses for able pupils are offered in all the academic fields. Separate sections in honors and college level courses are now scheduled. Representative courses are briefly discussed here, with regard to aims, content, and teaching methods.

First Year French Honors

The purpose of this course is to develop aural comprehension, oral expression, reading comprehension, and the ability to write simple French correctly. These are likewise the aims of our regular 1 French course, but in the honors classes much more material is covered, greater precision and accuracy in both written and oral work are required, and French is the language of the classroom to a greater extent.

The content of this course is richer and more varied than that of a regular section. The class should complete the first year grammar book by April, accomplishing in two days what the regular classes cover in three. The work in language fundamentals is supplemented by reading assignments which are approximately twice the length of those assigned to the regular sections. These assignments are treated in class in various ways. They may serve as a basis for conversation, as a source of cultural enrichment, or for intensive analysis of the structure and vocabulary of the text. In addition, the geography of France is thoroughly taught through readings, map study, slides, films, and class discussion.

Besides completing a standard first year grammar book and twice as much reading as is assigned to the regular class, the class will finish the first ten lessons of the second year textbook. To further develop reading comprehension, the teacher requires the more gifted pupils to read extensively outside of class and to submit written reports. Frequent use is made of records in order to give pupils the opportunity to hear voices other than that of the teacher.

European History—College Level

The course covers European history from A.D. 284 to 1939. The objectives are these:

1. To interest the student in the development of Western civilization from the collapse of Roman civilization to the present.

2. To introduce the student to the ideas and idea systems that have been important in Western civilization.

3. To give the student some knowledge of and some training in the method of writing history.

4. To give the student some appreciation and understanding of the interrelation in Western civilization of the humanities, the fine arts, the social sciences, and the natural and exact sciences.

5. To give the student an understanding of values to be derived from the study of history:

   a) A better understanding of human nature in both its individual and its social manifestations.
   b) Practice in the use of one's imagination in order to understand other times, other places, and other peoples.
   c) A better understanding of our own civilization and our own times.
   d) A truer perspective on the importance of events and problems of our times.

The method of the course is broadly the *analysis* of the complex phenomenon in human history called Western civilization. The method consists more specifically of applying three procedures to the principal events, the principal periods, and the principal institutions and ideas of Western civilization. These procedures are analysis, interpretation, and criticism. They are applied to the assignments, to suggest questions to stimulate and guide reading and study, to the comparison of historical accounts of a single event, and to the analysis of documentary materials. The same procedures are also followed in class discussions, in which the Socratic method is mainly employed. The criteria for written and oral reports also stress analysis, interpretation, and criticism. The few short-answer (objective) tests that are employed involve largely these three procedures. More use is made of the essay test, again with the same procedures in mind. In the case of written reports, essay tests and examinations, term papers, and even oral reports, the instructor comments in some detail on syntax and style. He also calls attention to misspelling, poor punctuation, and poor sentence structure and paragraphing.

Each week a short discussion (500–800 words) of an assigned specific historical problem, taken from the week's study, is written by each student. Sometimes students are asked to come prepared to write such a discussion in class, and sometimes they are assigned to write it outside. In both cases written discussions are read aloud to the class and are evaluated by students and the instructor. At six week intervals a somewhat longer paper (1,000 words or so) is written by each student. Once each semester a paper of 1,500 to 2,000 words is required, which demonstrates techniques of historical research. Attention here is given to the mechanics of preparing and form of a scholarly manuscript for publication, including proper form of footnotes, of quotations, and bibliography.

In order to give the students more time to read and to accustom them to the usual college schedule of three class meetings per week, an average of two class periods out of five is used for study. The instructor uses these periods to talk individually with the students about their work in the course, their progress in study skill, their written work, and their participation in class discussion.

Sophomore Physical Science Honors

This course is for the most able and highly motivated science student. Pairs of sections meet during the same period. One spends two days in physics, one 41 minute lecture period and one 87 minute double laboratory period. The other section has the same schedule in chemistry. Every two days these sections exchange classrooms and teachers.

These sophomores complete both regular one year courses in high school chemistry and physics in the sense of "getting through" the text and having the most important laboratory experiences. Most of them are also accelerated in mathematics. They are prepared for the college level courses in chemistry and physics which are offered in a two year sequence when they are juniors and seniors.

Immediate course objectives are about the same as in normal courses, with somewhat less mathematical rigor and greater emphasis upon the quality and implications of the major ideas. Another purpose is to make use of the very strong stimulation for the able sophomore which comes from his rapid encounter with an unusually wide variety of physical phenomena, from having less drill on specific facts and details, and from realizing that he is doing advanced work.

General classroom procedures feature films, lecture demonstrations, problem-solving sessions, student reports, *gedanken* experiments, and laboratory. The laboratory work is specifically planned to be "open-ended," almost sheerly exploratory, and wide ranging, with reduced emphasis upon verification, determination of constants, and routine laboratory skills. The *gedanken* experiments are exercises in the scientific method and take the form of class discussion of an imagined actual experiment, including procedures, apparatus, data obtained, analysis, conclusions, and general aspects. Actual laboratory work is recorded in a laboratory data book, and formal scientific reports are required periodically. When the students do experiments and record the results in their data book, they do not know whether a formal scientific report on the particular experiment will be required. Physical Science Study Committee materials are used in the physics section.

It is assumed that this course is the first in a three year sequence, although not all the students involved actually take the entire program. The most difficult single aspect of the teacher's daily preparation is the pacing, the effort to reveal the significant ideas pointedly enough so that they can be reasoned through without undue repetition or drill.

Senior Mathematics—College Level

This course includes a full year's study which integrates analytic geometry and calculus. It is the second year in a two year sequence offered to students gifted in mathematics, and it enrolls approximately 5 per cent of the seniors.

Mathematics content covers the following:

Cartesian co-ordinates—the straight line
Equations of curves
Derivative of a function
Differentiation of algebraic functions
Rates and differentials
Indefinite integrals—constant of integration
Definite integrals—the fundamentals of theorem and applications
Extreme values
The conics
Curve tracing
Exponential and logarithmic functions
Trigonometric functions
Theorem of mean value—indeterminate forms
Integration by standard forms
Table of integrals
Polar co-ordinates and applications
Parametric equations

The course is offered as a modified seminar of class discussion. Very few formal lectures are included. The class slogan is "Every student gets every problem." Daily work is recorded in a workshop notebook in chronological order. Although assignments vary in length, the average requires approximately one hour outside class. The students take pride in their notebooks and will carry them to the college of their choice as a guide for their placement in mathematics.

Approximately 12 period tests are given throughout the year, with emphasis upon the so-called "Big Three" the second semester: the school final examination (April, 2½ hours), the College Entrance Examination (March, 3 hours), and the Advanced Placement Examination (May, 3 hours). The achievements of former students in the Advanced Placement Program has been particularly gratifying. Most have started their college study in mathematics at the level of second or third courses in calculus. The average advanced credit received is six semester hours in mathematics.

Junior English Honors

Junior English Honors is one of a sequence of honors courses which start in the freshman year for pupils who are talented in English, and extend through the twelfth year.

In addition to the usual aims of any English program, specific objectives make these honors courses distinctive:

1. To become intellectual leaders by developing skills to verbalize, write, and act intelligently, and to think at a high level of abstraction.
2. To have a wide range of literary and language interests.
3. To develop a high level of critical thinking through an understanding of logic and semantics.
4. To move beyond essentials in developing communication skills.
5. To increase knowledge and use of a mature vocabulary.
6. To develop critical standards for judging the informative and aesthetic values of the mass media.
7. To appreciate and understand literature in depth through analysis and synthesis.
8. To develop critical acumen adequate to judge literature as a worthwhile use of leisure time.
9. To recognize the various forms of expression in great literary works.
10. To relate literary works to important periods of world culture.
11. To know and use grammar and its terminology.
12. To find rewarding outlets for creative talent.
13. To make effective use of library resources.
14. To develop skill in writing various types of expository material.
15. To develop ability to participate spontaneously and responsibly in discussion.
16. To understand the principles of and gain experience in formal speech situations.
17. To learn to listen critically and with concentration.
18. To increase skill in organizing auditory material for notetaking.

These objectives require a course different from the usual survey of American literature which characterizes most junior years in English. Teachers deal with significant whole books and plays, poetry in depth, and thought-provoking essays taken largely from *Harper's, The Atlantic Monthly, The Saturday Review,* and *The New Yorker.* Writing is an important part of the course, the emphasis being on synthesis and analysis of the literature read.

The literature has been chosen with such themes in mind as: The Nature of Man, The Dignity of Man, Man's Search for Individuality and Identification, The Vulnerability of Man, Man's Social Quest and Responsibility, The Nature of Tragedy, The Improvability of Man, and The Triumph of Man. The themes furnish an organization and make literature especially meaningful to able students, who are especially responsive to such timeless questions as: Who am I?, Why am I here?, Where am I going?, and How can I get there?

Great literature, dealing as it does with eternal verities, stimulates students' thinking in discussion and composition. It makes possible an integrated language-arts program in which reading, writing, listening, and speaking are all part of a natural, meaningful whole. Through such organization and methodology a teacher is able to emphasize the organic theory of literature—that form and content are inseparable. This approach enhances a pupil's ability to evaluate a work of art for he sees the relationships that exist throughout.

QUALITY OF LEARNING

The heart of the program lies in the quality of learning experiences expected of the talented boys and girls. The faculty at Evanston has not regarded objectives in the education of the very able as basically different from those for other students. All boys and girls need to learn to write clearly and effectively, for example, to think clearly about present-day problems, and to understand the physical world around them. Yet the program for the gifted must to some degree be different from that for other students if it is to accomplish its purpose. As time passes, a few basic ideas become more and more firmly embedded in the activities planned for these intellectually superior students.

The school encourages its talented students to work hard, and they do. Merely moving faster through ordinary material or working hard is not enough, however. The academically talented need to develop a higher quality of learning, a greater *precision and accuracy*. They can usually do so with less drill or formal emphasis.

Teachers must still require students to solve problems in mathematics, chemistry, or physics without careless errors. Students are expected to be competent in the mechanics of writing, not only in English themes but in social studies papers, science seminar reports, and bulletin notices. History teachers and others ask students to acquire a greater store of correct information as the base for sharper analyses and clearer concepts. Foreign language teachers emphasize exactness in meaning.

A better quality of learning involves not a mere collection of facts, but the development of abstract concepts and generalizations, the organization and integration of ideas, and a deep analysis of large and more complex phenomena. Ninth-graders can already go far beyond the narration of a plot to deal with the point of a piece of literature. Moreover, they are asked to read literature which has a point. They can begin a sophisticated concept of number in mathematics or of the free enterprise system in ninth grade civics. They can and will read magazines at the level of *Harper's, Science News Letter,* and *The Atlantic Monthly.* By the eleventh grade many courses require papers, sometimes 15 pages or longer, in which organized analyses of various topics are presented. Much help is given in English classes and elsewhere to the organization of writing and speaking. Those in college level courses use standard college level texts, but many other students make frequent use of books and articles at this difficult level.

Moreover, the concepts these academically talented develop must be integrated within ever larger wholes. One eleventh grade honors English class dealt with the meaning of tragedy when students read Steinbeck's *Grapes of Wrath* in the fall and continued to develop a concept of tragedy as they read Lewis' *Babbitt,* Benet's *John Brown's Body, Macbeth,* Hugo's *Les Miserables,* Sophocles' *Oedipus Rex,* Shaw's *Saint Joan,* and other examples of tragedy in literature during the year. Later they wrote papers of considerable length discussing the many aspects and meanings of tragedy in these and other books they knew. Another honors section at the same grade had similar experiences in developing ideas about the dignity of man. Others have worked on other concepts.

A college level United States history class during the year examined government's role in society, as seen by such men as Jefferson, Hamilton, Jackson, Bryan, Wilson, Hoover, and Roosevelt. In the spring they held an extended discussion of the changing ideas about the proper role of the government. College level physics students are more and more encouraged to learn both specific principles and the larger concept of scientific method from observation in firsthand experimentation, in contrast to seeing illustrations or clarifications of principles through their own laboratory demonstration.

A recently organized after-school humanities discussion group has tried to draw on both the humanities and the natural sciences in discussing relationships among human beings, one to another and as individuals in groups. Readings and discussion ran from William H. Whyte, Jr., to James B. Conant to Erich Fromm. A great arts course analyzes specific pieces of art in the contexts of their society and then develops comparisons among periods.

One of the chief differences between several courses for regular pupils and those for the academically talented is in depth of subject matter. The program in English shows the different approaches to content and method. An example is the unit of semantics, which is required in all regular, honors and college level (Advanced Placement) classes. Whereas regular and honors classes will study nearly all the basic semantic principles and apply them to their reading, writing, and listening, the college level class (the gifted) will extend the principles farther and apply them to a close analysis of their own literary background.

For example, in a major paper one boy related the semantic idea of extensional orientation to the concept of maturity and showed particularly that *The Adventures of Huckleberry Finn, Crime and Punishment,* and *War and Peace* increased a reader's extensional orientation and therefore his maturity. He showed first that a person's maturity is determined to a large extent by the nature of his extensional orientation and then, by close analysis of the works named, proved that literature aids us in obtaining an accurate extensional orientation and thereby helps us to achieve a mature attitude toward life.

A girl took the semantic idea of abstraction to prove that literature is an abstracting process. She started by proving first that any literature, whether modern poetry in free verse or ancient biography in Egyptian hieroglyphics, is abstraction and cannot reach below a certain level of the abstraction ladder. Through an analysis of such works as *Prometheus Bound,* the Biblical parables of the Prodigal Son and the Good Samaritan, *Romeo and Juliet, Hamlet, Les Miserables, Crime and Punishment, A Doll's House, Candide,* and *The Adventures of Huckleberry Finn,* she proved that literature can only go up the abstraction ladder and that it is the degree, rather than the fact, of its abstraction that determines its character.

In her analysis this student discussed the relationship of the creative process to the abstraction ladder, proving that the creative process in itself is an ordered climbing up and down the ladder and that literature generally attempts to make an idea concrete by personifying its characteristics. Speaking of the relationship of the reader to the literary abstraction, her conclusion was that "the relationship is that of a circle to a graph, the points are all there, arranged vertically and horizontally; the number of points the circle can encompass depends on its position and its size."

Other papers, all from a semantic point of view, have discussed the purpose of art as a combination of factors at various abstraction levels, the artist's responsibility to himself and his fellow men, taboos as a force in society, and others.

Similar depth approaches occur with other aspects of the English course. Much subject matter is different for gifted pupils, of course, particularly in the literary content. Many books read by them would prove too difficult for average pupils. More comparative or parallel analyses, both oral and written, are expected of the more able pupils. In essence, though, it is depth that distinguishes the classes of the gifted from those of the average.

The school is also giving increasing emphasis to critical thinking, problem-solving, and creativity. Able young people need to develop real understanding of the process and the purpose of thinking. Planned instruction in certain aspects of critical thinking occurs in virtually every course at all grade levels. While plane geometry classes work on the nature of logical proof, world history classes may evaluate historical evidence about the nature of an ancient civilization. Eleventh and twelfth grade English classes read Haya-kawa and Stuart Chase to apply some ideas from semantics. A physical science class learns to trust evidence from an experiment which seemingly contradicts an established principle. An extensive unit on critical thinking opens the senior American problems course, while critical analysis of influential documents takes place in college level European history.

English teachers encourage creative writing in the different forms of poetry, essays, and short stories. In the longer papers which students write in many courses, they are commonly required to make some interpretation which is, at the least, new to them. In the visual arts there are many opportunities for self-expression in many media. Entering their own writing or painting in local and national contests is a source of much satisfaction to many students—all the more so when, as often happens, their work wins some recognition.

In the science seminar all junior and senior students actually design and carry out a research project of their own. Budding scientists have worked long hours at turning up a new finding to be successfully reported to the seminar group, a science fair, or the Westinghouse Science Talent Search.

Coupled with ability to deal with problems must be capability for independent work. Able students in all grades are asked to handle more long-term assignments as distinguished from short daily homework. College level classes often meet four days a week and use the fifth for individual work and conference. To avoid using the instructor as a crutch, students in college level mathematics classes commonly explain calculus to each other in pairs or small groups. In many courses and extracurricular activities students organize and carry on their own discussion groups, publications, or programs with a minimum of faculty help. Students are encouraged to choose their own topics for individual investigation and presenta-tion in papers and reports and, at times, to choose learning activities and even major areas of class study.

Basic to growing independence are planned opportunities for students to undertake under guidance several kinds of projects, problems, or subjects among which sensible choices may actually be made. Also necessary in acquiring independent study habits is practice in defining and organizing, in notetaking, in selecting and evaluating reference materials, and in planning work. Helpful, too, is a sense of security in knowing that individual help is available and that success is possible. It is important to want and to enjoy independence in intellectual work.

Still another aspect of the curriculum is acquaintance with a wide range of values and critical awareness of those which individual students themselves hold. The science seminar, for example, has used such events as the launching of Sputnik as a basis for study and discussion of the comparative advantages of specialized versus general education. When a magazine asked its readers for judgments on true greatness, historically and in our times, the members of a ninth grade English class set themselves to reading biographies and to discussing and writing about the crucial values of living. United States history classes have dug into fiction to compare everyday values of the past with those they themselves hold. The annual three day Youth Conference afforded an opportunity to think through personal and spiritual values of many sorts. The enthusiastic preference of the humanities discussion group for a topic in the area of intensely human values bore out the belief of many staff members that it is worthwhile to develop the awareness of these values.

OTHER CONSIDERATIONS

Teachers

The staff members who teach the gifted need a good education themselves—usually more than a master's degree—outstanding competence in their subject fields, intellectual interests, ability to think, wide reading habits, and quick minds. It is sometimes said that a primary requisite for teaching the gifted is simply willingness to "get out of their way and let them learn." The school has not found this to be true. The gifted need positive help. What is more, teachers must give up notions that classes of gifted are simply "ideal" classes in which students "know all the answers." They must be able to create learning situations which are friendly and helpful but work-oriented and challenging. More than any other group in school, the academically talented have reported that they prefer this kind of teacher and such classroom situations.

Although college level classes usually have 15 to 20 or so students, honors classes more often have 25 or 30, as many as regular classes. Teachers of the gifted receive neither lighter loads nor extra pay. In return for what is often more work, however, they have found much rewarding satisfaction.

Instructional Materials

Books, films, records, laboratory facilities, maps, slides, and other learning materials suitable for other high school students are also useful for the talented, even though not used in the same way. The library and circulating book room, however, must carry a wide range of more mature titles primarily for them. Although high school texts are commonly used in honors classes and college texts in college level courses, much other reading material, special films, and the like are needed for almost every course. The science seminar teacher in particular can testify to a search for the most unusual material for laboratory work. Whatever is needed for gifted students must be just as available as materials necessary for other students. A large school is able to stock instructional aids which promote many kinds of interests and abilities.

Guidance

In a sense, the guidance program offers the talented the same kinds of opportunity available to all students. This includes help in making wise choices among the educational possibilities of the school, in planning for and choosing a college, and in considering a vocation for the years after school, and professional help with emotional problems. There are no special counselors for the talented. But the staff has identified points at which the talented commonly need help. These include developing awareness of their great abilities; choosing wisely among activities and courses rather than trying to do everything; selecting a college which offers sufficient challenge and appropriate social situations, rather than one which is merely famous, geographically near, or popular with other students; obtaining a college scholarship when financial assistance is needed; and thinking over vocational opportunities in the light of their unusual abilities. Counselors must also see that the honors course load is limited for students whose immaturity or temporary difficulties make such limitation desirable and that only those of very unusual ability elect two or more college level courses along with honors courses.

Counselors work with parents of the gifted as they do with all parents. Parents are informed not only of the potentialities of their sons and daughters but also of high school, college, and vocational opportunities open to them.

Research and Evaluation

Individuals and staff committees have been assigned to various research projects. One committee has participated in a study of school attitudes and self-attitudes of the talented, a project which furnished valuable information for the program. A group recommended higher criteria for placement in honors and college level classes. A comparative study of the achievement in tenth grade English of several ability levels, including the gifted in honors and regular classes, became the basis for a more challenging tenth grade English honors program. A subcommittee is now conducting a psychological study of the basic personality patterns of underachievers in the hopes of finding ways to help them. A study of patterns of achievement of high achievers, overachievers, and underachievers in high school and college is under way. Problems frequently encountered by the gifted have been identified for counselors. Another group has been working on more effective classroom learning experiences in several courses. Still another has been developing a humanities discussion group for advanced students.

Although the school continues to work at improving the program, it has been generally well pleased with its results. By national norms on standardized tests of such basic abilities as reading, making interpretations of material in the various subject fields, and effective writing, students score very high. Many also score high, and sometimes very high, on achievement tests standardized on more competent populations, such as the College Entrance Examination Board, the Illinois State-wide Scholarship, and the National Merit Qualifying tests. Every year large numbers win scholarships to colleges and universities and recognition of some sort in nation-wide searches for talent, such as the Westinghouse Science Talent

Search, *Scholastic Art* and writing contests, *Atlantic Monthly* writing awards, science fairs, and National Merit Scholarships. Follow-up of progress shows that Evanston students continue to do well in college.

Probably of more importance to teachers is the evidence, from boys' and girls' tests, discussions, papers, and other performances, of their maturity in understanding, competent thinking, and expressions of satisfaction in what they are doing. Students more often want to enroll in than to withdraw from honors classes. Moreover, the school has relatively few underachievers and almost none who either barely pass or fail their courses. Try-outs of these students in honors courses, or under special provisions within regular classes, have given Evanston reason to believe that their underachievement does not stem primarily from lack of stimulating opportunities.

The survey of school attitudes and self-attitudes carried implications for improving programs for the talented and for other students as well. On the whole, however, the talented expressed satisfaction with their opportunities and understanding of educational purposes. Those with intellectual competence generally recognized it in themselves. They reported that they had "enough" opportunities in their courses and extracurricular activities. They preferred challenging courses over easy ones. Typical of adolescents was the wish for more of what can loosely be called "social abilities," but they wanted "intellectual abilities" to just as great an extent.

Actually work on improving the program for the talented has stimulated faculty interest in other curricular improvements. A project for low ability students, for example, is getting under way. Moreover, work with the unusually able has probably made still another contribution to the education of all students—greater prestige for learning itself.

The program has been well accepted in the community. People who live or work in Evanston have spoken in many a classroom about their special competencies. All kinds of facilities in the area —libraries, factories, plays, municipal offices, concerts, exhibits— have enriched the program in one way or another. There is, however, no formal, cooperative arrangement for the education of the gifted between the school and any community group.

The talented are one of many groups of students for whom a comprehensive high school must offer challenging opportunities. These gifted boys and girls are entitled to the kind of education which encourages them to their fullest development as individuals. Their contributions are needed in our complex technological and democratic society.

Program for a High School of Science

Alexander Taffel
The Bronx High School of Science

THE Bronx High School of Science is a school for the gifted. It was established in 1938 by the Board of Education of the City of New York as a public academic high school for boys with particular interest and ability in the fields of science and mathematics. The resolution creating the school provided that the student body should be selected by entrance examination and survey of record and that the school should prepare its students for admission to liberal arts and technical colleges. In 1946 the school was opened to girls, who have since been admitted in the ratio of one girl to every two boys. The current population of the school is approximately 1,700 boys and 850 girls.

From its inception the school has taken a broad view of its educational purpose. Well-rounded liberal arts education, strong in the humanities as well as in the sciences, is the basis of its curriculum. The school provides special opportunities for gifted and interested students to develop their talents in the fields of science and mathematics. This training prepares candidates to meet the admission requirements of nearly all liberal arts and technical colleges in the United States. While special encouragement is given to those preparing for careers in science and mathematics, the school opens wide the pathway to any other careers its students may select.

The science orientation is better understood when it is noted that the role of science in human affairs is no longer merely a technical one. The methods, discoveries, principles, and inventions of science now invade and influence every field of human activity. Indeed, it is difficult to find a single area, whether government, politics, religion, ethics, economics, or education, in which a good grounding in basic science is not a prerequisite for a genuine understanding of the problems in that area. An educational program designed to prepare citizens for intelligent action and leadership must therefore include a thorough foundation in the basic sciences. This is the primary function of the required program in science.

There is, however, a second aspect of the school's science orientation. Recent history has dramatized the relationship between our national future and the development of our resources of human talent—particularly in the areas of science and mathematics. It now seems clear that early identification and development of talent must be a fundamental purpose of any sound educational program in a democracy. The full fruition of such talent requires long and arduous preparation, and the high school period certainly includes some of the golden years of greatest potential and fertility. These years must not be lost. With this in view the Bronx High School of Science accepts among its purposes that of identifying and developing outstanding scientific and mathematical talent. Special advanced elective programs, special facilities, and special guidance are offered for this purpose. But equally important is the school's atmosphere of high intellectual interest, in which talent stimulates talent to higher creative effort and achievement.

THE STUDENTS

A candidate for admission to the Bronx High School of Science must be a resident of the City of New York. Each year approximately 3,600 students apply for admission. About 85 per cent of them come from the ninth grade of the public junior high schools, while the remaining 15 per cent come from the eighth grade of parochial, private, and public elementary schools. Of all those who apply, only one in four can be admitted.

The selection process begins with an entrance examination of all candidates each January. The examination consists of two parts, one testing verbal abilities and the other, mathematical and reasoning abilities.[1] Three scores result for each candidate: a verbal score, an arithmetic score, and a composite score. These scores, together with the following data obtained from the pupil's application blank, constitute the basis for evaluating him: the intelligence quotient, the reading grade, the arithmetic grade, the average of all school marks to date, the current school marks, the attendance and character records, hobbies or special interests, extracurricular activities, the recommendations from the applicant's local school, and special attainments in science or mathematics, such as the winning of prizes at science fairs.

The selection process results in an entering class with a median I.Q. of 140, a previous history of high academic achievement, a reading and arithmetic level about two years beyond chronological age, a favorable disposition toward science and mathematics, and a high interest in academic success. The new entrants are about one year younger than the students in the same grade in other high schools, most of them having gained a year in the special progress classes of the junior high schools.

In all other respects the new entrants resemble their counterparts in other schools. They come from a wide range of economic and cultural levels and are interested in the sports, athletics, and social activities favored by their peers.

The effectiveness of the selection process is indicated by the fact that the overwhelming majority of those admitted to the school achieve success in its challenging program and graduate to go on to further success in college. While the comparative youth of the school and the intervention of two wars have made it impossible for the majority of its graduates to be firmly established in their chosen fields, a survey made in 1952 noted that some 80 per cent of the school's graduates were entering science-related professions.[2]

---

[1] The examination is prepared by Dr. Irving Lorge, Professor of Education, Teachers College, Columbia University.

[2] *Education for the Gifted*, the 57th Yearbook of the National Society for the Study of Education, a report by Dr. Morris Meister, Part II, 1958, pp. 274–275.

The Staff

The teachers of the Bronx High School of Science come from the general pool licensed by the New York City Board of Examiners for service in the New York City high schools. In general the equivalent of a master's degree, with a certain minimum distribution of courses among subject matter and education, is required. Most of the teachers at the school have taken many credits beyond the master's degree. The stimulation provided by an able student body has encouraged them to develop their own interest and competence in their subject areas through graduate courses, in-service institutes, experience in industry, and participation in professional organizations. The faculty includes a large number of authors of textbooks and professional articles and boasts an unusually large number of Ph.D.'s.

The average teaching load consists of 25 class periods per week, 5 periods of administrative assignment, and an official class period. Classes in the basic required courses average about 34 pupils, whereas elective course classes generally have about 25 or fewer.

The faculty is organized into the following departments: English, social studies, foreign languages, mathematics, physical science, natural science, art, music, industrial arts, and health education. Each department is headed by a chairman who assumes its professional and administrative leadership.

Building and Facilities

The school is housed in a new building, designed to meet its special needs, which was completed in 1959. It has an excellent library of some 20,000 selected volumes and contains 42 classrooms, 12 science laboratories (chemistry, physics, and biology), 12 science demonstration rooms, 10 shops and drafting rooms, and the following facilities to develop the special interests and capabilities of its students:

Four student project laboratories
Home technology laboratory
Three photographic laboratories and studies

Two greenhouses
Planetarium
Radio station
Weather station
Ceramics laboratory
Animal room
Mathematics laboratory
Band and orchestra room
Dramatics room
Speech clinic laboratory
Social studies laboratory
Language laboratory
Record listening lounge
Lecture hall for school forums and science demonstrations
Auditorium equipped for dramatics and science demonstrations
Two gymnasiums, one for boys and one for girls, including a recreation activities and apparatus room.
Playground with several basketball courts and tennis, volley, and handball courts. (Adjacent to the school is a large and fully equipped athletic field operated by the Park Department.)

GENERAL CURRICULUM

The basic purposes of the school are reflected in its curriculum. Balance is achieved by requiring a core of subjects made up of both the humanities and the sciences. In this respect the school differs sharply from other academic or comprehensive high schools. Approximately 90 per cent of its curriculum is prescribed, and only 10 per cent is elective.

Required Subjects	Electives
English—4 years	Advanced science
Social studies—4 years	Advanced mathematics
Science—4 years	Advanced industrial arts
Mathematics—3 years	Art
Foreign language—3 years	Social studies—techniques in public
Mechanical drawing—1 year	discussion
Industrial arts related to laboratory techniques—½ year	Creative writing
	Dramatics
The usual required courses in health education, art, and music appreciation	Journalism
	World literature
	College English

In the basic curriculum the school has from its beginning been meeting fully the recommendations made by the Conant Committee on challenging programs for the academically talented.[3]

ENGLISH[4]

The course of study in English has three main objectives: to develop high competence in the basic skills of reading, writing, speaking, and listening; to stimulate student interest in a wide variety of literary works, to sensitize the student to the wealth of human thought, feeling, and experience to be found in literature; and to encourage and develop individual creative talent. The composition work arises out of the students' own needs at home and at school and out of the experiences that come with the study of literature. Speech is emphasized in all English classes not only in class discussions but by way of dramatizations, panel discussions, practice of interview techniques, and specific speech drills. There is a minimum essentials syllabus in speech and a speech requirement for graduation.

The literature curriculum is rather full. In addition to required supplementary reading, students read five or six literature texts each year. They study classic novels (*Huckleberry Finn, A Tale of Two Cities, Silas Marner, Arrowsmith*); recent and contemporary plays (*An Enemy of the People, Cherry Orchard, Abe Lincoln in Illinois, Watch on the Rhine*); short stories (by Poe, Hawthorne, Conrad, Hemingway, William Sydney Porter, Katherine Anne Porter); as well as essays and poetry, both old and new. The twelfth year classes study *Macbeth* and *Hamlet, The Return of the Native,* and selections of the literature of England, from *Beowulf* to Dylan Thomas and from Francis Bacon to Winston Churchill.

By way of supplementing the textbook work, use is made of a library collection of records of the plays of Shakespeare and of readings by contemporary poets. There is also a cumulative file of tape recordings of literary material such as the META television program on which Archibald MacLeish discussed *J.B.* and the

3 James B. Conant, *The American High School Today* (New York: McGraw-Hill Book Co., 1959), pp. 57–76.
4 Prepared by Emanuel Bloom, Acting Chairman of the English Department.

prizewinning reading by one of our own students of T. S. Eliot's "The Love Song of J. Alfred Prufrock."

Special courses provide for the development of special abilities and interests. In the eleventh and twelfth years the department offers courses in journalism and creative writing, dramatics, world literature, and college English.

Creative Writing

This course is given to a selected group of about 25 juniors who have shown ability and interest. At the beginning of the year students begin journals in which they record the raw materials they will use later. Journal assignments point up the importance of feeling experiences as if they were unique and of reporting them in effective language.

In the course of the year every student is given several opportunities to read his manuscripts aloud for class evaluation. Rewriting of work along the lines of general critical agreement is encouraged. Too rigid emphasis on perfection of technique is avoided, however, to stimulate free expression and honesty of thinking and feeling. Creative writing classes have, during a typical year, written several short stories, formal and informal essays, biographical sketches, lyric and descriptive poems, short plays, mood pieces, parodies and satires, and magazine articles.

All the regular junior English textbooks are studied with special emphasis on the writing techniques which they embody. In addition, there is a special supplementary text, *A Collection of Readings for Writers* by Harry Shaw.[5]

Dramatics

The course in dramatics acquaints students with the literature of the theater from Sophocles to Arthur Miller and teaches them dramatic techniques through actual play production.

Members of the course are organized into committees to perform radio plays,[6] one act plays, scenes from Shakespeare, and scenes from

[5] *A Complete Course in Freshman English* (3rd ed.; New York: Harper & Brothers, 1951), Book III.

[6] M. W. Kaplan, "Radio Technique in H. S. Dramatics," *English Journal,* February, 1945, pp. 88–93.

full-length plays. Special casts give assembly programs and an annual show. In assembly and classroom productions the class presents original plays written by students, adaptations of radio plays to the shadow-graph technique,[7] and taped scores for musicals or operettas for which students develop the necessary pantomine.[8]

Regular English classes are generally invited to the dramatics classroom, which has a platform stage and 60 seats arranged in theater rows. Here they enjoy drama and learn to develop critical appreciation.

Journalism

This course is given on the junior and senior levels, both as a course in English for selected students interested in journalism and as a co-curricular activity training students to produce the school newspaper which appears eight times during the school year.

World Literature

The course in world literature aims to introduce students to some of the great books of the world. It requires the *intensive* reading of two novels, four plays, and a considerable body of poetry and *extensive* reading of six novels, four plays, and selected chapters of criticism. The broad trends and types of literature are explored. The sequence in reading is from contemporary literature, which is nearer the students' experience and understanding, back to Greek tragedy.

College English

This course anticipates the work of the freshman year in college and prepares the superior student for the Advanced Placement Examination of the College Entrance Examination Board. It emphasizes "close" rather than extensive reading of great works, and requires frequent substantial and carefully structured writing, often of the research paper type. The revised course of study has been

[7] M. W. Kaplan, "Stage the Radio Play," *Scholastic Teacher*, September, 1949, p. 21.
[8] M. W. Kaplan, "Make a Merry Musicale," *Scholastic Teacher*, December, 1953, p. 351.

published by the New York State Board of Regents.[9] Students who complete this course are eligible for credit in freshman English in many colleges that participate in the Advanced Placement Program.

SOCIAL STUDIES[10]

The Bronx High School of Science offers a four year program in social studies. The first year undertakes the study of world geography; the second is devoted to world history; while the third and fourth years represent a two year sequence in American history, American government, economics, and the history of New York State.

The department also offers techniques in public discussion, an elective course, which seeks to train students in the basic techniques of the communication of ideas, in the principles of discussion, in audience participation, in propaganda analysis, and in the planning, preparation, and conduct of public meetings.

Economics is taught formally during the second half of the junior year, after the students have completed the history of the United States from the colonial period through the Civil War. This gives them an understanding of economic terms and concepts needed in the study of the economic development of the United States since 1865. In the senior year a unit treating the current problems of American government is related to the earlier study of the basic principles set forth in the American Constitution. Some of the problems on which students do extensive research and reporting are:

The ideas Americans live by
Threats to American democracy
Color bar at the polls
The weapons of group influence
Congressmen as investigators
Science and security

The department makes wide use of films, film strips, recordings, and tapes, as well as magazine articles and television and radio

9 *Advanced Placement Program in English* (New York State Department of Education, 1959).
10 Prepared by Arthur J. Merovick, Chairman of Social Studies.

programs. It is currently engaged in drawing up resource lists of supplementary and enrichment activities suitable for each grade. These activities involve the school and community libraries, local museums, community agencies, public forums, the stock exchange, and local businesses. The school also has its own weekly forum at which current social and political issues are discussed by outstanding public figures.

Classroom procedures lean heavily on independent activities by students through committee work, panel discussions, student researches and surveys, and individual reporting. Students organize opinion polls, set up class bulletin boards, prepare exhibits, and take trips to study the business community, public housing, et cetera. In addition, the department guides and sponsors a very active student government organization, in which students have an opportunity to apply the knowledge and skills developed in the social studies program.

MATHEMATICS[11]

The teaching of mathematics at the Bronx High School of Science is directed toward the achievement of three main purposes. First, mathematics is taught for its intrinsic value as a logical discipline of remarkable innate beauty and simplicity. Second, mathematics is taught as the language and instrument of the physical and biological sciences. Third, mathematics is taught as a new, powerful tool in the social sciences.

Content and method have been adapted to accord with the needs of the times and the potential of a gifted student body. These students are generally highly self-motivated and eager to move ahead quickly. They respond enthusiastically to strict logical development of a topic and tend to show impatience with slow-moving psychological treatments. For them the interest is as much in the thinking through as in the end product, and drill is less essential than a critical analytic summary. Fast-moving, well-prepared lectures are frequently effective means of presenting new work to the advanced classes of these gifted students.

11 Prepared by Irving A. Dodes, Chairman, Department of Mathematics.

Class study is supplemented by differentiated homework assignments. These frequently include suggested readings from outstanding books such as *Principles of Mathematics* by Allendoerfer and Oakley, *Finite Mathematics* by Kemeny, Snell, and Thompson, *What Is Mathematics?* by Courant and Robbins; and from specialized books in the fields of non-Euclidean geometry and abstract algebra.

The challenge of the formal class program is broadened by a stimulating extracurricular program. The department publication, the *Mathematics Bulletin,* the Mathematics Society, and the Mathematics Team all offer exciting opportunities for probing deeply into unusual mathematical byways.

The differing abilities and life goals of the students make it desirable to have three academic levels of courses—a normal sequence, an accelerated sequence, and an honors sequence. They are described here briefly.[12]

The normal sequence in mathematics includes ninth, tenth, eleventh, and twelfth year mathematics, all of these being New York State Regents courses. The last of these is the experimental twelfth year course.[13] This is a modern course based upon symbolic logic, sets, groups, and fields and includes a strong sequence in functions, in vector fields, and in probability. It is suitable for students who are mainly interested in the biological or social sciences.

The accelerated sequence of courses includes the ninth, tenth and eleventh year mathematics courses, about half the twelfth year course, and approximately one year of calculus and analytic geometry. This is designed for students who are majoring in the physical sciences.

The honors sequence includes all the material of the accelerated level, but goes through one and one half or even two years' work in analytic geometry and calculus. This course is designed for students whose major interest is mathematics.

Additional enrichment is available in a special course on mathe-

[12] Detailed information can be obtained from the course of study and is available (as long as supplies last) upon request.

[13] Prepared under the aegis of Dr. Frank Hawthorne, New York State Supervisor of Mathematics.

matical techniques of science. This includes a thorough training in programing for an electronic computer (the IBM 650), linear programing, some theory of games, some operations research, some surveying, and some of the theoretical aspects of mathematical physics and biometry. Through the cooperation of the International Business Machines Corporation in New York City, students in this course have limited access to the IBM 650 computer. It is hoped that in the future some interested foundation will furnish an electronic computer setup for the school, so that this program may be enriched and expanded.

Some years ago the school experimented successfully with a seminar in mathematics and the sciences, conducted jointly by the mathematics and science departments. It is hoped that at some time in the future a course like this, tying together the loose ends of mathematics and science, will be a regular elective for students interested in research problems.

In September 1959 the department of mathematics began to experiment with a new course in geometry (tenth year) based upon sets, unions, intersections, and half-planes. It is an integrated course in plane and solid geometry and goes far beyond the recommendations of the Commission on Mathematics of the College Entrance Examination Board.[14]

PHYSICAL SCIENCE[15]

In physical science there are two basic courses and seven advanced elective ones in chemistry and physics.

The elementary chemistry and physics courses, which are required of all students, are based upon the New York State Regents syllabuses but go considerably beyond the minimum requirements of these syllabuses. They are given for one year for six periods per week, four recitations, and a double laboratory period.

In basic physics the school has been a participant in the Physical Science Study Committee program since its inception and has taken a direct part in the development of the new approach. An evalua-

---

14 Publication of the College Entrance Examination Board, 1959.
15 Prepared by Herman Campsen, Jr., Chairman, Physical Science Department.

tion of this innovation in physics teaching will come in due course from the Physical Science Study Committee.

The emphasis in four of the regular elective courses in chemistry and physics is on the development of laboratory skills and methods. Each of these courses is given for one year for five periods a week, two double periods of laboratory work, and a single period of recitation:

Advanced General Chemistry. A course covering selected topics in fields of descriptive physical, colloidal, and organic chemistry.

Analytical Chemistry. A course devoted to the basic techniques of qualitative and quantitative analysis.

Radio Physics. A course covering the theory of electronic circuits and their application to radio, cathode-ray systems, sound systems, and television.

Automotive Physics. A course covering basic principles and testing procedures related to the operation of the automobile and the airplane.

Another elective, the history and development of science, is given five periods a week to students interested in the development of fundamental concepts in astronomy, physics, chemistry, biology, and earth science from ancient Greece to the present.

Selected outstanding students are permitted to undertake the advanced placement courses in college chemistry and college physics. The content is based upon the Advanced Placement syllabuses developed by the College Entrance Examination Board at Princeton, New Jersey. Successful completion of these courses entitles students to claim credit for first year chemistry or physics in the colleges participating in the program.

Several experiments have been conducted in recent years to improve the quality of the laboratory work in the basic courses through the introduction of the "open-ended" type of laboratory exercise. In this program the usual laboratory experiments in chemistry and physics are presented as classroom demonstrations. The laboratory time is then devoted to learning basic laboratory techniques and to open-ended experiments that offer real challenges to the pupils. Here is a brief account of some of the work done in chemistry.

A class which so elected was permitted to take chemistry in the sophomore year. The class was given five recitation-demonstration and two laboratory periods per week, the recitation and laboratory periods being conducted by different teachers.

In the laboratory during the first semester the class did experiments designed to teach basic laboratory techniques. During the second semester a series of open-ended experiments illustrating basic principles of chemistry were performed and discussed. Some of these experiments were designed for a more intensive development of basic theory than that covered in the regular classes, while others went into topics not ordinarily covered. The conventional course-connected experiments were done as demonstrations in class.

LIST OF LABORATORY EXPERIMENTS

1. The Bunsen burner and its use in the manipulation of glass tubing
2. Preparation and collection of gases
3. Separation of liquids from solids
4. Separation of miscible and immiscible liquids
5. Purification of solids
6. Melting point determination (capillary method)
7. Use of the chemical balance
8. Per cent of H_2O of crystallization in an unknown hydrate
9. Titration
10. Preliminary experiments for the analysis of group I cations
11. Simplified semi-micro procedure for the analysis of the Group I cations
12. Factors affecting the speed of a reaction
13. Mechanism of reaction
14. Chemical equilibrium
15. Corrosion and electrochemistry
16. Time-cooling curves and the eutectic point
17. Freezing point depression in electrolytes and nonelectrolytes

The titles of Experiments 1 to 11 are self-explanatory. They are essentially experiments designed to develop laboratory techniques, although problem-solving elements are introduced in each. Experiments 12 to 17 are open ended in the sense that they are designed to lead to further discussion and experimentation.

In Experiment 12 the student determines quantitatively the effect of temperature and concentration on the speed of reaction. A qualitative determination of the effect of state of division and catalyst is also performed.

Experiment 13 consists of a series of short experiments designed to point up the elements of the kinetic theory of reaction, i.e., molecular movement, number of contacts per unit time, energy of activation, and possible intermediate catalytic reactions.

Experiment 14 deals with Le Chatelier's principle as applied to changes of concentration and temperature. Discussion is designed to lead to the over-all generalization.

The series of experiments included in Experiment 15 is designed to integrate the concepts of activity, oxidation-reduction, primary and secondary cells, and corrosion.

In Experiment 16 the class acts as a team to construct a freezing point-composition curve for a simple two component system. Each group plots a time-cooling curve and correlates it with visible freezing points of aqueous solutions of electrolytes and nonelectrolytes to elucidate one of the bases of the Arrhenius theory.

NATURAL SCIENCE[16]

The offerings in natural science consist of a basic course in general biology and these five advanced elective courses:

Microbiology. A study of bacteria, protozoa, fungi, and phages.

Blood and Urine Analysis. A course including qualitative and quantitative analysis techniques, blood typing, and Rh determination.

Field Biology. A study of the ecological relationships of local fauna and flora and other biological problems in the field.

Home Technology. A course designed for girls who wish to pursue careers as nutritionists, food analysts, and technicians in testing laboratories.

College Biology. A course in general biology, equivalent to that taken in the freshman year at college. Successful completion of the course makes a student eligible for credit for first year biology in colleges participating in the Advanced Placement Program.

The elective courses lay heavy stress on laboratory techniques and experimental biology. In general, they provide for a minimum of four periods of laboratory work per week, usually as two double periods.

The basic course in general biology provides for four recitation

[16] Prepared by Jerome Metzner, Chairman of the Biological Science Department.

and two laboratory periods per week. The course is required of all students and goes well beyond the requirements of the New York State Regents syllabus in biology. The essential characteristic of the course is that it is flexible in content to meet the special capacities and interests of the pupils. It provides for extensive required reading beyond the basic text and for laboratory experiences that give students opportunities to perceive and formulate scientific problems and to devise procedures for solving them. Activities include pupil reports and demonstrations; field trips; creative project work; visits to museums, zoos, botanical gardens, hospitals, and research laboratories; and participation in school biology clubs and science fairs.

The department has experimented with laboratory work for the purpose of developing laboratory experiences that are genuine challenges for the student. In one approach, laboratory work begins with basic biological techniques and procedures, such as use of the microscope; culturing and methods of studying microorganisms; preparing culture media; and caring for and maintaining plants and animals. As pupils learn these techniques, they are encouraged to discover problems and propose methods of investigating them. A pupil may begin by studying the extrusion of trichocysts in paramecium and go on to study the feeding reactions of an organism with localized trichocysts, such as Dileptus. He may then go farther and perform merotomy experiments to discover the reactions of specialized parts of a unicellular organism. The essential orientation of these laboratory experiences is to have the student engage in activities that a biologist would normally pursue in his daily work. Furthermore, these activities are highly motivated because they relate to a problem which the student has chosen and defined for himself.

Another development of the basic biology course is the contract plan. During the past two years we have tried out a plan in which a selected class of students completed a year's work of tenth year biology in half a year. In this time students were given enriched class and laboratory work in the topics normally covered in the first half of the course. Concurrently they were given teacher-prepared contract plans for extraclass study of basic subject matter in the remainder of the course. Special instruction was given in areas in which weakness or lack of understanding was revealed in tests given after completion of contracts. In January 1958 State Regents examinations in biology, 18 of the 28 students in this venture received grades of 90 per cent or better. None of the remainder received grades below 80 per cent.

During the second half-year this same class was organized on a seminar basis. Topics previously studied under contract were now expanded and studied in depth. For example, to supplement the unit on reproduction among living things, special reports were made and discussions were held on such topics as viral reproduction, sexuality in bacteria, bacterial transformation, and present concepts of the nature of the gene. When the group did not meet as a seminar, students could make use of the unusual facilities of the department for their projects. A twofold purpose was served by this organization. By giving students responsibility for guided self-instruction in certain topics, time was gained for intensification of learnings in these topics and for engaging in creative research and project work.

A wealth and diversity of facilities and materials provide real, firsthand experiences in biological science, in addition to learnings acquired through readings, demonstrations, and discussion. There are special laboratories for elective courses and project work, greenhouses, photographic dark rooms, animal rooms, and laboratory preparation rooms. The equipment goes well beyond the requirements of basic biology. Stereoscopic microscopes, microscopes with oil immersion lenses and condensers, microtomes, photomicrographic apparatus, pH meters, colorimeters, incubators, ovens, autoclaves, centrifuges, stills, refrigerators, and other specialized equipment are available. Furthermore, there is ready access to a library that includes up-to-date books in the biological sciences, biological journals, biological abstracts, reprints of research papers, and magazines such as *Science* and *The Scientific American*.

Formal instruction and course work is supported by a rich cocurriculum and extracurriculum, where students may engage in activities that give expression to their talents and satisfy their interests. A variety of student biology squads function under teacher sponsorship: Drosophila squad, protozoa squad, histology squad, scientific illustration squad, animal squad, plant squad, bacteriology squad, field biology squad. Each squad has two main activities.

Materials are prepared for school use, and in addition, pupils of each squad utilize the material in connection with individual or group projects. Thus the Drosophila squad maintains cultures of various types of Drosophila for class genetic studies. At the same time the squad members may be studying the changes induced by the addition of a radioisotope to the culture medium of the fly.

The club program functions to meet certain specific needs. In the Experimental Society students engage in experimental work. The members of the Field Biology Club prepare and classify exhibits of specimens collected on frequent field trips. The Biology Society caters to those students with generalized interests in biology. The program of the society includes pupil reports and demonstrations, panels, film showings, and talks by members of the faculty and by outside speakers.

Under expert teacher leadership science weekend trips, co-sponsored by the biology department and the school Fathers' Club, make the biological resources of the outdoor world available to students. Trips are usually scheduled for Saturdays to wooded areas in or near New York City. The program for the day includes a morning theme, such as a fossil hunt, followed by lunch, rest, and recreation. The afternoon may be devoted to the investigation of life in a fresh water pond.

Finally, opportunities are provided for students showing unusual promise to be apprenticed to practicing biologists. Our students have worked during vacations and after school with members of the staffs of the American Museum of Natural History, the Haskins Laboratory, Montefiore and Mt. Sinai hospitals, Columbia University, and Sloan-Kettering Cancer Institute.

Talented students have been guided to special opportunities for summer scientific study at such institutions as the Jackson Memorial Laboratory in Maine and the Worcester Foundation in Massachusetts.

THE SPECIAL SCIENCE ACTIVITIES PROGRAM[17]

The establishment of the Special Activities Program represents an innovation in the teaching of the gifted in science. The purpose of this program is to identify highly motivated students in science and to provide opportunities for them to participate in creative

[17] Prepared by Zachariah Subarsky, Co-ordinator of Special Science Activities.

research projects. Preliminary experience has shown that gifted pupils can successfully undertake the study of a specific problem in depth and can do respectable research projects on the level of their development.

Heading the program is a Co-ordinator of Special Activities. He has at his disposal four specially designed project rooms equipped for individual work in biology, chemistry, and physics. In addition, there are two greenhouses, a weather station, and a radio shack. During the current year three teachers of biology, one teacher of chemistry, and one teacher of physics are assigned for one period a day to the program. Each teacher has a group of 15 to 25 students whose work he directs and supervises. The students have been screened by the Co-ordinator and have been programed to a project class as a regular five periods a week assignment.

The general atmosphere of the science project room is comparable to that of a professional research laboratory. Appropriate literature is available. The student works at his own pace, keeps notes, and is free to leave to go to the library for extensive library research whenever necessary. Periodically the teacher organizes a group into a seminar session, where individual students report on work accomplished or in progress. From time to time outside professional consultation becomes necessary. Such consultation is generally obtained through the Co-ordinator of Special Science Activities.

Some typical areas of investigation taken from student application forms are listed below. Some of these are exploratory in nature, others experimental.

To build an infrared indicator for the detection of heated objects

To study local radioactive fall-out

To construct a Kilowatt Linear Amplifier

To construct a ½ MEV Linear Betatron (well under way)

A new approach to an Electronic Teletype Machine

To construct a polarimeter and study the specific rotation of optically active substances

Comparison of particles of rayon fibers produced by varying laboratory processes

To study conditions under which complex ions are formed

Chromatographic analyses of pigment in sea shells from various parts of the world

Extraction of rare metals
Visual conditioning in fish
Two aspects of the stimulation of bird migration—vision and time sense
Effects of thioguanine when given before and after the introduction of Sarcoma 180 in mice
To develop radioautographic techniques on a cytological level
Effects of Potassium Gibberellate on Euglena
To develop a heat-resistant strain of *B. subtilis*
Effects of thymus hormone on secretion of pituitary hormones

Another important phase of the Special Activities Program provides opportunities for students interested and able in science to explore and experiment under the guidance of outstanding teachers and professional scientists. It is hoped to expand this program into the regular school year, but at present it functions mainly in the summer programs supported by the National Science Foundation and by private foundations.

To promote student participation in these programs, the Coordinator of Special Science Activities gives them wide publicity, encourages students to apply, helps evaluate applicants, and orients them to problems that can be pursued later on in project rooms through the school year. During a recent summer, students from the High School of Science were working in the following institutions:

Science Institute of Northern Michigan College
Cooper Union
Jackson Memorial Laboratory, Bar Harbor, Maine
New York Botanical Garden
University of Oklahoma
The Rockefeller Institute of New York
Manhattan College
Columbia University
Yeshiva University
The Sloan-Kettering Institute for Cancer Research
Animal Behavior Laboratory, American Museum of Natural History
The University of Bridgeport, Connecticut
Florida State University
The Hayden Planetarium (Satellite Research)
The University of California—Berkeley

Foreign Language[18]

The school offers five foreign languages: French, German, Spanish, Latin, and Hebrew. Before graduation every student is expected to complete three years of one of them.

The objectives of the foreign language program are twofold: to introduce the student to a rich foreign culture, and to develop in him an ability to use a particular language—to understand it, to speak it, to read it, and to write it.

As early as possible the spoken language is used in the classroom and the student is accustomed to hearing it and encouraged to use it. Systematic formal instruction in basic grammar and syntax gives the student a sense of the structure of the language and lays a sound foundation for competence in reading and writing.

This oral-aural approach is designed to avoid the degeneration of understanding and using the foreign language into a process of slow decoding. The objective is *direct* understanding, speaking, reading, and writing without the intermediate step of deliberate translation.

Among the class techniques used to attain this objective are creative dialogues. Here students create and memorize the dialogue suitable for any one of a variety of life situations. This approximates the natural use of the language and gives students a ready functional vocabulary for everyday use.

Formal class teaching is supported by the use of many aids that bring the living language to the students: transcription of foreign language radio and television programs, foreign language records, motion picture films, tape recordings, and local language newspapers. Further direct contact with the foreign language and its culture is obtained in the foreign language clubs, where students hear prominent invited speakers, learn songs and dances, and produce playlets and skits in the foreign language.

Industrial Arts[19]

In the tenth year all students take basic technical drawing for two terms, meeting four times a week for single periods of about

[18] Prepared by Charles Hodes, Chairman of the Foreign Language Department.

[19] Prepared by Abraham Calmus, Chairman, Department of Industrial Arts.

40 minutes each. This course attempts to develop understanding of and ability to use a number of standard procedures and techniques which are basic in the graphical language of engineers, architects, and technicians in science and industry.

In the eleventh year all students take basic science techniques laboratory for one term, meeting each week for two double periods of shop work on projects and one demonstration period devoted to basic shop techniques. Each student is required to do an independent project. All projects are based on or exemplify principles of science and involve the use of several materials. Working drawings, an essay discussing the scientific principles involved in the project, a well-organized notebook, and an essay of evaluation are required. Typical projects include Van de Graaff generators, spectroscopes, stroboscopes, and various electronic devices.

In the twelfth year students may elect advanced technical drawing or advanced science techniques laboratory. During the first term of advanced technical drawing, which meets five periods a week for two terms, each student makes the basic working drawings for a house of his own design. In the succeeding term those interested in architecture make the basic drawings for larger projects, such as a public library, a school, an office building, or an air terminal. Those interested in engineering make drawings for various types of cam and gear and a set of working drawings for a project in machinery.

In advanced science techniques laboratory, which meets for five double periods a week for one term, the technical applications of the different sciences are learned through projects and group demonstrations. Projects involve metal turning, pattern making, heat treatment of metals, foundry work, glass blowing, and the grinding, polishing, and silvering of lenses, mirrors, and prisms.

THE GUIDANCE PROGRAM[20]

The guidance department is headed by an administrative assistant to the principal and consists of 15 teachers who devote part of their teaching programs to guidance work. Parents, teachers, and community agencies of all kinds are also involved in the program. Continuity is maintained by having each teacher-adviser move up

20 Prepared by Bernard Manson, Director of Guidance.

with his group from the basic orientation in the school to graduation and college entrance. The work of the department falls into
the following categories:

The Admission Program

This includes acquainting lower schools, prospective students,
and their parents with the philosophy, curriculum, and admissions
requirements of the school; administering the admissions examination; studying the qualifications of each candidate for admission
and making a selection; and evaluating the records of the successful candidates for purposes of course guidance and placement.

The Orientation of New Students to High School

Meetings with new entrants and their parents are held preceding
their admission, in June, and again in the fall when they are already in attendance, to present essential information and to get new
students off to a good start. This is followed up during the remainder
of the student's first year by an intensive homeroom guidance program. Among the topics discussed in the homeroom are: School
Routines You Should Know About; Study Efficiency; Budgeting
Your Time; Requirements for Graduation; Extracurricular and
Service Activities; Electives; and You and the Honor Society.

Individual Guidance

Each student is interviewed periodically, as well as by ap-
pointment, by his adviser to obtain aid in planning his educational
program and to review his progress to date. The adviser also
supervises the student's extracurricular activities and assists him with
his personal problems. Unusual personal problems are referred to the
guidance social worker who arranges for assistance from out-of-school
agencies as required. Parents are consulted and kept informed of
every step in the individual guidance of their children.

Group Guidance Program

Throughout a student's stay in school, he has the benefit of a continuing group guidance program in his homeroom which systemati-

cally takes up subjects of common interest to all. Typical of the topics presented are: Boy Meets Girl; College Purposes and Problems; Importance of Character Training; and Parent-Student Relationships.

The guidance department and the Parents Association sponsor Alumni College Guidance Day each December and the series of Career Guidance Conferences each February. On Alumni College Guidance Day those returning are grouped according to the colleges they are attending, and meetings are arranged with students interested in these colleges.

The major purpose of the Career Guidance Conferences is to orient students to the opportunities available in different professions and occupations and to inform them of the preparation needed to qualify for vocations. Conferences are arranged by subject as follows: Engineering and Mathematics; Scientific Research; Medicine, Nursing, and Dentistry; Teaching; Law, Accounting, and Business. Experts in each field are invited to address the students and are available afterward for questions.

The College Bureau

This special unit of the guidance department concerns itself with all aspects of the problem of college admission and scholarships. The work of the College Bureau includes providing information to parents and students, advising individual pupils on college choices, preparing individual applications for admission, arranging for students to take necessary College Entrance Examination Board examinations, arranging for college interviewers to meet student applicants, visiting colleges attended by our students to establish better liaison with the former and to follow up the performances of the latter, acquainting students with scholarship opportunities and arranging for them to take the qualifying examinations for those scholarships (i.e., New York State Regents Scholarship Examinations and National Merit Scholarship Qualifying Examination).

The importance of the College Bureau is underlined by the fact that some 800 seniors apply for college admission each year. Of these, approximately 500 qualify for various kinds of scholarship.

Student Activities[21]

Student activities at the Bronx High School of Science are an integral part of its program. Through student government they provide natural opportunities for pupils to exercise the knowledge, skills, habits, and attitudes basic to active, intelligent citizenship. They provide opportunities for the development of special interests and talents in such areas as sports, creative writing, science project work, art, and music appreciation. They have guidance value in extending the areas that pupils can explore beyond the confines of the curriculum in such activities as the Chemistry Club, the Mathematics Club, the Student Forum, and the Astronomy Club. They offer recreational activities in which pupils can find relaxation and enjoyment in each other's company. They provide a natural setting in which pupils can learn the social graces and acquire poise in their associations with their peers and their elders. And finally, they provide many opportunities for building lasting friendships.

Student activities fall into six categories, as follows:

First are those associated with student government. The Student Organization (S.O.) is directed by three elected officers and the elected Student Council. It assumes responsibility for all student activities and collects, budgets, and disburses the funds needed to finance them. The S.O. also participates in the formulation of school policies as they apply to the students and legislates regulations to control all student activities. Subordinate to the S.O. are the class governments, which control the special activities of each of the four classes: freshman, sophomore, junior, and senior. These have their own elected class officers.

Second are the sports activities, which include interscholastic as well as intramural sports. The interscholastic program features varsity teams in baseball, basketball, golf, track, cross-country, handball, bowling, tennis, and swimming. The students on these teams participate regularly in scheduled games with other high schools. The intramural program offers an opportunity for all other interested students to take part in sports such as baseball, basketball, and volleyball and to compete against teams of their peers within the school.

21 Prepared by Doris Eliazon, Faculty Adviser of Student Organization.

Third are the club activities. The school features clubs in the following areas:

Drama Workshop	Astronomy Club
French Club	Camera Club
Spanish Club	Chemistry Club
Hebrew Club	Radio Club
Math Society	Forum
Girls' Chorus	Bridge Club
Orchestra	Chess Club
Record Club	Newman Club
Biology Club	Science Techniques Laboratory Club
Experimental Biology Society	Technical Drawing Club

The programs of these clubs often supplement and expand the curricular program in the various subject areas.

Fourth are the publication activities. The major publications are the school newspaper; *Dynamo,* a literary magazine; the *Mathematics Bulletin;* and the *Journal of Biology.* In addition, the Senior Club publishes its yearbook, and each of the grades publishes a newspaper which appears several times during the year.

Fifth are the social and recreational activities. These include student dances, concerts, skating parties, theater parties, the student lounge, the presentation of an annual show, picnics, boat rides, and excursions.

Sixth are various service activities in which students provide clerical, messenger, mimeographing, patrol, and other services needed by the school and its departments. Some of these service activities, like the laboratory squads and the school store squads, offer pupils special opportunities to obtain experience of great practical value.

Perhaps the best objective evaluation of the effectiveness of the Student Activities Program is the fact that practically every student is enrolled in one or more activities. Furthermore, there is evidence that students are accepting responsibility and are making decisions in governing themselves, that their interests are being developed, that they are forming good attitudes and many friendships, and that their school life is generally being made more pleasurable and interesting as the result of participation in student activities.

Parent Activities

All school activities are strongly supported by an exceptionally large and active Parents Association. The association provides funds for many special activities and services. These include additional clerical services to support the college admissions program, professional guidance by a trained social worker, scholarship aid funds and other financial assistance as needed, and a social lounge in which students meet weekly under parent sponsorship. Parents also volunteer to chaperone student functions, to provide transportation for student trips, to offer medical and psychological consulting services to the school, and to act as resource persons in areas of their special training and competence. They take a very active part in placing the school's needs before the New York City educational authorities.

In the area of general guidance the Parents Association brings outstanding experts to its meetings as speakers, arranges annual Career Guidance Conferences, sponsors Alumni College Guidance Day, and sends the school's college advisers on exploratory trips to make contact with the colleges and to gather information.

A monthly newspaper published by the Parents Association reaches every parent. It gives timely and accurate information about all aspects of the school program as well as about current parent activities.

PART IV
CONCLUSIONS

I3

Ideas for Programs

Samuel Everett
The City College of New York

AVAILABLE resources and the climate of opinion at any particular time determine and limit what can be done in education. The climate in America is today more favorable for educating the gifted than it was a few short years ago. Amazing technical advances requiring ability and training of a high order, commitments abroad, and Russian achievements in science and productivity have roused us to the crucial need of educating our able youth to their maximum potentialities. National survival and our way of life may well be at stake.

A number of accepted social ideals and habits of mind are favorable. The cherished tradition that every individual be given the opportunity to develop to his potential capacity is accepted by citizens and educators alike. This ideal clearly includes our unusually able as well as less able youth. Moreover, we still have faith in the future, that we can mold it to suit our desires.

Schools represent the road to success in our developing society. The picture of America as a land of opportunity for all, however, is currently being challenged. An alarming percentage of our most intelligent youth are leaving high schools and colleges for a variety of reasons. Among these are insufficient funds, lack of strong incentives, and failure of educational programs to meet their needs.

Evidence that cherished democratic ideals are being inadequately implemented and that militant communism threatens national survival has moved citizens, members of boards of education, school administrators, and teachers in innumerable American communities to seek to improve school programs at all levels for the more talented students. Particularly is this true at the high school level, since it is here that decisions regarding vocational and life plans are made.

Because of our sincere concern to understand clearly the nature of the task we face, a number of the authors of this Yearbook have stressed certain social factors that make difficult the development of programs for the gifted in our high schools. Our habits of mind and our use of resources are clearly not all favorable.

Visitors to American shores, through much of our history, have noted a widespread distrust of intellectual pursuits, of creativity in the arts, and of scholarship in general. The three authors of Part II, "Programs from Abroad," find that intellectual life is much more highly respected in the U.S.S.R., in Germany, and in England than in the United States. Sports, the poorer television programs, concern for making money, and nonintellectual recreation set the tone in the typical middle class American home. When the goals of life and habits of mind of economically secure youth develop in such a climate, it is most difficult, even under favorable school conditions, to present a convincing case for the values of another way of life.

Chapter 1, "The Gifted in American Society," covers those conditions in society and in schools which basically determine the social aspects of our problem. Glaring inequalities discourage able Negroes from continuing their education. Extensive economically and culturally deprived areas, both rural and urban, also condition youth poorly for intellectual and creative endeavors.

The national disposition to conform, rather than to challenge popular beliefs and established ways of doing things, discourages attempts to lead youth to think for themselves. It is particularly disadvantageous in programs for able youth who feel a golden future is theirs for the asking. Such primary goals as making money, seeking security, and an early retirement devoted to personal pleasure, lead to conformity rather than to bold thinking, a creative life, and devotion to the social welfare.

These materialistic goals affect teachers and administrators as well. We, too, need to establish qualitative, rather than conforming, goals. Everyone must struggle to reorient his habits of thinking, his personal ideals, and especially his directing democratic values.

To move wholeheartedly toward the development of programs for the gifted, teachers and administrators will have to rethink their directing democratic values. Some educators fear that to build a program for our more able youth is, in fact, to promote a class concept in society. This is a real danger if we are led to respect only the gifted, and not all children, for their potential worth as people. But the needs of the gifted must be provided for in the same spirit as slow learners now are.

Conformity, in the guise of democratic cooperation, has too often destroyed creativity. Greater respect for originality, uniqueness, and nonconformity is needed if teachers and administrators are to carry out their task effectively.

Inequalities of financial support among neighboring communities within states, and among states, limit what can be done for gifted students, as for all others. Salaries must be raised to attract larger numbers of superior people to the teaching profession. Money must be found for buildings, equipment, teaching materials, and scholarships for talented, needy youth. In Germany and England scholarships at the secondary school level have long been available.

Considerable evidence is presented in Part III, "Programs in Operation in the United States," that adequate provision for superior students is expensive. The extensive use of school trips, found in the Lyons Falls experiment to be so important for rural youth, is expensive, involving transportation and staff time. Regional and European trips, which enlarge the perspective of youth, must have some public financing.

Portland supports a larger supervisory staff in programs for gifted students. In Evanston Township High School a research and counseling staff, along with college-bound classes of 15 to 20 students each, greatly increases the costs, as do the numerous laboratories and special rooms in the Bronx High School of Science. Smaller classes, which improve the effectiveness of teaching and guidance, and adequate counseling are especially costly. Really adequate programs should have classes as small as those in the last two years of secondary school in England and Wales, which average 15 students.

The currently growing concern about the inadequate development of our able students highlights the need for the improvement of educational programs for all youth. Proper subjects for exploration include: inadequacies of finance in this, the wealthiest country of the world; unequal opportunities for millions of our citizens due to differences in race and socio-economic background; selfish social values inimical to excellence of mind and character; parochial conceptions of the place of America in the world today; and misconceptions of the essential nature of democratic values.

LEARNING AND THE GOOD LIFE

Dr. William Heard Kilpatrick's statement of the democratic faith in terms of the maximum development of the individual, in Chapter 3, "A Philosophic Viewpoint and a Suggested Program," is not new. Indeed, seeking the welfare of the individual has become a cardinal principle in the education of all youth. The significance of his *further major aim . . . to improve our civilization* is not as well understood nor is it accepted in practice.

The first aim without the second has led, and still leads, to emphasis on rugged and sometimes ruthless individualism. Where social purposes—achieving the good society—are not continually present, the materialistic goals all too often remain primary. The learner's major goals become money, leisure, and perhaps an early retirement to follow private pursuits, irrespective of what may be happening in the larger society.

Probably the greatest danger in the development of programs for the gifted is that our able minds are stimulated to achieve excellence in science, mathematics, history, and other specialized fields without being challenged, at the same time, to accept the welfare of others—the progress of our civilization—as worthy of effort and allegiance.

In the U.S.S.R. the welfare of the state and responsibility for its development are primary, and there is comparatively little concern for the individual. The cooperation of abler youth in aiding the less scholarly is stressed in order to build responsible citizens within the Soviet ideology. Outside of school, participation in the Young Pioneers (ages 9–14) and Konsomols (Young Communist League, above 14) gives practically all youth citizenship training and practice.

In connection with the necessity for emphasis upon social goals, we can all learn from a closer look at secondary education as developed by the Society of Friends. One Friends high school presents the numerous ways in which it promotes social awareness and personal responsibility. Social values are ever present in the minds of this faculty. Activity groups, leadership in assemblies, and housekeeping chores promote responsibility.

The Germantown Friends Schools Council, made up of ten neighboring institutions, publishes a newsletter and promotes Saturday work camps, conferences, and interschool visits. An Advisory Committee is elected within the school. Without a faculty adviser, the members are available to help students—(usually with troubles of a social nature). The Faculty-Student Selection Committee, chosen by the Student Council, recommends representatives to go to conferences of Friends, where the life of service to one's fellows is the dominant theme. Student weekend and summer work camps give experience in community fact finding and responsible action. Students travel in groups abroad. They regularly participate with adults in religious and community projects.

Here is Quaker creed, applied to our special problem:

> It is relatively easy to develop in bright people a critical spirit. Too often, however, this spirit is not translated into action; and the result is cynicism. One of the most important functions of a school fortunate enough to have a high proportion of gifted students is to try to develop in these privileged individuals both a critical spirit and the feeling of obligation to serve their fellowmen.

The fullest development of the individual and the improvement of society are the first two major aims. Dr. Kilpatrick's third aim is the development of those traits of character needed to attain the good life. A fourth is finding and using those materials and activities most likely to achieve the preceding aims.

In our Western culture any conception of personality and of learning must accord with scientific facts. The Soviet assumption that all people are equally educable is not a finding of research. People have different capacities for learning. A varied and rich curriculum, therefore, is necessary to meet all needs.

Habits of mind inculcated in years of education in which experimental and creative conceptions of learning have not been accepted make our task exceedingly difficult. New experiences lead students to ask significant questions and to incorporate new and old learnings in meaningful ways. Furnishing such experiences is a requirement for guided learning. This enrichment is especially needed for the underprivileged.

Unfortunately there is in this Yearbook a regrettable lack of exploration into the nature of the learning process involved in creative work in the arts. If we are to meet the needs of the gifted and build the good society, much more attention must be given to artistic values and ways of developing them in drama, painting, sculpture, music, and the various crafts. Distinctive work is being done in these areas in the high schools described in Part III. Yet there is little probing into the process involved.

The personal, socially responsible, and experimental way of learning which can give basic orientation to educational programs for gifted students, as for all others, is possible in classrooms and all-school activities devoted to both special and general education. Dr. Kilpatrick prefers a core type of curriculum, supplemented by specialized subjects. But he specifically states that the type of learning he advocates is applicable to special courses such as mathematics as well as to the more socialized core program. He favors the comprehensive American high school, as do most of the authors of this Yearbook. It is his belief, however, that it may be possible for us to learn things of value through the study of such specialized institutions as the Bronx High School of Science, a description of which is found in Chapter 12.

NATURE AND NEEDS OF THE GIFTED

Our concern for both the individual and the improvement of society leads us to include *all* who have unusual talent. Early studies which relied primarily on I.Q. test results assumed that only those having I.Q.'s of 130 or 140 and above were gifted. A very select few, therefore, were involved.

Today a broader conception of giftedness is recognized. It is explored, with supporting data, by Paul Witty in Chapter 2, "The Nature and Needs of Gifted and Superior Adolescents." *The talented or gifted child is one who shows consistently remarkable performance in any worthwhile line of endeavor.* This conception is appropriate to democratic education and is most useful in building curriculum programs.

James B. Conant has included in the academically talented group "15 to 20 per cent of an age group who have the ability to study —effectively and rewardingly—advanced mathematics, foreign language, physics, and chemistry." This generalization does not include all who show "consistently remarkable performance in any worthwhile line of endeavor."

Witty explores four types of giftedness: (*a*) high abstract intelligence and unusual competence in a wide range of activities, (*b*) special promise in science, (*c*) creativity in the arts, and (*d*) ability in social leadership. The point is stressed that creativity in the arts and social leadership are consistently recognizable only in performance.

In a study of creative writing reported by Witty there seems to be only a slight relationship between I.Q. and creativity, though the most superior work comes from pupils with an I.Q. of 110 and above. Studies of creativity in drawing, painting, sculpture, and music might be consulted by program makers to determine the characteristics closely correlated with talent in these areas.

Though high performers on tests often demonstrate social leadership, many people showing these qualities do not rate high on the usual evaluative instruments. Indeed, little is known of the relation of intelligence to the various types of social leader. This is a most promising area, therefore, for future exploration in high school situations.

Studies of unusually able youth seem to indicate that they are no different from their fellows in the need for sympathetic understanding. They must feel that they are accepted, appreciated, and loved if they are to do their best. There are, however, many examples of genius operating without such emotional support. Though on the whole those of superior ability are unusually well adjusted to others, able students from time to time experience difficulties and require the help of discerning adults. Those who for a variety of reasons are not demonstrating their potential abilities require special attention. Able students are subject to feelings of inadequacy and of loneliness, resulting from the knowledge that they are different from their fellows, and they may be depressed at times at being unable to solve academic or personal problems. Common needs and real problems call for understanding and guidance.

Where school programs offer little challenge to those of unusual ability, apathy and lack of incentive result. On the other hand, able students who are challenged to do their best intellectually, artistically, and socially usually desire to continue in school. In this respect, the goal of going to college is a stabilizing and constructive influence.

TEACHERS OF THE GIFTED

The teachers of gifted students are unusually able and well prepared. In England, grammar school staff members are university graduates, which means that academically they are among the upper 5 per cent of the population. Teachers in German Gymnasia are highly select and well qualified.

In the American programs described, teachers of able students, for the most part, have studied beyond the B.A.; many have the M.A. or its equivalent; some hold Ph.D. degrees. As a group they know their subject fields unusually well. They have more than cursory knowledge of adolescent problems, evaluative procedures, philosophic issues, and teaching methods. Thus, students are led to think in depth, to relate fields of knowledge, and to do individual research of high quality.

These teachers are devoted to their jobs beyond the call of duty. They work many hours examining student records, meeting to establish common purposes, considering the needs of the able students, making composite evaluations of individuals, guiding research, and developing appropriate courses of study. It is their business to educate youth in self-awareness, emotional balance, precision, conceptual thinking, the integration of ideas, and the making of informed choices.

Those who engage in such a wide variety of learning activities achieve a self-respect which is the mark of the professional. Colleagues not so engaged, discerning parents, and the lay public in general should respect their efforts when made aware of them. Certainly one way to gain more public support for the intellectual life and for those who engage in it is through the publicizing of all such "good works."

Teachers of gifted students are rarely paid higher salaries than others of equal tenure. Presumably, like all teachers, they receive regular increments within their salary ranges and for advanced course work. Often they are rewarded for excellence by being made administrators and, tragically, are thus removed from the teaching jobs they do so well. And frequently they leave education for much better paying positions in industry.

Clearly, if we are to recruit and keep able, well-prepared, and devoted teachers, ways must be found to pay them adequately. This need not mean that we depart from the democratic principle of similar increments to all teachers. It may mean considerable increases in salaries across the board. It may mean enlarging, and increasing the number of, special increments for graduate and other work. In any case, the description of the teacher's task in Part III raises the basic question of incentive. Better solutions must be found in a great many communities if programs for the gifted, or indeed, any and all special school programs, are to achieve excellence.

Teachers of gifted children, in addition to being students of their subjects, must also be students of society. With one notable exception there is a paucity of evidence that a majority of faculty members are consciously aware of the special need in modern American society, and therefore in American schools, for the development of keen social criticism and a sense of personal responsibility in building the good society. In working for the best development of the individual, there must be a clear realization of the supreme importance of democracy as a way of life. At this crucial point of social responsibility Soviet education seems to be superior to American education. Their Young Pioneers and Komsomols are doing an efficient job, as are their schools, in promoting responsibility, communist style, in all youth.

Deeply rooted in Western economic and political theory is the assumption that if you concentrate on the individual enough, increase his skill and knowledge enough, society will inevitably be served. Sanctioned in America by generations of rugged individualists, this conception worked reasonably well in an earlier, simple agrarian age. Its day is past, however. For better or for worse, we all are now our brother's keepers. The realities of an interdependent world and an interdependent America require that major efforts be made to see the individual in his social setting and, conversely, to see the social setting in terms of its meaning for developing individuality.

SELECTION AND EVALUATION

The selection and evaluation of talent in youth is exciting and important. This is especially true where giftedness is broadly defined as "consistently remarkable performance" in a variety of pursuits—academic, scientific, artistic, and social. Furthermore, the realization that an individual may be gifted in only one area enlarges the problem.

Two of the smaller high schools, Germantown Friends and Ohio State University High School, report two advantages: that they are the upper years of twelve year institutions, and that children of unusual ability continue on into high school. These factors greatly simplify the problem of selection. Students and their parents are personally known by staff members. Extensive use is made of personnel records from elementary grades. The program is further coordinated through faculty consultation on a variety of problems.

Standardized evaluative instruments are utilized in different degrees. In some schools three or four basic instruments are relied upon. Evanston Township High School uses a variety of tests covering reading ability, mathematics fundamentals and reasoning, vocational interests, academic ability and personality traits.

In the smaller high schools teachers meet formally and informally to evaluate each student in terms of academic progress, health, and emotional and social development. Thus, all those working with each individual student are made aware of his achievements, potentialities, and difficulties. Records are kept and used for guidance.

Evanston Township High School uses a number of promising evaluative procedures other than scientific testing. Classroom instructors and sponsors of student activities define talent in their several areas. Teachers use both quantitative and qualitative data after determining goals and familiarizing themselves with appropriate evaluative instruments. The rich and varied programs in this school stem in part from the involvement of many people, not merely of "the experts."

In the Ulysses S. Grant High School a co-ordinator is released one period a day for testing, compiling test data, and preparing tentative class lists for advanced seminars and other advanced classes. Even this limited time allotment is invaluable.

In larger schools, having more specialized personnel, studies of value can be more easily initiated. An underachiever study at Evanston Township High School is one example. Research promises both to advance the quality of education and to provide new knowledge on the education of the gifted.

Useful evaluation devices are reported. At Germantown High teachers rate each student five times a year on the following six point basis:

1. Outstanding achievement in every area of the course
2. Highly competent performance
3. Good achievement
4. Work clearly better than just passing
5. Work just passing
6. Failure

Personal comments are included on unconventional report cards which go to parents and are attached to college and transfer records.

In the Ohio State University High School students must choose and utilize appropriate criteria in the selection of both content and methods. Moral and social, as well as intellectual, qualities are regularly tested in the core program.

In Lyons Falls the students participating in the Talented Youth Project also evaluate their own achievements. They try to discover fully for themselves what the year's experience has meant to them.

The American high schools described here use evaluative techniques appropriate to various purposes—factual knowledge, concepts, skills, personality growth. As far as academic learning is concerned, external evaluation includes examinations by the College Entrance Examination Board, state agencies, individual colleges, and universities. Newer external examinations, such as those set by individual higher institutions for advanced standing and various merit scholarship awards, also are thought to be useful in evaluating programs.

It is necessary to point out here, as in other sections of this analysis, that selection and evaluation of student achievement in the creative arts, at least in definitive detail, are not included in any of the descriptive accounts.

ADMINISTRATIVE PROVISIONS

In the Soviet Union Marxist doctrine leads to the assumption that differences in ability are traceable to environmental factors, not to innate ability. The separation of students on the basis of ability is there believed to promote a class society.

In Germany and England secondary schools were established historically to conform to the classes of society. Separate schools, Gymnasia and grammar, were established for the intellectual aristocracy. A variety of other schools were developed for the less able. This class pattern, with its attendant social distinctions, still persists in these countries.

The American public high school developed in the mid-nineteenth century in response to social needs in a more equalitarian society. Children of all intelligence levels attend our comprehensive high schools. Curriculums have been differentiated to accord with vocational interests and carefully compiled knowledge of innate differences in ability. Course requirements guarantee a considerable exposure to liberal arts subjects along with elective specialization.

In the development of curriculums for gifted students, the administrators of the six American schools reporting have sought to meet various needs and abilities. Accepting an experimental concept of learning, rather than a static social and political dogma, they have utilized and tested various methods. Individual scheduling, grouping, and nongrouping have resulted from a combination of theory, tested knowledge, and hard facts.

The Germantown Friends School cannot group homogeneously on the basis of ability since the student body is too small. Instead, ingenious ways have been found to provide for individualization for all students. In English, for example, eleventh-graders meet in class three times a week. In addition, they meet once a week in small groups. Each senior has four scheduled English periods a week. He may also join one of many voluntary reading groups. Flexibility frees the teacher for individual and group guidance. The programing of students in this school is in relation to personal needs. In a class of 60 seniors 50 are likely to have individual schedules.

In the Ulysses S. Grant High School most required classes are heterogeneous. Where the need for special groups is obvious, however, they are established—for instance, classes for the very retarded and special seminar-size ones for the advanced.

In Portland heterogeneity was a factor in leading the general public and those in charge of secondary schools to seek new ways of working with gifted students. Four other social factors moved high schools toward homogeneous grouping: the rapid growth of population, the requirement that all youth stay in high school until the age of eighteen, America's need for more and better prepared leaders in domestic and international affairs, and a shortage of adequately prepared high school teachers who were expert in teaching a wide range of ability in one class.

In the Ohio State University High School heterogeneous grouping is favored for social reasons. In the core program the more able students come to realize that they are not superior in everything, that academically poorer students often have other qualities which merit personal respect, and that ability to do advanced work is not always equated with ability to deal with one's personal problems. Homogeneous grouping is little used in this school. Yet at the upper level students segregate themselves as they move into classes with more specialized and difficult subject matter. Also, some students take classes in the university.

A large comprehensive institution such as the Evanston Township High School can develop an abundance of administrative ways of scheduling to meet the varying needs of its high school population. This school of 3,300 pupils has definitely taken advantage of its size to do just this. With a view to attaining the intimacy which small units make possible, the student body is divided into four separate, complete divisions. There are honors classes in all academic departments. At the top, college level classes of from 15 to 20 students are provided. A continuous study of the work of individual boys and girls makes it possible to re-allocate them in accordance with potential and actual achievement.

The Evanston program is obviously organized with a view to the establishment of homogeneous groups, though attention is given in regular classes to providing for abler students. In the core curriculum program, fine arts, business education, practical arts, and physical education students are not grouped on the basis of ability. A number of procedures are used to recognize and develop special talent.

The highly select Bronx High School of Science has most to offer in quality of content and high level of intellectual achievement, but not in unusual administrative procedures.

Curricular Content

The liberal arts tradition predominates in American high schools, as in German Gymnasia and English grammar schools. In the U.S.S.R. nearly half of the time is devoted to science and mathematics. Soviet teachers of these subjects maintain close relations with local agricultural units and industries. Farm and factory experts lecture in classrooms, while students observe practical situations. This marriage of education with the practical world has recently been extended to include early work in industry.

The close association of the theoretical and the practical in the mathematical and scientific education of Soviet youth may well have strengthened the quality of education in these areas. Similar cooperative relationships could presumably be worked out in our country without lessening the general requirements we believe necessary for a liberal education.

The school day in these three European countries is much more rigid than in the United States. This is especially true in the U.S.S.R., where all youth, regardless of ability, study the same curriculum. In England requirements are somewhat less rigid. This is particularly true in the last two secondary school years, when sixth-formers give most of their time to the specialized study of two to four subjects in preparation for university examinations.

In America requirements in the first two years of higher education have increased, with more freedom being granted for special study later. In our high schools freedom of election and of substitution, in accordance with ability and needs, varies widely. In the Bronx High School of Science 90 per cent is prescribed—an unusually high proportion. An important consideration in relation to freedom of choice is that in American high schools quite different types of courses are available in the academic subject areas. This allows for election within required subjects.

Even in a school devoted to science education, such as the Bronx High School, there are special courses in creative writing, dramatics, journalism, world literature, and college English. Nature of proof (geometry), radio physics and automotive physics are samplings of other adaptations.

To meet the many needs of students, core programs are provided at the Ohio State University High School and Evanston Township High School. There are workshops at Ohio State and advanced seminars in Portland. Honors and advanced classes in the various subjects are also numerous. When one adds enriched offerings, as described in the Talented Rural Youth Project, the German-town Friends School, and in the other schools reporting, one cannot fail to be struck by both the quality and the richness which freedom has stimulated and made possible in American schools.

The depth of learning required in foreign secondary institutions, however, is most impressive. Extensive experience in essay writing in English grammar schools makes for excellence in the use of the mother tongue for which well-educated Englishmen have long been noted. Both the Germans and the Russians expect their better students to use at least one foreign language in research projects at the secondary level, in addition to having a speaking knowledge of at least one language. In Germany, the U.S.S.R., and England subjects are required for sufficient years to develop competence comparable to that found in the first year or two of college in the United States. This is especially true in the sciences and mathematics. We are told that in Moscow all tenth year students are now given trigonometry, binomial theory, combinations, and permutations, and are soon to be expected to master calculus. The biological sciences (biology, botany, zoology, anatomy, physiology, and psychology) begin at age eleven and continue for seven years. Physics begins in the third grade and continues for seven years. Chemistry runs for six years.

Mathematics and the sciences are studied for comparable lengths of time in English grammar schools. The work in calculus is incredible. Those who have passed examinations in biology at advanced or scholarship levels have done work of the quality of at least an elementary college course. *Examinations ostensibly require enormous knowledge of theoretical and factual material, and also the ability to integrate this material, to organize it, and to think about it.* The six or seven years of physics preparation placed the student *about two years ahead of his American counterpart in topic coverage. More important, however, is the fact that he already has had a number of years of deep digging and hard serious study.*

The advanced classes of one German Gymnasium studied these two questions from various vantage points: "What are the operating forces of the eighteenth century?" and "What is enlightenment?" The thoroughness of their analysis, their intellectual depth, and their integration of ideas are shown in the summary report in Chapter 5.

The extent and the quality of thought in secondary schools abroad is worthy of examination. Comparable examples of quality in American high schools can be found. The quality of study in run-of-the-mill American schools, however, cannot approach that usually found in programs for gifted students in the three foreign countries on which reports have been made. A major attempt must be made to develop courses of study for the gifted which will have the quality and depth of the best examples of secondary education both at home and abroad.

STUDENT ACTIVITIES

American high schools are rich in student activities, for the social aspects of education, in contrast to the intellectual, have long been stressed—councils, clubs, societies, publications, sports, and other recreation. The superior student has many opportunities to develop excellence. He enters activities with enthusiasm. Indeed, he may have to be restrained from taking part in too many. Numerous clubs—mathematics, foreign language, science—furnish opportunities for delving more deeply into academic learning. However, because entire high school programs are described most student activities are not presented in great detail.

In the Bronx High School activities in science are given in considerable detail. These should be of special value to schools contemplating further development in this area. A co-ordinator of special science activities stimulates many projects. Biology squads, protozoa squads, animal and plant squads, and other comparable groups prepare material for class use, as well as for group and individual research. Such organizations as the Experimental Society and the Field and Biology clubs make reports and demonstrations and produce special programs. A number of project rooms are equipped for work in biology, chemistry, and physics. The list of individual research projects is imposing. Students are encouraged to obtain summer positions in science institutes and higher educational institutions to further their knowledge and experience.

The fine arts play a considerable role in several programs. Fortunately they are not considered mere handmaidens to social studies, but are recognized as an important means of expression requiring skill and imagination.

Extracurricular art activities are nourished by electives, not merely by the conventional art and music classes. These electives include special music courses, drama, speech, stagecraft, creative writing, and journalism. A public speaking course in one school, for example, is elected by virtually every senior. Fine and industrial arts are housed in adjoining rooms at the Ohio State University High School so that individual interests may be more easily developed during free periods. Evanston Township High School has outstanding productions in band, orchestra, and chorus. Portland schools consciously utilize extracurricular activities in personal advisement.

Student government organizations supposedly give experience in representative government and responsible conduct. It is pertinent to ask whether they in fact do this, or whether they are often used by able students as instruments for the advancement of their own prestige or of the prestige of certain social groups. Are the areas in which student organizations have advisory, or more complete, authority well defined? Are limitations of student authority clearly understood? Are students in fact given freedom within recognized limits to develop special artistic and intellectual interests? Do sports and recreational activities draw off too much of the energy of able students from hard digging and superior scholarship? Do "service" activities, even when supplemented by a leadership training course, inculcate devotion to the public good in a democracy as effectively as youth groups of the Soviet Union prepare for communism?

These are but a sample of the questions which must be raised in order to build activity programs for which able students provide much of the leadership.

GUIDANCE

Guidance involves teachers, parents, courses of study, student activities, administration, special personnel, college requirements, and community expectations.

The authors of Part III, without exception, conceive of their task as one of personality development—to stimulate a student to achieve the best that in him lies. Individual teachers in the several programs discussed play active roles in guidance and counseling as well as in the acquisition of knowledge.

The Talented Rural Youth Project was inspired by the guidance idea. The program stresses extending the experience of the participants by means of community resources, intellectual exploration in depth, and thinking about values—aesthetic and moral. The Germantown Friends School faculty meets regularly to share information about students. Each faculty member with special guidance responsibilities cares for approximately a dozen students. The guidance possibilities in a core-centered program are explored in the Ohio State University High School. In the larger and more formally organized programs in Evanston, Portland, and New York, specialists in guidance and counseling assemble records, give standardized tests, determine individual student programs, and advise on college selection as well as on other personal problems.

The philosophy of the school and the resulting programs determine the possibilities. Portland has special group provisions for less than 13 per cent of the student body. Evanston programs a much higher percentage of unusually able on the basis of ability. In the Bronx High School of Science all students are in the higher ability range.

At Evanston counselors see that individuals do not attempt too heavy honors and college level course loads. They advise on personal problems. They consult with parents. The staff has identified certain points at which gifted students commonly need guidance:

developing awareness of their great abilities; choosing wisely among activities and courses rather than trying to do everything; selecting a college which offers sufficient challenge and individually appropriate social situations, rather than one which is merely famous, geographically near, or popular with other students; obtaining a college scholarship when financial assistance is needed; and thinking over vocational opportunities in the light of their unusual competencies.

It is pertinent in the context of this Yearbook to add to such a list *developing a sense of personal responsibility for achieving the good society*.

Critical awareness and social responsibility are themes appearing frequently in descriptions of programs. Such purposes must be implemented in much greater detail in hundreds of American high schools if we are to prepare gifted youth adequately for the troubled and new world in which they are destined to live.

BASIC IDEAS FOR PROGRAM MAKING

The following is a summary of major points discussed in this Yearbook:

1. The gifted show consistently remarkable performance in any worthwhile endeavor.

2. Many show giftedness in only a single area of activity.

3. The academically gifted, comprising 15 to 20 per cent of the age group, have the ability to study academic subjects effectively and rewardingly.

4. Program development should be considered in terms of academic, scientific, artistic, and social giftedness.

5. The maximum development of the individual is our goal.

6. In our avowedly democratic society critical awareness of social issues and personal concern for community welfare are paramount.

7. Creativity is to be sought in all subjects and activities.

8. Materialistic goals and unquestioning conformity must be fought if excellence is to be achieved.

9. All those who educate youth must consciously strive for excellence in order to escape mediocrity.

10. Constant experimentation in all aspects of program making is necessary to achieve excellence.

11. Educating our ablest youth involves educating all youth in a democracy.

12. Provision should be made for special groups of gifted students, in addition to their participation in common experiences with all high school youth.

13. The comprehensive school is the appropriate institution for educating gifted youth.

14. Identification and guidance are primary functions of teachers and administrators, as well as of specialists.

15. Both individual and social needs require a broad liberal education.

16. Within the context of a broad liberal education vocational preparation is desirable in secondary schools.

17. There is real danger at the present time that manpower defense needs may lead many gifted students, whose abilities lie primarily in other areas, to specialize in mathematics and science, thus depriving them and our society of unique creativity.

Index